Basketball
Trafficking

Basketball Trafficking

Stolen Black Panamanian Dreams

Javier
Wallace

Duke University Press   *Durham and London*   2025

Project Editor: Liz Smith
Designed by Courtney Leigh Richardson
Typeset in Merlo and New Century Schoolbook by
Westchester Publishing Services

Library of Congress Cataloging-in-Publication Data
Names: Wallace, Javier, [date] author.
Title: Basketball trafficking : stolen Black Panamanian dreams /
Javier Wallace.
Description: Durham : Duke University Press, 2025. | Includes
bibliographical references and index.
Identifiers: LCCN 2025009628 (print)
LCCN 2025009629 (ebook)
ISBN 9781478032809 (paperback)
ISBN 9781478029342 (hardcover)
ISBN 9781478061557 (ebook)
Subjects: LCSH: Discrimination in sports—United States. | Racism
in sports—United States. | Basketball—Social aspects—United
States. | High school athletes—United States—Social conditions. |
High school athletes—Abuse of—United States. | High school
athletes—Legal status, laws, etc.—United States. | Student
passports—United States. | Immigrant youth—Legal status, laws,
etc.—United States. | Immigrant youth—United States—Social
conditions. | Hispanic American high school students—United
States—Social conditions. | Panamanians—United States—Social
conditions.
Classification: LCC GV706.32 .W34 2025 (print) | LCC GV706.32
(ebook) | DDC 796.323092—dc23/eng/20250615
LC record available at https://lccn.loc.gov/2025009628
LC ebook record available at https://lccn.loc.gov/2025009629

Cover art: Basketball court at night. Courtesy Adobe Stock/Jesse
Morrow/Stocksy.

This publication was made possible in part by a publishing
subvention grant from the Tara Coyt Publishing Fund for
Scholars Chronicling the Black Experience.

To all the young people in pursuit of their dreams

Contents

Introduction

"¡Saca rápido!" (Get it in quickly!), the coach yelled from the sideline, hoping the players would inbound the ball quickly after giving up another bucket. His pleas, however, were lost on the players, who passed the ball sluggishly back in bounds, eating time off the clock in a game that was over before it began. The opposing team, Las Panteras (the Panthers), had destroyed their will to even finish the competition.

"Ball!" Tito, one of the star players of Las Panteras, a longtime Panama-based private basketball academy, called out to his teammate as he leaped into the air in front of his opponent. Since joining the academy years before, Tito had played basketball in more parts of the country and the world than anyone in his household could ever have imagined, including going on a trip to Washington, DC, in 2017, when he and I first met, that ultimately transformed his life. Tonight, in 2020, back in Panama City, his teammate answered the call by throwing the ball high in the air with such precision that Tito easily grabbed it and laid it in the rim for the final victorious alley-oop.

Summertime in Panama City was nearing an end, and the evening crowd at a popular public park on Via Argentina, one of the city's liveliest streets, was still energized as Tito and four of his teammates hurried to change out of their sweaty uniforms postvictory. They were rushing to catch the metro headed to Albrook National Transportation Terminal, the capital's biggest bus terminal, to take the evening's last one-hour bus ride across the isthmus to their Atlantic coast city, Colón.

Seeing Tito play at the park that evening reminded me of when his mother jokingly told me, "He is your son." He was not my son. I was less than twelve years his senior. Tito had grown up with both of his parents and had a great relationship with his father. However, I was proud to see him play and felt a sense of responsibility and love as if I had known him my entire life.

Maybe the two years we had spent in each other's lives from morning to night, between Panama and eventually Austin, Texas, made me feel this way. Looking at the now legal adult standing in front of me evoked these emotions. The peach fuzz I remembered sprouting on his sixteen-year-old face was starting to darken and thicken around his jawline, and the muscle mass on his body was increasing.

"Una foto," I requested of him, capturing the moment on my cell phone's camera the same way I had when I last saw him in December 2019 at the Dallas airport, with hopes that I would soon see him back in Texas with a new F-1 student visa to attend junior college. Two years before that, in September 2017, Tito had first arrived in the United States on an athletic scholarship to play high school basketball, an experience that eventually became marked by exploitation and abuse. Ultimately, Tito's scholarship at the private school was revoked by his coach, supposedly based on his academic performance. After that, Tito moved in with my family in Austin and enrolled in public school, slowly piecing his new life and basketball career back together until we were surprised by President Donald J. Trump's 2018 Memorandum on Combating High Nonimmigrant Overstay Rates. With so much uncertainty looming on the horizon, my family and I supported Tito by helping him search for a college basketball scholarship that would allow him to stay in the United States. He received an opportunity to attend a junior college on a new student visa. However, this never happened: When he returned to Panama for the visa adjudication, he was denied reentry to the United States.

Our paths had reconverged tonight. Tito stood there drenched in sweat, his light blue uniform sagging from his shoulders and waist. As usual when he was being photographed, Tito did not smile. Instead, he clenched his lips tighter, trying to hide the new braces aimed to correct a childhood issue. For me, the simple act of photographing him at this moment reminded me of what we shared and why I had decided to become a part of his life.

Before I met Tito, I met his mother, Katia, at a basketball tournament I organized as the athletic director of an elite international high school in Panama City. Katia worked the statistics table at that tournament, keeping track of all the vital points throughout the games. Besides the official statistics sheets, Katia also carried a small packet that included a letter detailing how her son's Panama City–based basketball academy, Las Panteras, had been invited to a recruiting camp in Washington, DC. Accompanying the letter were pictures of Tito, who attended the basketball academy on a scholarship, in the many different uniforms he had donned during his relatively short but highly successful teenage basketball career. There was even a photo of him with "PANAMA" displayed across his chest from when he was a member of the national Panamanian juvenile basketball team. Katia handed me the packet, and as I flipped through it, she interrupted me to show me a cell phone video of her son dunking a basketball. Despite my amazement at all the recorded accomplishments, I kept returning to one picture of Tito dressed in a celestial blue uniform with gold trim. It read "COLÓN" across the chest.

"The kids from Colón are the best players, but they never get to travel for these showcases and special trips," she said, highlighting how rare the opportunity Tito had been granted through his academy was.

I nodded my head, deeply understanding the truth in her statement. My own father is from Colón, and when I first moved to Panama in 2012, I lived in Colón as well. After only a year, however, I abandoned the life I had carved there in search of more money and opportunities in Panama's capital city.

In that moment I made my decision. I wanted to support Tito with not just this first trip to DC but his continued basketball career by donating funds for him to become spatially mobile and increase his opportunities of being seen by coaches in the United States.

I was excited to call my father, who had left Panama for Texas in 1974 on a tennis scholarship and an F-1 student visa, and tell him about Tito. On hearing Tito's story, my father reminisced on his youth playing tennis in Colón before attending Huston-Tillotson University, a historically Black university in Austin. He detailed how athletes in Colón were underfunded by the Panamanian sports ministry compared to those in Panama City and faced many financial barriers that prevented them from accessing similar opportunities to travel. He recalled how his uncles and family friends pooled their resources to buy him an airplane ticket because his parents could not afford to send him to *el norte* (the north, that is, the United States). There was an almost fifty-year gap between his time in Panama and Tito's, but the narratives were strikingly similar. Seeing himself reflected in Tito's story, my father decided that he also wanted to support Tito and funded his trip to Washington, DC, in a gesture to pay it forward.

Tito had a great time at the camp in Washington, DC, where he and Yohanis, one of his best friends, were treated like special guests. This trip was not the first time their athletic talents supplemented the less talented paying members of their Panama City–based youth basketball academy.

In the months after he got back from DC, I met with Tito several times, mainly at Gimnasio Kiwanis, the gym where I first met his mother. He practiced there with his basketball academy twice a week in the evenings before returning to Colón. After the camp in DC and a successful international basketball competition in the Dominican Republic shortly after, Coach Barrigon (a pseudonym), the head basketball coach at Tech Prep (also a pseudonym), a private high school in Texas, offered Tito a basketball scholarship.

Katia ensured that I was among the first to know about this new development in their lives. We were thrilled. The excitement was short-lived, however, when we discovered that the scholarship would cover only 80 percent of the tuition. Tito's family would need to contribute the remaining balance plus an additional $100 per month for living expenses. Once again, limited economic resources surfaced as a barrier to Tito's developing US hoop dream.

After I conferred with my father, we decided to support Tito's family with the additional costs. With that, Tito was off, and so was I. Traveling to La Frontera ("The Border," a pseudonym I use for the city to preserve anonymity) brought Tito to Texas for the first time. I would also be traveling back to Texas to pursue a doctorate at the University of Texas at Austin and reunite with my father after living in Panama for more than five years.

In mid-September 2017, on a scorching central Texas day, I picked up Tito, who arrived in the United States some days after me, from the Austin airport. Tito and I decided that before heading to La Frontera, he would make a two-day stop in Austin. After meeting my parents, visiting the Texas state capitol, and sitting in on several university lectures with me, he was en route to his new home.

For a while, things seemed to go well, but in retrospect, there were warning signs from the beginning, particularly surrounding academics. Within Tito's first month at Tech, academic performance became a point of contention for us since I believed that he was wasting his opportunity, per the information I received from Coach Barrigon. Before leaving Panama, Tito and I had had numerous conversations about him using this basketball opportunity to get a US education. Coach Barrigon reached out to me when Tito was not performing up to par academically in his new all-English advanced placement school. My tipping point came when I received a text message from the coach informing me that he was revoking Tito's scholarship due to poor academic performance. Following an argument, I decided to listen to Tito's version of events. On the tense phone call, Tito reluctantly explained how Tech was not providing him with any of the promised additional support. Moreover, he explained that Coach Barrigon's real gripe was with his *athletic* performance. Coach Barrigon expected Tito to become a leading point scorer immediately on his arrival at Tech. However, Tito could not meet the unrealistic expectation of scoring eighteen points per game, a quota set unfairly by the coach. Tensions continued to rise when the coach described Tito as a "damaged" player. Coach Barrigon accused Tito's Panamanian coach and his mother of sending him to La Frontera with secret hopes that Tech would cover the cost of a knee operation.

Tito's hesitant confession, which clearly eased a burden he was carrying, completely stunned me. I was transported back to my collegiate athletic days when I had witnessed something similar. Per National Collegiate Athletic Association (NCAA) rules, coaches could not get rid of a player because of their athletic performance. However, through surveillance, they could use other infractions such as poor academic performance to justify getting rid of a player or revoking their athletic scholarship (Comeaux 2018). It became clear to me that Tito was in a similar situation as an F-1 student visa holder. While there are no provisions for removal based on lack of athletic talent, a sponsoring institution can revoke a student's visa if they are not passing their classes.

Less than three months following Tito's arrival in Texas, I was on the phone with Katia, who was asking me to take care of her child and bring him to live with me in Austin. Things continued to spiral out of control. We soon discovered that Tito was not just struggling to keep up with his schoolwork in the new all-English academic environment. We also found that he was enduring deplorable living conditions, being fed inadequately, living under threats of being forcefully removed from the country, and being verbally and psychologically abused. All this was being done to him by the same person we had entrusted with his care and advancement: Coach Barrigon. Tito was almost completely alone, and losing his scholarship also meant losing his legal status in the United States.

From that fateful day, basketball trafficking became our lived reality and redirected the course of our lives. I first encountered the term in news stories, but I have come to define *basketball trafficking* as the exploitative and unregulated migration of youth to the United States through international interscholastic athletic programs, which, in many instances, begins with being awarded an F-1 student visa. I could have never imagined that Tito would travel from La Frontera back to Austin with a newly acquired "out-of-status" immigration classification. More important, he was not alone. As other news stories reported, there were many more young people like him across the United States with similar out-of-status classifications who had entered the United States on F-1 student visas to pursue their American hoop dreams, which, on arrival, turned into nightmares. Even at Tech, Tito was not alone. In the housing where Tito lived in La Frontera, there were eight international noncitizen teenagers in total. Two were from Panama, another two from Mexico, and four from Costa Rica, all living in deplorable conditions in near silence. We found out only when Katia's childhood friend from Panama, who was living in La Frontera, informed us about the kids' real living conditions. When asked how things were going, Tito always answered simply "bien" (good).

According to the US Department of Homeland Security (2013), "Human trafficking involves the use of force, fraud, or coercion to obtain some type of labor or commercial sex act." Yet, once Tito acquired his out-of-status classification and we sought assistance in the pro bono immigration space, most officials who work to protect migrants and trafficked persons could not think of someone like Tito as a victim of trafficking. They were puzzled by the notion that basketball could be a form of trafficking, and this limited the legal relief Tito was qualified to receive.

I was exhausted and nearly at my wit's end in the search for help before—seemingly following a divine intervention—we found someone who could help. At a nonprofit resettlement service in Austin, two caseworkers with decades of experience immediately recognized Tito's plight. Their professional experiences working with countless victimized individuals made it clear that Coach Barrigon's control over Tito's cell phone, the long abusive late-night tirades, the points-per-game quota, the threats to send him back to Panama, and the offers to work in his auto body shop in exchange for shoes and other necessities indeed represented a form of human trafficking.

The caseworkers even submitted Tito's application for assistance to the Administration for Children and Families' Office on Trafficking in Persons. The office determined that through basketball Tito may have been subjected to a severe form of trafficking in persons and that he was entitled to seek federal relief. However, this assistance came just a bit too late, as Tito had already left the country due to Trump's 2018 memorandum, forfeiting relief, as defined by the administration, to attempt to get a new student visa and attend junior college.

This book follows Tito's narrative to shed light on basketball trafficking. First and foremost, *Basketball Trafficking* demonstrates that young, healthy, strong Black males can be the victims of trafficking, even if they do not fit the typical image of a trafficking victim (gendered female and sexually exploited). It is urgent to contend with these realities because similar cases of kids being trafficked on basketball dreams have surfaced in the mainstream media, such as that of Souleymane Doumbia from the Ivory Coast. Souleymane was one of over seventy kids trafficked by the Evelyn Mack Academy in North Carolina, shuffled around the country without proper migratory status, and deported from the United States. It is harder for young Black men who do not fit the constructed image of a human trafficking victim to get relief.

In a contemporary sense, Tito represents the large number of youth who have become spatially mobile at younger ages to fuel the growing athletic industrial complex (AIC), which depends on the athletic labor of Black boys to function (Runstedtler 2018). Historian Theresa Runstedtler argues that big businesses such as Nike, the NBA (National Basketball Association), and other media companies not only benefit from young Black American boys' athletic labor but also take advantage of Black boys' lack of access to good-quality public education, their diminished job prospects, and their early exposure to the criminal justice system, which often pushes them into certain sports, such as basketball, as a way to achieve upward social mobility. Strategic marketing by these companies presents rags-to-riches stories that make it seem like hard work will allow these boys to overcome their circumstances.

As the game of basketball becomes more global, targeted efforts to capture the attention of young Black boys and their families all over the world present an American hoop dream as a viable option to circumvent their social positioning. For instance, the Jordan Brand commercials set in Parisian suburbs featuring Black youth use similar imagery and messaging: the rags-to-riches narrative and the idea that hard work in basketball will help them overcome marginality in French society. There is also the multiyear, multimillion-dollar exclusive rights deal that the International Basketball Federation (FIBA) struck with Nike to clothe players head to toe at official competitions. Additionally, there are the NBA's efforts to expand its presence through NBA Academies, where they identify, train, and house top talent in one of three academies located in Mexico City (NBA Academy Latin America); Saly, Senegal (NBA Academy Africa); and Canberra, Australia (NBA Global Academy). The NBA also hosts a vast array of Basketball Without Borders camps globally to identify talent and funnel them through their pipeline, all the while introducing the game to a larger audience and creating fans through a development lens.

In this book I make sense of how Tito navigates the complexities of migration, legal status, exploitation, and athletic recruitment from my experiences with him both in Panama and in the United States. I also look at how he makes sense of himself, particularly his racial and athletic identities as a transnational youth athlete from Latin America. I contextualize why Tito's subjectivity is used to represent the issues that impact many Black Panamanian boys. Particular attention is placed on the criminalization, surveillance, and policing of their bodies and neighborhoods. As in the United States, the construction of Black Panamanian boys as "superpredators" in Panama—heartless, senseless criminals with no morals—informs policies, programs, and interactions that negatively impact them (Rios 2011). They experience and witness different forms of institutionalized violence daily. The Panamanian police force often appears in photos at charity events supposedly aimed at helping intentionally marginalized communities. Yet they engage with Black communities in riot gear, wielding deadly assault weapons, and institute *toques de queda* (curfews) where they routinely and selectively round up Black boys and carry them off to police stations, causing confusion and worry among their parents. When the police reports on these efforts, they often present them as a necessary security measure. Yet the parents' and communities' complaints of ill treatment are often ignored (Lowe de Goodin 2014).

"And1"

"How was the game?" I asked Tito and his sweaty teammates after the Via Argentina match in Panama City.

"Trash!" Chambers, one of Tito's teammates, yelled back in English, making everyone laugh. Tito and Las Panteras had controlled the game from every aspect, dominating their opponents by forty points.

Tito's near six-foot muscular body forcefully, but seemingly with ease, drove the ball down the paint, laying it up in the hoop. The dark brown skin that is Tito's badge of *negritud* (Blackness) closely matched his teammates' but collided against the lighter hues of his mestizo opponents. Throughout the evening Tito's teammates exclaimed "#Money" when someone made a clean shot and "And1" when someone drew a foul on a point driving to the basket.

Las Panteras had a competitive advantage because they had been strategically pieced together over the years by Panamanian basketball coaches and basketball academy owners. Tito and a few others had been selected as members of the national Panamanian juvenile basketball team beginning in their early teens. They were the country's best basketball athletes in their age group in an academy of their own, and they traveled around the region competing against high-level opponents. But they were in Panama and not in the United States, where the real money for basketball is.

That evening match on Via Argentina was like many others for Black Panamanian teenagers searching for class mobility through sports. They hustle up and down basketball courts across the isthmus getting better, winning games, and receiving recognition in order to create more economic opportunities in their lives. They are willing to play the game nearly anywhere, as long as it creates the desired opportunity. Sometimes that means traveling to play in neighborhood parks hours away from home, like on the evening described in this introduction or moving to another school across the country to be on a stronger basketball team. For years, they battle early morning traffic jams and extremely late returns home to leave it all on the court.

Tito came to love basketball at the age of eleven. His first athletic passion was *fútbol*, as for many youth in Panama. Soccer reigns supreme in the country, and it occupied Tito's thinking until his father introduced him to basketball, where he excelled immediately and found a variety of opportunities, including transferring from Colón to a school in Panama City on an athletic scholarship. Coach Mendoza, Las Panteras' owner and principal coach, noticed Tito's talents, recruited him to the national youth team, and facilitated his move to Panama City. It was in Coach Mendoza's best interest to bring Tito to Panama City so he could be with the other team members who also had athletic scholarships. Being in the same building made it easier to develop the team's talent.

At seventeen, Tito was one of the top five players in Panama in his age range. However, the three-pointers he became famous for sinking across the Central American nation did not matter in the sea of over half a million boys in his age range fighting for top rankings in the United States. If Rivals or MaxPreps, the premiere US-based high school sports ranking sources, ranked top basketball prospects in Panama, Tito would surely have been on that list. His years competing on Panama's national team made it clear that he had a level of talent and prestige, but those accolades were not recognized in the United States. When Tito attended Tech Prep on an F-1 student visa, he became one of the many unknown student-athletes included in the over eighty thousand students holding F-1 visas at the K–12 level (US Immigration and Customs Enforcement 2020). His basketball prowess became invisible, like his new life in *el norte*.

Despite his relative invisibility in US basketball circuits, Tito was nonetheless "getting known," which Scott Brooks (2009, 23) describes as a complex process and network where labor, spatial movement, and luck are necessary to gain exposure and recognition. Gaining international recognition at the 2017 FIBA under-seventeen (U17) Centrobasket Dominican Republic tournament enabled Tito to transcend his borders and try his luck in the world's pinnacle basketball locale: the United States. However, basketball also became the source of his exploitation and victimization once stateside.

Throughout the Via Argentina match, Tito and his Black Panamanian teammates, mostly monolingual Spanish speakers but with historical connections to the English language because of their Black West Indian roots, exclaimed basketball terms in English. *And1* was the term that most caught my attention. When they yelled it out on the court, I was immediately transported back to my childhood days, when my brother and I would find ways to get copies of the *AND1 Mixtapes* on VHS. The *AND1 Mixtapes* were entertaining and instructive compilations of streetball highlights featuring primarily Black males with nicknames such as Skip to My Lou, Hot Sauce, and Escalade. Many said that the AND1 players violated the sport's official rulebook. They blurred the thin line between an infraction and a legal move. I, however, thought that they inventively remixed the rules of basketball like the rap mixtapes playing in the background. It was riveting. That night on Via Argentina, when Black Panamanian youth barely old enough to know what a VHS tape is exclaimed "And1," I was forced to confront what it means to be a Black basketball player defined by geopolitical borders that require passports and visas to play the game beyond where one is born.

Being a Black basketball player of West Indian ancestry in Panama is especially important to highlight given West Indians migrated to Panama by the thousands to labor in the construction of and around the Panama Canal. They navigated questions of citizenship and belonging between Panama and one of the United States' neocolonies, the US Panama Canal Zone, known locally as the Canal Zone, in the country's capital. Established in 1903, the ten-mile stretch of land cemented divisions within the nation. The near-sovereign US territory imposed a racial hierarchy relegating Black folks, the majority of West Indian origin, to performing the most dangerous forms of labor as well as staffing the railroad, dock facilities, and low-level clerical and administrative positions (Frenkel 2002). However, the movement and meeting of the Black diaspora in the Canal Zone, including many Black Americans, would eventually shape Tito's twenty-first-century basketball pursuits and American hoop dreams.

An article headline detailing famed American basketball coach William "Bill" Yancey's arrival in Panama in the April 3, 1937, edition of the *Indianapolis Recorder* read "'Bill' Yancey Is Idolized by Youth of Panama as Work Begins to Shape." The Black-owned newspaper further elaborated on Yancey's reception by Black Panamanians: "His first introduction to Panama colored society was in the form of a stag party given in his honor and sponsored by George Washington Westerman, sportsman, writer and author of the 'Passing Review,' a weekly column."

On March 1, 1937, about a month prior to the publication of that article, ss *Virginia* had anchored in the Port of Cristóbal, carrying Yancey and his wife. A small group of friends welcomed them, including the local representative of the Negro Associated Press and George Westerman, who was described by the West Indian News section of the *Panama American* newspaper as "one of the men responsible for his tour of duty down here" (1937b). In the preceding months, the West Indian News and the News of the Colored Community sections of the *Panama American* newspaper had built the excitement leading up to Yancey's arrival. And rightfully so: Panama had secured the talent of the renowned athletic standout from Philadelphia. On March 7, 1937, in the West Indian News section of the *Panama American*, George Westerman wrote:

> This new comer to Panama has become famous in North America. Entering the ranks of professional basketball with the Renaissance Quintet in 1928, "Billy" Yancey is said to have developed into one of the greatest Negro guards in the history of the floor game. With his refreshing speed and great effectiveness, he rose to stardom almost in a split second and his continued successes enabled him to remain in the rarefied atmosphere of basketball greats, irrespective of color, right up to January 18 when he left his team at Cincinnati to accept the proposition which caused him to be at present on the Isthmus.

Yancey was both a baseball and basketball legend and former team member of the New York Rens, considered to be "the colored Champs of basketball of the world" (*Panama American* 1937a). George Westerman and other Black Panamanian coaches and leaders principally recruited him to Panama to coach the multiracial Panamanian Olympic baseball and basketball teams. Yancey was a hit among local youth and found immediate success, as reported by the Black press. When the 1938 Central American and Caribbean Games rolled around, he coached Panama's women's basketball team to their first international gold medal. In addition to leading

FIGURE I.1. The New York Rens, a dominant 1930s Black professional basketball team. *Left to right:* Clarence "Fat" Jenkins, Bill Yancey, John Holt, James "Pappy" Ricks, Eyre "Bruiser" Saitch, Charles "Tarzan" Cooper, Wee Willie Smith, and team founder Bob Douglas (*inset*). Bill Yancey later moved to Panama to develop basketball, baseball, and other sports in Panama. Biblioteca Nacional de Panamá.

the Panamanian squads to victory, Yancey was a conduit connecting Panama's Black sporting networks with those of the United States, particularly the sporting congregations of historically Black colleges and universities (HBCUS) (White 2019).

To be clear, Yancey was a conduit, not the creator of these diasporic networks. On his arrival in Panama, he joined the Black coaches and physical educators across the Canal Zone and the broader republic, who were already using sport to determine their places within Panama and forge better opportunities beyond the isthmus, mainly in the United States.

Aston M. Parchment was one of the physical educators and coaches already actively developing Panama's Black sporting scene and connecting local youth to international opportunities before Yancey's arrival. Born in Jamaica but raised in the Canal Zone, Parchment became a physical education teacher and activist in the Canal Zone. He also started Club Mercurio, one of Panama's top private athletic clubs that trained the republic's first international champions, particularly in track and field.

FIGURE I.2. Coach Aston M. Parchment, pictured in 1941 with an athletic trophy at his desk in the former US Panama Canal Zone. Parchment was the founder of Club Mercurio. Aston M. Parchment Scrapbook, Museo Afrocaribeño de Panama, Ministerio de Cultura (Panamá).

Not only did Club Mercurio secure Olympic medals; it also facilitated educational and athletic opportunities beyond the isthmus for Black youth. Parchment successfully sent Black Panamanian athletes to HBCUs. He coached track stars Jennings Blackett, Clayton Clarke, and other Black Panamanians who went on to Xavier University of Louisiana. Once at Xavier, they were coached by renowned African American Olympian and professor Ralph Metcalfe. Parchment also coached Charlotte Gooden, who obtained a track scholarship to Tuskegee University and became one of the first women in Panama's history to participate in a Summer Olympics. She did this alongside Lorraine Dunn, Jean Holmes, and Marcella Daniel, who all went from the Canal Zone's racially segregated schools to Tennessee State University's legendary Tigerbelles women's track team.

Parchment welcomed Yancey to Panama in 1937 and must have been ecstatic that Yancey would improve the community's basketball prowess.

Cecilio Williams, a standout Black Panamanian basketball player and originator of the famed Panama Pipeline at Briar Cliff College (which sent nearly thirty Panamanian basketball players to the small college in Iowa starting in the late 1970s, leading Briar Cliff to reach national prominence in basketball), further strengthened the sport that Yancey helped develop on the isthmus. Coach Williams eventually formed some of Panama's strongest basketball teams and standout players.

Williams's tall stature gave him an advantage in the game, where height matters, but maybe more advantageous than his height was his connection to the Black sporting pipeline between Panama—more specifically the segregated institutions in the Canal Zone—and HBCUs in the United States. In the early 1950s, Williams left Panama on a scholarship to attend Savannah State College (now Savannah State University), an HBCU in Georgia, where he competed on the university's basketball team. Following his time at Savannah State, Williams returned to Panama and became a mathematics teacher within the Canal Zone's segregated school system. He continued to strengthen the pipeline of majority-Black youth going to the United States and became the central piece for the Panama Pipeline that emerged at Briar Cliff University in Iowa. Williams established Operación Tamaño (Operation Height), a basketball program in Panama City and Colón City, aimed at supporting positive youth development. Williams also intentionally sought out tall players who could potentially become great basketball players and be sent to the United States. In total, twenty-eight Panamanian basketball players, the vast majority of them Black, went on compete at Briar Cliff during the 1970s and 1980s, leading the tiny school to eleven trips to the championship game under Coach Ray Nacke's direction (Briar Cliff University 2023). By the 1980s the NBA had drafted four Black Panamanian youth that Coach Williams had sent to Briar Cliff.

From Williams's success with the Panama Pipeline in the 1970s and 1980s to Las Panteras' 2020 evening victory in the park on Via Argentina, conditions have changed drastically in Panama. The country's sovereignty is no longer dictated by the former US Panama Canal Zone or by a US-controlled Panama Canal. The Panama Canal Treaty, signed in 1977, ended the Canal Zone as of 1979 and solidified the return of the canal itself to the Panamanians on December 31, 1999.

By the time Tito was born in 2000, the Canal Zone and the American-occupied Panama Canal existed only in the memories of his elders, in school textbooks, and in some of the lasting infrastructure in the *areas*

FIGURE I.3. Profes-
sor Cecilio Williams,
yearbook photo from
Paraiso High School
in the US Panama
Canal Zone, 1970.
Williams, hailing from
Colón, was known for
founding Operación
Tamaño in Panama.
Biblioteca Nacional de
Panamá.

revertidas (reverted areas) within the former US neocolony, such as Gimnasio Kiwanis (Kiwanis Gym), where we first met. The US military once called it Reeder's Gym back when it was situated within Fort Clayton. Now the gym is part of Ciudad del Saber (City of Knowledge), the renovated US military base, which is a business park and technology hub hosting some of the region's largest international organizations, such as the United Nations. Albrook National Transportation Terminal, where Tito and his teammates rushed to catch their buses following the Via Argentina victory, was once Albrook Air Force Station. Now it was not just a transportation terminal but also a domestic airport and the second-largest shopping mall in the Americas. This is Tito's new Panama.

Tito and his teammates recognize their ancestors' journeys primarily from the British- and French-controlled Caribbean, but they see and understand themselves as *panameños* (Panamanians). Historically, becoming *panameño* was a long process that called for a collective amnesia that would absolve the Panamanian nation of the hurtful and discriminatory practices that targeted Afro-Caribbean people in its recent past (Corinealdi 2022), which included an emphasis on speaking Spanish and not their ancestors' languages. As previously noted, the young Black athletes' on-court vocabulary is peppered with English words, but they speak Spanish, a direct result of the process of *ser panameño* (being/to be Panamanian). The collective amnesia involved in becoming or being Panamanian also included attempts at destroying the athletic pipelines that tied Black Panamanians to US colleges and universities on athletic scholarships.

One of the most significant blows to these pipelines was the transfer of the Canal Zone's segregated schools for Black people to the Panamanian government's control in 1956 and their ultimate closure by the United States in 1978. For decades, these Black-centered schools had created, nurtured, and facilitated opportunities for Black youth to try their luck at US colleges and universities, particularly HBCUs. Once the United States in conjunction with Panama phased out (that is, closed) the former colored schools turned Latin American schools in the Canal Zone, many Black Panamanian stronghold educators like Coach Williams were denied opportunities to continue teaching in their same capacity in the newly integrated Canal Zone schools. As the US government reported in 1977, "There have been, however, strong objections raised by U.S. citizens against having their children taught by non-U.S. citizen teachers. Thus, placement of the teachers from the Latin American schools as those schools are phased out, is very sensitive and requires special care and attention" (US House of Representatives 1977, 105). Similarly, like elsewhere throughout the US South, many Black Panamanian educators, and coaches, were dismissed, demoted, or forcefully encouraged to retire. Consequently, the sporting networks and pipelines connecting Black Panamanians to HBCUs and Black sporting congregations in the United States began to disappear.

Tito and his teammates' style of play and their jargon have been influenced by the diasporic flows that nurtured basketball in Black communities across the diaspora. However, we cannot overlook that the Black art of basketball is deeply connected to the AIC. Athletic technology, ideas, and apparel, among other things, can now travel with ease, but Black people and their bodies, depending on their nationalities, are not afforded the same privilege. These Black bodies are bound by their nations' borders and geopolitical relationships with other countries. Heidy Sarabia (2015) asserts that passports and visas issued in the Global North award different rights and privileges from those granted in the Global South. American nationality and citizenship mean mobility for many Black athletes, whereas their peers in the Global South find it more difficult to become spatially mobile across different nations due to discriminatory visa processing practices.

Basketball Trafficking does not stop at critiquing the AIC's exploitative use of Black youth labor within the United States. I argue that the movement of Black basketball culture around the globe without the free movement of Black migrants pushes us to consider how the AIC is also a nonstate actor and enforcer of race- and class-based US immigration policies. Tito's individual story as a young Black Panamanian male who believes he must make it to the United States to achieve class mobility and basketball success is like the stories of many others. Tito and others like him must navigate the combined efforts of the AIC, the US immigration system, and local anti-Blackness to exploit their labor until it becomes disposable and they are deported back to their countries of origin. *Basketball trafficking*, as defined in this multisited, person-centered ethnography, proves that citizenship matters within the unequal dynamic of sports migration and has material consequences in the lives of some of the youngest members of the African diaspora. Tito's experiences provide a tool of comparison to understand the subjugated colonial position that Black people share around the globe regardless of whether they are in the Global North or the Global South (Coleman-King 2014), or moving between them.

Chapter Overview

I have divided the book into seven chapters tracking Tito's journey from Panama to the United States. Chapter 1 introduces the concept of basketball trafficking by looking at the regulations behind the F-1 student visa. The chapter opens with a narrative of the 2017 Centrobasket tournament in Santo Domingo, Dominican Republic, with Tito securing Panama's third-place victory. I depart from Tito's story to analyze the trajectory of many aspiring Black male Central American basketball players like him, highlighting how language, race, class, and nationality are determining factors in their ability to pursue international athletic migration to the United States. Speaking English, for instance, is a requirement for participating in US intercollegiate basketball and securing an F-1 student visa. For non-English-speaking youth like Tito, even with their immense athletic talent, the absence of English proficiency can be a barrier to entry to the United States. These English language requirements push non-English-speaking students to enter the United States at an earlier age, rendering them more vulnerable and at risk for exploitation and trafficking. As there is less regulation and virtually no oversight at the high school level, the power dynamic of coach and student can further complicate how these youngsters fare. This chapter explains why an earlier departure through interscholastic athletic migration, usually in early high school, at about fifteen to sixteen years old, provides an opportunity to overcome the strict language requirements of US colleges, universities, and intercollegiate athletic governing bodies, such as the NCAA.

Chapter 2 is entitled after the Panamanian pejorative *chombo*, which historically means a Black English speaker of West Indian descent. Tito is a Black boy from Colón City, a historic West Indian city, and the chapter seeks to connect the history of surveillance, policing, and exploitation of Black West Indians in Panama to the present by looking at Tito's visa adjudication journey. The chapter's opening scene begins with consular officers at the US embassy in Panama City denying Tito an F-1 student visa based on a "lack of English proficiency" despite the fact that Tito had won a hard-earned US basketball scholarship. I center my analysis on how the English language has a racialized character within the Panamanian context, and this often becomes one of the many challenges that young Black men encounter when applying for educational visas to the United States. The Panamanian government and elites historically viewed English- and French-speaking West Indians and their descendants as an unassimilable, anti-Hispanic criminal population, concentrated in certain neighborhoods, and took steps to diminish the use of English. Today, I argue, these dynamics play themselves out in the migratory process, and this is not just because of the US immigration system's anti-Blackness. Also at play is the local anti-Blackness in Panamanian society, informed by these histories and displayed by consular officers whose job is to make interpretations about which "aliens" to deny entrance to the United States.

Once Tito finally secures his US F-1 student visa, chapter 3 follows him to Tech Prep, a private American high school in La Frontera, Texas. Tito spends three months at Tech Prep before Coach Barrigon, the coach who saw him play at Centrobasket and recruited him to the US high school, revokes his scholarship and terminates his lawful right to remain in the United States. This chapter examines the experiences of not just Tito but also his mostly Black teammates/housemates from Costa Rica and Panama. They are often called *los becados* (the scholarship players) by coaches, school administrators, and other students. Central to this chapter is examining the anti-Black discourse present within Latinidad at Tito's majority-mestize (gender-neutral term) private American high school, which I argue contributes to the racialized and classed singling out of Tito and his other Black teammates as *becados*. I demonstrate that stereotypes applied to Tito and his Black teammates, including racialized nicknames that evoke tropes about Black athletic superiority, are pervasive within Latinx communities. I further argue that these racialized nicknames and other racist ideology that marks Tito's time at Tech are masked by Latin American *mestizaje*, which silences the racialized and anti-Black logics commonly employed in Latin America and its diaspora in the United States and elsewhere. I identify how anti-Black discourse around "helping" the *becados* was actually employed by school officials to exploit the student-athletes' labor and deny them promised opportunities, such as access to an English-language education and safe living conditions. In news articles and school fundraising opportunities, Tech made it seem as if it were "saving" *los becados* from their impoverished backgrounds, and any condition they found themselves in in the United States was an upgrade to their lives at home. According to this logic, Tito and his teammates should be grateful for being in the United States and should not have any gripes. Looking at the United States, Panama, and Costa Rica, this chapter demonstrates that the *desire* for Black athletic labor is fluid beyond national borders but that these young Black *men* of specific nationalities are not, and they face material and symbolic acts of anti-Black discrimination.

Chapter 4 more closely follows different types of relationships that affect Tito's life, including the hierarchical coach-player relationship with Coach Barrigon, which limits Tito's ability to protect and advocate for himself. Positive nonathletic relationships thus become essential to Tito's survival in La Frontera. He unexpectedly develops a relationship of support with Aunt Sonia, a Panamanian immigrant woman living in La Frontera who was a childhood friend of his mother and provided him a much-needed respite from the coach and sport that so negatively affected his well-being in the States. Their relationship is central to the chapter because Aunt Sonia helps Tito forge opportunities to escape abuse by revealing Tito's true living conditions, exposing his relationship with Coach Barrigon, and ultimately participating in the ploy to safely remove him from Tech. Last, the chapter explores Tito's more abstract relationship to the US immigration system as a Black noncitizen teenager and F-1 student visa holder. This is Tito's most significant relationship during his life in the United States, but it is also the one he has the least control over. At its core the chapter demonstrates that athletic governing bodies effectively render athletic eligibility an extension of lawful immigration status in the United States, and this leads to the surveillance and punishment of F-1 student visa holders like Tito. These punitive measures manifest in different athletic governance agencies at various levels and with conflicting international student-athlete recruitment regulations.

Chapter 5 extends from the previous chapter's focus on relationships to explore how my own father's athletic migration from Panama to the United States is part of a larger historical Black West Indian Panamanian sport migration. Departing from this history, the chapter continues to make sense of Tito's arrival in Austin, Texas, following his removal by Coach Barrigon from Tech Prep. Tito subsequently enrolls in Turner High School, a public school protected by *Plyler v. Doe* (1982), a historic ruling that allowed young people to enroll in a US public school without revealing their immigration status. However, as explored through other mediated basketball trafficking cases in the chapter, the ruling also set a precedent of enabling coaches and US public school officials to evade and cheat immigration rules by using the *Plyler v. Doe* protections to get international basketball players into public schools. This chapter reveals the interconnectedness of the AIC and US federal policies by highlighting the complicity of the athletic governing bodies in different states, the NCAA, and the US Immigration and Customs Enforcement (ICE) agency. These institutions work in tandem to surveil, police, punish, and forcibly remove Black male athletes once they are no longer useful to the system, and this reality cannot be divorced from the disproportionately racialized and gendered nature of the US deportation machine.

Chapter 6 addresses the (il)legibility of noncitizen Black male athletes to be considered victims of human trafficking in the United States. I address Tito's basketball trafficking victimhood and the material consequences of being read as illegible to pursue and obtain immigration relief in the United States. The stories in this chapter emerged in the fall of 2018 when Tito was in his second academic year at Turner High School in Austin following his removal from Tech Prep. On the verge of turning eighteen, Tito navigated illegality and the fear of deportation as he transitioned into adulthood, all while trying to achieve his US hoop dreams. Ultimately, Tito returned to Panama in 2019 to readjudicate a new visa in preparation for enrolling in a junior college in Texas, where he had been granted a full scholarship. However, he was interrogated for two hours by US consular staff and denied a new visa. He decided to remain in Panama and forfeit the scholarship.

The book's conclusion provides an update on Tito's life after his second visa denial, when he decided to remain in Panama. I explain how Tito and his family navigated his return to life in Panama and his continued desire to leave for basketball opportunities. Tito ultimately decides not to return to the United States because of his adverse experiences. Instead, he decides to go to Mexico and participate in the growing university basketball scene near the US-Mexico border. This chapter poses questions about how the growing Mexican basketball scene mirrors the dynamics of US intercollegiate basketball, particularly with the emphasized recruitment of Black Central American players. I leave these questions as departure points for further research to interrogate the role of race and the sports industrial complex in Latin America. I also provide recommendations on identifying and mitigating instances when basketball trafficking is occurring.

1

CENTROBASKET AND ENGLISH

The Importance of English in US Basketball Recruitment

With three minutes and twenty-eight seconds remaining on the game clock, the crowd in Santo Domingo, Dominican Republic, had chosen a favorite. Perhaps it was Lopez's three-pointers that closed the more-than-twenty-point gap, tying the game at 69–69. Or maybe it was the hard drive down the lane and powerful dunk by Panamanian American Robert Bello that drew the crowd to favor the Panamanians. Ultimately, though, it was Tito's two consecutive trips to the free throw line with five seconds left in the game that sealed the third-place victory over Mexico.

Tito's knees were slightly bent, giving him the perfect amount of momentum. He looked down to ensure the tips of his Nikes stayed behind the line. Focused, with determination in his eyes, "PANAMA" boldly printed on his chest, Brown (his surname) across his back, and the weight of his country on his shoulders, he drove up and released the ball. It went right into the basket. It was good. Roars erupted from the bench and the crowd. The referee handed Tito the ball again, and he stood at the line, maintaining the same focused intensity as before. This was his chance to *dejar en alto el nombre del país* (leave the country's name on high). He bent his knees and carefully spun the ball in a reverse motion toward himself, his knees released, and he pushed up, launching the ball. With a perfect arc, the ball reached its highest point before descending into the basket. The swoosh of the net would have been audible if not for his teammates' screams as they swarmed the court. The mostly Dominican crowd, along with the few Panamanians waving flags and cheering with noisemakers, added to the hysteria. The young players, all under seventeen years old, screamed with joy. They had won third place. They embraced each other. Tito ran until he found number 19, Josue, the other guard. Josue jumped on him, wrapping his legs around Tito, forcing him to bear their combined weight. The two screamed in unison, their voices blending with the chaos of the moment. This was not the first time they had celebrated a basketball win like this one together.

Tito's Win Story

One year before this game at the 2017 International Basketball Federation (FIBA) under-seventeen (U17) Centrobasket tournament in Santo Domingo, Tito and Josue were making the long bus ride from their home on Panama's Atlantic coast to Panama City to study and play basketball at a private school and basketball academy. They had known of each other within the country's basketball circuits, especially because they were both from Colón. However, it was not until they transferred from their respective public high schools to the private Colegio Bolivariano in Panama City that they truly developed a close connection.

Since becoming teammates at Bolivariano, Tito and Josue had experienced both victory and defeat together. But during Centrobasket they were in Santo Domingo, not Colón or Panama City. After their win they quickly embraced each other, a moment of celebration before they rushed to clear the court as the Dominican and Puerto Rican teams entered for their championship warm-up. The Panamanians scurried to the sideline to shake hands with the defeated Mexican team. The dark brown hands of the mostly Black Panamanian squad collided against those of the mainly white and mestizo Mexican players, a contrast that spoke to the histories of their countries and the complex dynamics of who gets to represent them on public stages like Centrobasket. The opportunity to represent a country on a national team does not always result from a meritocratic process. It is called a *selection* for a reason. National teams represent a country and its public.

Tito and Josue's time together was dwindling. Maybe the emotion they shared meant something more than the third-place victory they had secured for their country. Their victory guaranteed Panama's spot in FIBA's under-eighteen (U18) Americas Championships, to be held in Canada in 2018. But when they returned to Panama, they would not have much time to relish each other's company.

Josue was slated to return to La Frontera, where he had spent the last year laboring on a basketball scholarship and attempting to learn English at a private high school on an F-1 student visa. Tito knew that one day he, too, would need to go to the United States if he was to achieve his dream of becoming an NBA player. It was an idea he had heard repeatedly in Panama.

It was around this time that Tito and I met. After my father funded Tito's international basketball trip to Washington, DC, we started to develop a closer relationship. About once or twice a week, we would text each other. Our connection grew, and occasionally, after attending school at Colegio Bolivariano, Tito would stop by my office on his way to basketball practice. My private school was located in the former US military installation Fort Clayton, which had been converted into the Ciudad del Saber. Since the conversion, Ciudad del Saber is now a business and technology park that houses academic institutions, nongovernmental organizations, and other businesses. Both the school building and the gym where Tito had his after-school practices were housed in the remnants of the base. The security guards and front desk staff at the school knew Tito was welcome to come by my office without an appointment.

He usually stopped by my office before changing out of his seafoam-green school uniform into his practice clothes. As odd as the color of his uniform was, it made him look like the thousands of school-age children around the country. However, his hair placed him in a more diasporic uniform, one shared by other young Black men of his age around the globe. Once in his basketball clothes, Tito was nearly indistinguishable from the Black youth featured in the perfectly edited highlight reels pinned on X (formerly Twitter) profiles by hopefuls just like him, searching for their next basketball opportunity. These highlight reel mixtapes, often created by the players themselves, have become a fundamental part of the recruiting process. They allow players to exercise agency in how they present themselves to coaches and scouts, deciding which parts of their game should be showcased. Additionally, these mixtapes are an opportunity to see the latest styles of play and fashion trends from around the world. Tito wore his hair in an Afro tapered on the sides, free on top, and made curly with a small hair sponge he carried in his backpack. The X world named this style the "Duke Starting 5" because the all-Black male starting lineup at Duke University in North Carolina had made the hairstyle visible and legible to mainstream audiences.

"What's up! How are you?" I would always begin our exchanges in English.

"Bien," he always replied, indicating he was doing well in one word.

I intentionally spoke English with him because I knew from his English surname that we shared a similar heritage. More than that, I knew the importance of English within Panama and understood that if Tito wanted to attend a US university—like the one whose players could have influenced his hairstyle—he needed a command of the language.

English

The 2017 Centrobasket win also secured Tito's recruitment to a US high school. For a Panamanian, going to play high school basketball in the United States means more than just evading the country's underdeveloped basketball infrastructure. It's a crucial step toward eligibility for intercollegiate basketball. Panamanians without access to quality English-language education face significant challenges in meeting the academic eligibility standards required by the United States' National Collegiate Athletic Association (NCAA). The NCAA places a heavy emphasis on English language proficiency within its requirements. The NCAA defines a *qualifier* (qualifying athlete) as "a student who, for purposes of determining eligibility for financial aid, practice and competition, has met all of the following requirements (see Bylaw 14.3): (a) Graduation from high school; (b) Successful completion of a required core curriculum consisting of a minimum number of courses in specified subjects; (c) Specified minimum grade-point average in the core curriculum; and (d) Specified minimum SAT or ACT score" (NCAA 2020, 167). Additionally, for prospective international student-athletes, the NCAA also required that "all qualifying SAT and ACT tests must be taken in English" (2021, 11). The centrality and constraints of a standard Anglo-centered English education within US intercollegiate basketball can be read through the standardized admission tests. The Scholastic Aptitude Test (SAT), American College Testing (ACT), and Test of English as a Foreign Language (TOEFL) serve as barriers to entry.

Even though there are sliding scales for grade point averages (GPAs) and other necessary test scores, youth like Tito who lack access to an English-medium education—where English is the primary mode of instruction—and who have limited test preparation opportunities face significant challenges in securing a high-enough score on these entrance exams. While English-medium education and standardized tests are available in Panama, the ability to access them is deeply linked to race and class across the Central American isthmus. Only wealthier individuals, most of whom are white, can afford the resources to prepare for these exams and attend the types of schools that offer such opportunities.

Tito and many of his Black teammates, hailing from some of the country's Blackest regions and neighborhoods, did not have access to the resources needed to succeed in US admissions processes. For students in Panamanian public schools, English was merely a foreign language credit, and Tito had never even heard of the SAT, ACT, or TOEFL. Tito needed to access English-medium education in the United States, which is ironic given that his father and paternal grandparents are native English speakers. Tito's father, like thousands of other Black Panamanians, is a descendant of Black West Indian people from the anglophone Caribbean who migrated to the Central American isthmus beginning in the 1850s (Newton 1984; McGuinness 2016).

Anti-Black racism within Panamanian nationalism has long cast Black West Indian migrants and their cultural manifestations as English (or French) language pariahs who diverged from Hispano-Panamanian ideals. Black West Indians, or Afro-Antilleans, and their descendants were positioned in opposition to the Afro-colonial population, which is largely constructed as descendants of enslaved Africans trafficked to the isthmus during the Spanish colonial period. Over a century later, Tito—a descendant of both groups, with his Anglo surname linking him directly to his Black English-speaking West Indian heritage—found himself in a similar position to his ancestors: needing to leave Panama in search of upward mobility. However, the English language that necessitated his departure from Panama was also the same force that truncated his path forward. While language is undoubtedly important, this situation is not just about language—it's about a Black boy from a marginalized area of the country, an area often associated with deviance and violence, trying to navigate and circumvent the structural barriers that have historically plagued Black Panamanian youth. Like many Black Panamanians before him, Tito had to use sport, his Blackness, and the English language as tools to leave Panama and achieve upward social mobility.

Decades before Tito began traveling for sport, my father, a Panamanian hailing from Colón, did the same. He was my first introduction to the concept of needing to become spatially mobile for a chance at transcending one's circumstances. Tennis was his way to *el norte*, the colloquial name given to the United States, and it became his saving grace. Like Tito, he would travel on public transportation from Colón to Panama City to compete in sports, primarily tennis. In the many athletic tournaments organized by the famed Carlos Eleta in the 1950s and 1960s, my father and his teammates would literally traverse multiple borders, both national and cultural (Ariail 2017), moving from their racially segregated, mostly West Indian enclaves within the US Panama Canal Zone into the Republic of Panama's capital city. Their all-white tennis uniforms, which their mothers had stitched together from "cheap white fabric from the [US] Commissary," as my father recalled, contrasted sharply with their slender, dark brown frames. Their journeys would lead them to some of Panama City's most exclusive hotels and venues. They had one goal: to win.

"The *rabiblancos* always wanted to play against us and get their kids to try and beat us," my father recalled. *Rabiblanco* is Panamanian slang, which translates literally as "white tail." It is reserved for the rich, and *blanco* indicates the white citizenry within the Panamanian republic. My father recalled how these players would show up in nice, store-bought white tennis uniforms, but they never managed to secure a victory against the Black youth from Colón. Despite all his victories within Panama, he, like Tito fifty years later, knew he could not remain in Panama. *El norte* was his goal. Tennis would eventually get him there. Staying in Panama would keep him tethered to possibly working at the Panama Canal, the very industry that had drawn his Jamaican and Barbadian grandparents to the isthmus.

Black Panamanian youth, particularly those of West Indian descent, have historically encountered limited access to employment opportunities (Priestley 2004). The US Panama Canal was one of their many sources of employment but only within the most labor-intensive and menial positions. My father decided he would not continue life in a neocolony (Corinealdi 2013). English would be one of his most powerful tools to assist him with leaving.

"One of the *rabiblanco* families wanted me to go to school with their son in the United States because I spoke better English and could help him with his school," my father shared with me as he reflected on his youthful days. "I wasn't going to be anybody's nanny or tutor! I told them no."

My father, like Tito's father, is a native English speaker. He did not officially learn Spanish until he was old enough to enroll in elementary school. However, being an English speaker during those times was considered anti-Panamanian. More precisely, the Panamanian government determined that being a Black English-speaking person was anti-Panamanian and took deliberate measures to limit such people's migration to the country. Even in 1952, the year my father was born, nearly four decades after the completion of the Panama Canal, there was still considerable contention surrounding the large, primarily English-speaking West Indian community and their descendants living in Panama. Since the arrival of Black migrants in the isthmus, the Panamanian government had taken intentional measures to direct their assimilation into the country. Many people of English- and French-speaking West Indian descent faced discrimination in most aspects of their lives and, in many instances, would forgo using English and French in public spaces to avoid negative consequences. However, the connection between English and race in the Panamanian context provided these individuals with opportunities to become part of a larger Black diaspora, particularly among those from the anglophone Caribbean and African Americans in the United States. This situation highlights the transnational connections that Black people within the Circum-Caribbean, or the Black Global South, were able to forge despite the pervasive anti-Blackness in the Americas. In Panama, especially within the segregated athletic spaces of the former US Panama Canal Zone, Black physical educators and coaches built relationships with historically Black colleges and universities (HBCUs) in the United States (J. Wallace 2023). The *Panama Tribune*, from the 1930s and beyond, is filled with stories of Black Panamanians who received athletic scholarships to HBCUs, opening doors for others to follow.

My father benefited from the connections his coaches had forged with African Americans during very intense legal segregation. In 1974 he received a full tennis scholarship to Huston-Tillotson University, a historically Black university in Austin, Texas. His coach and physical education teacher, Mr. Stanley Loney, who had been an international Panamanian athlete in the US Panama Canal Zone in the 1930s–40s, utilized his connections and his knowledge of the English language to grant opportunities for youth like my father, his two siblings, and a host of neighborhood kids to venture to *el norte* on full athletic scholarships with F-1 student visas. Most of them were placed at HBCUs throughout the United States, schools where at least one Panamanian had been before. They formed part of a network of HBCUs and Black folks in the Global South that were looking toward each other to forge opportunities. Just as Frank Andre Guridy (2010) described Afro-Cubans writing to Booker T. Washington to gain admission to the Tuskegee Institute in Alabama, the same was happening in Panama within the sporting realm. International athletic competitions in the past, like Centrobasket in 2017, became fertile ground for diasporic recruiting and opportunity making that allowed Black diaspora athletes to transcend borders through sport.

Centrobasket

Centrobasket is a tournament where the best youth players from the region come together to represent their countries, including those who have left in search of opportunities or have ancestral ties to the area. Sponsored by FIBA, it is an event where national teams from Central America and the Caribbean compete. Centrobasket is the place to be seen—not just in your country's colors but by scouts or others who can provide more exposure. Scott Brooks (2009), in his ethnography entitled *Black Men Can't Shoot*, emphasized the importance of gaining exposure and "getting known" in US high school basketball.

Getting known, a process that is both meritocratic and subjective, requires significant work, and organized ball and tournaments like Centrobasket are essential to gaining exposure (Brooks 2009). Brooks states that players must create a name for themselves:

Exposure is the opportunity to compete with high-status persons and play in settings where college coaches, recruiters, and scouts are present. Positive exposure affords the best players the opportunity to be recruited by Division 1 college coaches and private high school coaches in addition to being promised playing time. The consequences of the contrary, playing in places with low exposure and low competition, are how kids remain "unknown" even when they are talented. They may be able to outperform known players in one-on-one contests or in informal settings, but a player needs to be able to play organized ball. Organized ball provides wider exposure. (2009, 23)

The gym in Santo Domingo, Dominican Republic, is no different from the playgrounds and gyms that Brooks traces behind a couple of African American teenagers in pursuit of hoop dreams. The best place in the world for men to play basketball is the United States, largely because the NBA is considered the pinnacle of the sport. While systemic and discriminatory pay inequities mean that women players can often earn higher salaries in European and Asian leagues, the United States remains an important locale for women as well. Basketball in the United States is dominated by Black people. They constitute the majority of players at the highest level of college and professional ball. Black males have become the preferred laborers of the sport. African American males, regardless of their socioeconomic backgrounds, hustle up and down courts trying to get known and make it to the next level. However, it's not just African American youth who must play in big events to gain exposure with the hopes of improving their athletic careers.

The Nike-sponsored tournament in Santo Domingo, like other FIBA-organized events, serves as a key site for international youth to gain exposure and potentially secure a spot on a US roster. Founded in 1932 in Geneva, Switzerland, FIBA is the global governing body for basketball, dictating the trends of the game, deciding the rules and punishments, organizing competitions, and popularizing the sport. Its international tournaments also showcase youth of dual citizenship. During the 2017 Centrobasket tournament in Santo Domingo, there were US citizens playing for different national teams. Players like Tito's teammates Robert and Josue, as well as several Dominican players, had spent time on North American courts alongside African American players. Many members of the Dominican Republic's championship-winning team were enrolled in US high schools. Additionally, some players, like Robert, had been born and raised in the United States but represented their parents' home countries. This diversity of nationalities within a single roster and the strong ties to the US basketball scene reflect the diasporic connections that have long shaped the sport. However, more important, it underscores the basketball industry's dependence on Black male labor.

All the teams at the 2017 Centrobasket tournament were draped in new uniforms, each adorned with the unmistakable Nike swoosh on their shoulders. From the top of their uniforms to the soles of their sneakers, the athletes were fully branded by Nike. The court itself was surrounded by Nike advertisements, making it clear that this was a Nike-sponsored event. Nike, the largest brand globally by revenue, and one of the most recognizable, had secured a prominent presence in international basketball. Months before the tournament, FIBA had announced an eleven-year strategic partnership with Nike. In a press release, FIBA highlighted, "It is a natural partnership between the number one basketball brand in the world and the sport's governing body, which counts 213 National Member Federations all around the globe." The release clearly showed the mutual benefits of such a partnership: "Nike, the number one sports brand in the world, will benefit from long-term global marketing rights related to the major FIBA national team competitions. FIBA's ambitions to grow the game will be supported by Nike contributions in the areas of promotion, marketing communication and the engagement of top players and ambassadors" (International Basketball Federation 2017).

Nike was heavily represented in Santo Domingo, thousands of miles away from its North American headquarters in Beaverton, Oregon. Athletic apparel companies like Nike have built an empire by capitalizing on the star power of African American male athletes. These companies' financial successes and brand placement have not been confined to the United States. Instead, Nike, along with its Jordan Brand, has expanded its reach globally, including to Santo Domingo. While Michael Jordan's rise from the University of North Carolina at Chapel Hill might be far removed from the minds of youth playing in the Santo Domingo gym, his image is plastered on basketball shoes that resonate even in Central America and the Caribbean. The aspirations of Black boys in Santo Domingo are not much different from those of youth in New York City. Though articulated differently and complicated by history and geography, they all play with the same goal in mind: to escape challenging conditions and reach a better life—*para llegar* (to make it). Nike and other athletic brands, along with the broader basketball industry, depend on their labor and the lack of access to upward social mobility for many of these young athletes (Runstedtler 2018). Black men and boys, no matter their nationality—whether African American, Panamanian, Nigerian, or Black British—have become prime brand ambassadors for companies like Nike. These companies are less concerned with the politics of Blackness and its articulation as a real or not real racial identity. What matters is their ability to sell a product. They care about the *aesthetic* of Blackness.

The 2017 U17 Centrobasket tournament featured squads from Panama, the Dominican Republic, Guyana, Jamaica, Puerto Rico, and others. Each nation-state, or colony in Puerto Rico's case, has its particular history of how race has been articulated and promoted in the national and public discourse. Nonetheless, all of these places share a history shaped by the trafficking of Africans for enslavement, which continues to manifest in structures of racialized labor, including within basketball. Centrobasket is where racialized discourse comes to a head with the athletic industrial complex (AIC) (E. Smith 2014).

In return for offering racialized youth opportunities, FIBA gains access to talented players to keep its organization running, and many of these players come from countries with few resources or opportunities that offer a comparable level of competition. Additionally, FIBA's global partnership with Nike ensures that Nike will dominate both established and emerging markets. Nike can rely on emerging stars like Tito and his crew, plastered on the front pages of Panamanian newspapers following their win, to advertise its products and create brand awareness in Panama. Tournaments like Centrobasket are also spaces where people like Coach Barrigon recruit players like Tito, offering them scholarships to play abroad, though, as I have begun to unearth, there are limited protections for these youth. It is important that Centrobasket is part of the AIC, which funnels talented players and their labor to the NBA and other professional basketball leagues. The pageantry of international athletic competitions and the spirit of nationalism are used as key components to get countries to excitedly support these types of tournaments.

The absence of visibly African-descended players on Mexico's team at the 2017 U17 Centrobasket tournament highlights the role of international sporting competitions as places where ideas about the nation are reinforced through the intentional inclusion or exclusion of certain individuals. Afro-Mexicans and Indigenous people have been excluded from sports due to geographic isolation and racism. In 2021, after constant agitation by activists, Mexico passed legislation to include Black and Indigenous groups in sporting spaces and redistribute resources (Senado de la República 2021).

On the court, racial discourse and identity politics matter. Centrobasket and FIBA understand these kids as Black and depend on Black labor for their machines to work. For them, these tournaments are a way to obtain, show, develop, and exploit Black talent for a fraction of the cost compared to African American males. At the same time, FIBA does not care about the racial politics of the different countries. However, racial politics do matter and have material consequences for how these boys come to participate in the competitions representing their countries and for what challenges they encounter as Black males attempting to migrate from their countries.

Centrobasket's Importance to Tito

"If you are a basketball player and over the age of eighteen and you haven't left Panama, you don't have much of a future in the sport," Tito once told me.

He had heard it repeated over and over by his coaches. In 2017 he was turning seventeen, and his clock was ticking. Panama was his home, the place that had shaped him into who he was. He had traveled within and outside its borders, representing his province at both national and international tournaments. By age sixteen he had already left the country, something neither his father nor his mother had ever experienced. While Panama was his home, it was not where he envisioned his basketball future. His eyes were set on *el norte*, the United States. He knew he had to go. Although the United States did not compete in Centrobasket, it was still heavily represented. Many US blue-chip recruits with ties to Central American and Caribbean nations played for various national teams.

Tito was seen by Josue's US coach, Coach Barrigon, a Mexican national, during Centrobasket, and he was offered an opportunity to play basketball at the same private school in La Frontera, Texas. Time was not on his side. He was promised the scholarship on the condition he could pass the English admission test. Tito's potential to enter and succeed in the US basketball system was never in doubt due to his basketball skills. However, his main concern was whether he could triumph in the system given his lack of English proficiency. More important, his future success in the United States was tied to whether he could meet the academic standards required to qualify for the NCAA.

Tito knew this well. His coach in Panama, Juan Mendoza, who had orchestrated the deal with the coach in Texas, was fully aware of the constraints. In a text message conversation, Coach Barrigon explained the conditional nature of the offered scholarship and the centrality of English in the process: "And all conditional on him being able to pass the entrance exam because I doubt that in 2 years, he will be able to learn enough English to go on to graduate and go to university. . . . Josue is in the same process. If he DOESN'T learn English, it will complicate everything. His size and his little offense that this year I want him to produce more. But coach you know they have to focus on English if they want to succeed in this country" (personal communication, October 2017).

Going to La Frontera was not the first time basketball had enabled Tito to change schools beyond his borders. Basketball had already taken him to a private school in Panama City. He was recruited to Colegio Bolivariano by Coach Mendoza, who not only was the school's coach but also ran a basketball academy in which most of the school's players, including Tito, participated. However, it was not enough. Besides lacking the level of basketball competition he needed to showcase his abilities to US coaches, Bolivariano was a Spanish-language school. A Spanish-language education holds very little weight in becoming eligible to compete at the NCAA Division I level. The NCAA required all SAT and ACT exams to be taken in English, and Tito didn't speak English. US high school basketball lowered the bar of entry for Tito. By entering the United States in high school, he would face fewer regulatory barriers. Ideally, he would spend enough time in the United States to learn English, achieve a decent SAT or ACT score, and become eligible to play college basketball. At the very least, he would circumvent the TOEFL or other exams measuring academic English skills, required for college admissions, provided he graduated from a US high school. The TOEFL is a standardized test that assesses the English language proficiency of nonnative speakers wishing to enroll in English-language universities. However, by receiving a US high school diploma, Tito could, in theory, demonstrate his English proficiency and bypass the TOEFL. The NCAA eligibility rules are virtually the same for all aspiring international student-athletes, but they do not impact all populations equally. For certain youth like Tito—Black youth and other youth of color from the Global South, particularly those from non-English-speaking countries—entering the United States earlier can be advantageous. However, their earlier entry into a less regulated system also makes them more vulnerable to exploitation due to their status as minors. The NBA, NCAA, and US college basketball dictate the movement of global basketball (Chepyator-Thomson et al. 2016).

How Eligibility Rules Lead to Migration

Not only did Panamanian youth like Tito have to travel to the United States to be seen by coaches and compete against better talent, but they also needed a way to navigate the US intercollegiate athletics eligibility standards. Waiting until they graduated from high school was not an option—they would not qualify or be eligible to play intercollegiate basketball in the United States. Where would Tito have learned English to the level required to achieve a decent score on the SAT, ACT, or TOEFL? Many youth from the Global North, particularly those who are English speakers or have been academically trained in English, do not face these barriers. However, in Panama Tito lacked both the exposure to a developed youth basketball program and the academic infrastructure necessary to make him eligible to compete in the United States.

The US intercollegiate basketball system, particularly the NCAA, is complicit in pushing international interscholastic migration and producing basketball trafficking among certain groups. The NCAA helps establish the standards and flow of migration for basketball talent worldwide, serving as a natural and consistent feeder system for the NBA. However, new pathways are emerging as alternatives. For example, programs like the NBA G League Ignite and Overtime Academy now provide viable options for highly talented NBA prospects. These pathways allow a select few to hone their skills, receive compensation, and gain other educational benefits. These models have emerged alongside the NCAA's adoption of an interim Name, Image, and Likeness (NIL) policy that went into effect July 1, 2021, which refers to the rights of college athletes to control and profit from their name, image, and likeness (Hosick 2021). The NCAA is a business, and so are its more than 1,200 member conferences and institutions, which provide tens of thousands of athletes roster spots annually. The changing legal landscape, including California's 2019 Fair Pay to Play Act, which prohibited the NCAA from punishing athletes who benefited from their NIL (Wetzel 2023), has forced the NCAA to adjust its policies to remain competitive and maintain its revenue streams. As of 2021 NCAA student-athletes have been able to profit from NIL deals, marking a significant departure from the NCAA's long-standing stance on amateurism.

Additionally, as of 2023 the NCAA has officially removed the SAT and ACT from eligibility requirements, though individual schools can still request them. Removing the exams as eligibility criteria is another way for the NCAA to be competitive in this changing world. It widens their recruiting pools and attractiveness to prospective athletes as it removes a barrier to those who may not obtain the necessary scores to be eligible for NCAA-governed athletics.

However, NCAA student-athletes and prospective college athletes stand to benefit greatly from participating in traditional intercollegiate athletics. Many NCAA basketball players go on to secure professional contracts overseas, with European leagues often serving as prime destinations. It serves as the guaranteed exposure that players need, and it is a vetted system. Yet the NCAA—and, more broadly, most athletics in the United States—is deeply intertwined with the US education system. That's the added layer of complexity that most other professional sports do not contend with (Sekot and Pětivlas 2014).

Tito did not fully understand the complexities of being a college basketball player in the United States beyond the simple fact that he needed to be in school. His ignorance of the United States' intricate interscholastic and intercollegiate systems prevented him from realizing that his need to become spatially mobile before his eighteenth birthday was being shaped by the very system he saw only on television during the occasional NCAA March Madness broadcast in Panama.

Much later, in 2019, Tito and I discussed the departures of Josue and his other Panamanian friends and teammates who had gone to the United States. A bit flustered as he tried to recall the details, Tito ran through the timeline of all the players who had traveled from Colón to Colegio Bolivariano in Panama City and then to *el norte* to pursue their American hoop dreams.

"Sí, mira cuando llegué al Bolivariano el mismo año acabándose el año, Salazar se fue a los Estados Unidos y Jaron y Josue también" (Yes, look when I got to Bolivariano that same year as it was ending, Salazar went to the United States and Jaron and Josue also), Tito said.

"And what about Yohanis?" I asked Tito, inquiring about Yohanis Zavala, one of Tito's good friends I had met in Panama City.

With a look of teenage annoyance, he responded, "Sí" (Yes).

"But wasn't he there when you were there?"

"Sí, pero él no estuvo en el Bolivariano cuando estuvo Salazar, Jaron, Josue, ni Overton" (Yes, but he was not in the Bolivariano when Salazar, Jaron, Josue, or Overton were there), Tito replied.

Jonathan Salazar Young, as Tito mentioned, was already on his way out of Colegio Bolivariano by the time of Tito's arrival. He had secured an opportunity to go to *el norte*.

"But not long after, a high school coach watched him play in Panama. Two weeks later, that coach approached Salazar with an offer to play high school ball in Las Vegas," a Long Beach, California, newspaper reported about Salazar's discovery (Grosbard 2018). Contrary to what was reported in the newspaper, however, Salazar's story was more like Tito's. He was not simply discovered or randomly spotted playing basketball somewhere in Panama. Instead, ever since his mother had encouraged him to try basketball, Jonathan Salazar had been hustling up and down both Panamanian and international courts, perfecting his craft. Since his preteen years, the Federación Panameña de Baloncesto (FEPABA; Panamanian Basketball Federation) had selected him to compete in international competitions like

Centrobasket. He, too, made the daily trek across the isthmus to Colegio Bolivariano in Panama City. By the time he was on his way to Las Vegas with an F-1 student visa in hand, migrating for basketball and educational opportunities had already become his norm. He was deeply embedded in the North American basketball industrial complex.

"At first I thought it was just basketball. And then I changed my mind and said, it's not only basketball. It's basketball, school, your personality. Basketball has changed me. Playing soccer, that was another Jonathan," Salazar said in his more developed accented English in a media interview (Grosbard 2018). He went on to explain that being in a US high school had helped him improve his English and increase his chances of being recruited to play college basketball.

Ironically, Salazar did not first encounter English when he arrived in Las Vegas. He inherited his second surname, Young, from his mother, an English teacher in Panama's public schools. Like Tito Brown's, their surname also pointed to a history of West Indian migration to the isthmus dating back to the previous century. She encouraged her son not only to try basketball but also to learn English. However, like many youths of his generation who were connected to the language through heritage, Salazar dismissed the importance of learning English, largely due to the predominance of Spanish in the country.

I have never spoken with Salazar, so I do not know the extent of his experience at that first Las Vegas high school. But as I looked through the online content I found about him, it appeared that Salazar had stayed in Las Vegas for only one year before transferring to another private high school, this time in California.

Was he not getting what the school had promised? Was he having problems with his coach? Or did he want more exposure or a different opportunity? These are questions we do not have answers to at this moment. What is certain, however, is that for whatever reason, he felt the need to leave the school and transfer to another.

"I am working hard for my mother, that I finished high school and I am about to start college. I know she's very happy," Salazar said in a news report profiling his time in California (Lago 2018) as he signed his NCAA Division I letter of intent.

Salazar's migration to the United States proved to be a success, if success is measured solely by making it to a US college team and, more specifically, securing an NCAA Division I basketball scholarship. His accented English, evident when he responded to reporters' questions, showed that he had acquired the level of English needed for NCAA eligibility while in the United States. After receiving an NCAA scholarship, he spent some time at the Division I level before transferring to a community college. At the time of this writing, Salazar is competing at an HBCU in an NCAA Division II program. I hope he receives a degree from one of the colleges he has attended. His story is still unfolding.

Then there's Iverson "El Fenomenal" Molinar Jones.

"Everyone was like, we need to see this 'phenomenal,'" Leyza Jones de Molinar, Iverson's mother and an acquaintance of Tito's mother, Katia, said.

Leyza and Katia knew each other from Panama's youth basketball scene. Their children, less than one year apart in age, were and are heralded as some of the best basketball players in the country. At the time of this writing, Iverson is one of the most successful basketball contemporaries of Tito, who also journeyed from the Panamanian isthmus to pursue his American hoop dreams. Iverson now competes in the United States and Mexico City in the NBA G League.

Before he departed Panama, as a preteen, Iverson earned the nickname "el fenomenal" (the phenomenal) because of his exceptional talent on the basketball court. Much earlier than Tito, Iverson also donned the Nike-branded Panama uniforms in youth tournaments and competitions sanctioned by FEPABA and FIBA. According to a news report, unlike many other Panamanian kids, Iverson first picked up a basketball instead of a soccer ball. His parents had already destined him to play basketball. His full name is Iverson Latrell, chosen in homage to NBA Hall of Famers Allen Iverson and Latrell Sprewell, a reflection of the cultural influence of basketball among Black communities worldwide.

Iverson's early entry into basketball proved to be a positive force in his career, as he gained exposure early on and was getting known in basketball circuits. Tito, in contrast, faced more limited opportunities because he entered Panama's basketball networks as an older teen. However, both Iverson and his family knew that to achieve his basketball dreams, he couldn't remain in Panama. Like Tito, Iverson moved to *el norte* on a basketball scholarship, understanding that the path to success in the sport lay in the United States.

Iverson also struggled with English when he first migrated to the United States to play interscholastic basketball but not due to a lack of contact with the language. His heritage in Panama is similar to Tito's and Jona than's, and it is reflected in his surnames, Molinar Jones. His mother speaks English, and in her youth she left Panama to play high school volleyball in the United States. Because of this, she was more familiar with the United

States and its systems. She traveled to the United States and visited Iverson at his US high schools.

"He played a few other high schools, including the one that he graduated from in Marietta, Georgia, before getting back to California to play for Coach Zedan at Veritas. There were various reasons for his constant shuffling, none of which matter now," read a news article about Iverson. "What matters is despite the relatively rocky road, Iverson still made it to a Division I university. He's having success in his first season, and anybody that has ever coached him believes that the Bulldog can make it big at the next level" (Horka 2019).

I cannot speculate what made Iverson's experience "rocky," as stated by the journalist. However, jumping straight to him making it to a Division I university does not adequately address the "constant shuffling" and the issues this reveals about international hopefuls attending high school on F-1 student visas.

In four years, Iverson attended four different high schools in the United States. He went from a school in Los Angeles, California, to the school in Las Vegas, Nevada, that Jonathan Salazar first attended. Then he journeyed across the country to a school outside of Atlanta. Finally, he finished high school at a prep school back in California, where he ultimately signed a letter of intent with Mississippi State University, a major NCAA Division I basketball program. He was successful.

Nevertheless, gaining recognition in the vast world of US high school basketball is a tricky endeavor. As the journalist alluded to with the reference to Iverson's "relatively rocky road," the desire or need to move between high schools as an international player is fraught with challenges and risks. If not managed carefully, transferring between schools can lead to migratory and eligibility issues. While it might seem alarming that Iverson attended a different high school each year in the United States, constant movement has become the norm in US prep basketball. College basketball prospects often switch schools annually, and it's not uncommon for a high school player to have attended three, four, or even five different schools or programs before graduating.

Even though constant shuffling is common and accepted in the world of US prep basketball, I contend that we are neglecting an underlying issue. We don't always know why kids leave one school for another. The general assumption is that these athletes are migrating to get known or increase their exposure in order to secure the next opportunity. Yet that is not always the case, as we see with Tito. Some players are moving schools for reasons of safety and well-being, but there are limited mechanisms in place to assess or address those experiences when they change schools. This lack of oversight raises important questions about the vulnerabilities and challenges these athletes face as they navigate an often unstable system.

We must also consider how constant shuffling impacts the schooling experiences of these international youth. Elaine Allard (2015) argues that the 1.25 generation international high school students in the United States—many of whom can be categorized as global youth—have unique educational experiences and needs. Who is attending to these learners' needs as they move through different schools? In Iverson's last school, for instance, they received virtual education before the global COVID-19 pandemic. The question becomes: Do these schools have the resources to adequately support English language learners? Very little scholarly research has attempted to make sense of the interscholastic experiences of Black male athletes in the United States (May 2007; Brooks 2009; Adeyemo 2022, 2023), and there is even less about the experiences of international Black male athletes in migration in US secondary schools.

Salazar and Iverson are one year older than Tito, but they were involved in Panama's official basketball networks, getting known, before Tito. Their earlier entries into these networks made a significant difference, as they had more time to make it to the United States before turning eighteen. They entered US high schools at fourteen and fifteen, whereas Tito was nearly seventeen years old. Coaches from around the globe had seen Salazar and Iverson at international competitions since 2014, when they competed on the Panamanian under-fifteen national team (U15). Despite this exposure they still needed to leave Panama to compete at the heart of the game in the United States. English was a principal reason for this need to migrate during high school.

However, historically, they are all connected to the English language and had some familiarity with it before needing it for NCAA eligibility. For these athletes, English appears not only on the back of their Panamanian jerseys but also on their birth certificates and report cards through their surnames, which trace back to their Black English-speaking ancestors who migrated to the Panamanian isthmus due to earlier waves of US imperialism and neocolonialism. Their use—or lack of use—of English in Hispanic Panama reflects a deeper, ongoing struggle they continue to face as descendants. This struggle is tied to navigating issues of race, upward mobility, and connection to the US empire, now manifesting in barriers like NCAA eligibility standards. These athletes' lives highlight how the legacy of colonialism and race continues to shape their experiences and opportunities in the present.

US high schools and basketball academies attracted athletes like Salazar and Iverson stateside because of US basketball's global neocolonial hegemonic positioning. Salazar and Iverson dreamed of competing in college basketball; the earlier the entry, the better. I argue that their success was partially due to timing, combined with the fact that they were on official basketball pathways sponsored by FIBA earlier than Tito and entered the United States at a younger age. This gave them more time to be seen, face challenges in "bad" schools, have rocky experiences, and shuffle between schools to find better opportunities. By the time it was Tito's turn, he was nearing the age of seventeen and graduation, with little to no formal English training. He did not have the time or flexibility to navigate the complex world of US high school basketball. Instead, he jumped at the first opportunity that came his way through Centrobasket.

English and the Panamanian Nation

"Alcanzamos por fin la victoria [We finally achieved victory], / en el campo feliz de la union [in the happy field of union]; / Con ardientes fulgores de gloria [With blazing blazes of glory] / ¡Se ilumina la nueva nación! [The new nation is illuminated!]" slipped from their mouths as they stood on the baseline in a line singing Panama's national anthem. As they stood draped in their country's colors, Tito was singing for a country where he knew he could not remain. They were singing to the nation they were all striving to leave in pursuit of their basketball dreams. Centrobasket represented one of the few opportunities when Black youth could step outside the shadows of being marginalized within their own country, even if only for a limited time. It's one of the few times and spaces where their citizenship is not questioned because it benefits national interests. Scholars (see Hawkins 2017; Gill et al. 2020) have elucidated that Black athletes are afforded full rights to citizenship only when the larger society stands to gain more. Centrobasket was an opportunity to evade what Panamanian society had constructed Black males from Colón to be. But even as they celebrated the victory of raising Panama's name high, that moment could not shield them from the anti-Blackness that awaited them in the United States. For the lucky few like Tito, heading to *el norte* still meant navigating the US im-

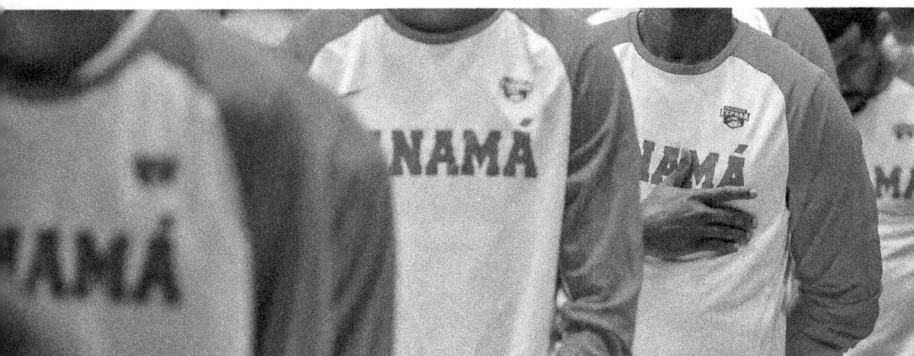

FIGURE 1.1. Panama basketball players in shooting shirts during the playing of the Panamanian national anthem at an international competition.

migration process and confronting the realities of being Black male Spanish speakers in a foreign land.

Panama's national stance on the English language has never truly been about the language itself but rather about what English represents racially. English has represented a racialized Black Other, a barely tolerated foreigner. The irony is that Black Panamanian basketball players, particularly those of West Indian descent, need to know English to achieve upward social mobility. It would seem from the way English has been framed that no one would want to speak the language. However, that is not the case either historically or in the present. Some Panamanians believed that West Indians were stealing jobs from them that emerged from the North American imperial project, which was supported by the mostly white Panamanian elite, *los rabiblancos*. My father was propositioned for servitude by the white Panamanian family for his English abilities. They were just as invested in obtaining opportunities within the US Panama Canal Zone and taking advantage of opportunities in the United States. Olmedo Alfaro's (1925) *El peligro antillano en la América Central* (The dangerous Antillean in Central America) highlights that white and mestizo Panamanians held Black West Indians in contempt not because they spoke English but rather because they were Black. Alfaro states that Panamanians were denied the opportunity to learn English and obtain these positions. He was not against US imperialism. He was against Black migrants who immigrated to Panama because of US imperialism. Many Panamanian presidents and members of elite society, both past and present, have studied at US colleges and universities. Many never considered remaining in Panama to be educated at the post-tertiary level.

The historical discourse surrounding Black West Indians "taking over" or colonizing parts of Central America, as promulgated by figures like Olmedo Alfaro, played a crucial role in fueling violence against Black people in Panama. This hysteria or moral panic deeply impacted the lives of all Black people. It was never about the English language. The same way that Justo Jaén was murdered by Panamanian police because he was perceived as a West Indian, the violence continues to impact the lives of all Black Panamanian youth regardless of their Black ethnicity (De Paulis 2007). Jaén was understood as a subject to be killed because he was a foreigner, he was a thief of the nation, he was not the nation. This discourse legitimized and justified state-sanctioned abuse, which continues into the present, as Black boys and young men like Tito are marked as the criminal Other and, as such, have less access to opportunities to improve their lives.

The irony is that Black Panamanians, many of whom have Black West Indian ancestry, like Tito, fill the rosters of the most visible teams on international stages. However, this has not always been the case. During the large Black West Indian migration to the country, there were barriers that sometimes made it difficult and other times impossible for Black migrants and native-born Black Panamanians to represent the country in international competitions. Such was the case for Delmira Pierce, a Black woman basketball player. She became known as the *ciclón del Caribe*, or the Cyclone of the Caribbean, for her dominant skills, which led Panama to its first gold medal in basketball at the 1938 Central American and Caribbean Games. Subsequently, Panamanian officials barred her from representing the country in following international tournaments because she was *negra* (black). Today Black Panamanians constitute the majority on the basketball rosters. They leave it all on the court for a country that makes it challenging to carve out dignified lives for themselves. Basketball is a tool for highly talented Black Panamanian players to achieve upward social mobility for themselves and their families. Still, the other irony that surfaced, at least in Tito's life, is the centrality of the English language. His Black West Indian heritage associated with English was one of the things that mainstream Panamanian society ostracized, targeted, discriminatorily called *chombo* (a Panamanian pejorative used against Black Panamanians, specifically those of anglophone West Indian descent), and historically forced other Black West Indians and their descendants to relinquish to be falsely part of the Hispanic nation. But English is the exact thing Tito needed to make it to the United States, and it dictated his subsequent entry and experience there.

Conclusion

The Centrobasket tournament sponsored by FIBA played a pivotal role in Tito's journey. He and the dozens of other youth representing their countries benefited from playing on a large international stage organized by the sport's official governing body. This tournament propelled him from being known locally in Panama, with its poor basketball infrastructure, to the United States, the pinnacle of high school basketball. As much as Tito benefited from gaining exposure and ultimately getting his opportunity to play high school basketball in the United States, FIBA and its partners benefited more. Through partnerships with FIBA, apparel brands such as Nike gain market share and increase brand awareness through their presence on participating athletes' backs, chests, and feet. Centrobasket and other tournaments are critical parts of the AIC, which utilizes Black males as its preferred laborers in the sport of basketball.

Sojourning to the United States to compete in basketball at the high school level is vital to success for youth like Tito. However, this form of athletic migration presents various challenges for noncitizen and international players headed to the United States. One of the primary challenges is English. To qualify for NCAA eligibility and gain admission to one of its member institutions, prospective athletes must prove they are proficient in academic English. In Tito's case, as a young, Black, predominantly Spanish-speaking Panamanian youth with the surname Brown, his need and ability to be competent in academic English is tied to a more extensive history of race, ethnicity, migration, imperialism, and anti-Blackness enacted through language practices. His paternal side, where he inherited his surname, comprises people of West Indian descent who spent the past century fighting to become and be recognized as full citizens in the Panamanian republic. The Panamanian state used the English and French language practices of Black migrants to construct these individuals and their descendants as pariahs and perpetual foreigners to its mestize nationalism project. Over the decades, in many historic Black English-speaking communities in Panama City and Colón, the use and teaching of English became less prevalent, as English schools were closed, and anti-Black sentiment assimilation tactics forced people to forgo the use of English in many settings.

Today Tito's story reflects the contradictions and complexities faced by many youth of West Indian heritage, particularly in Panama. Many of them do not speak English anymore. This irony is pronounced when considering

Tito's position in 2017, representing Panama in the Centrobasket tournament. As a Spanish speaker, Tito was playing for the nation his father's and grandparents' generations fought to be recognized as true citizens of. The historical struggle for recognition of Black West Indian descendants in Panama has long been tied to language, with the use (or nonuse) of English often serving as a marker of one's eligibility for full citizenship. However, knowledge of the English language is also the same thing Tito needed to access the life he desired outside of Panama.

2

CHOMBO

Language, Race, and Black (In)visibility in Panama

"¡Colón! ¡Colón! ¡Colón! ¡Hay puestos! ¡Hay puestos!" screamed the *pavo* (lit. turkey; a Panamanian idiom for bus assistant) as the brightly colored bus pulled up to the *parada* (stop). The loud plena music shifted my attention away from the boys *birriando* (casually playing with) a soccer ball on the concrete-floored court, which serves as both a basketball court and a soccer pitch. It is clear that soccer is the dominant game played on this court. Waiting for the bus at the entrance to Santa Rita, a neighborhood within one of Colón's fifteen districts that make up the urban city, is always suspenseful, since you can never be sure how many people are actually on board. The young bus assistant, hanging from the door, will always assure passersby that seats are available, whether they are or not. He'll shout, "¡Pidan permiso, señores! ¡Pidan permiso! ¡Hay espacio! ¡Córranse pa'tras!" (Say excuse me ladies and gentlemen! Say excuse me! There's space! Move toward the back!) A few people exited as we lined up to board, searching for a seat and safe passage down the *carretera* (highway). The final destination is always Colón, which people from Colón know means the central part of the city.

Before arriving at Sabanitas, one of Colón's largest districts, and making a right to enter the road leading to the province's city center, we pass the Irving Saladino housing projects. The twenty-five pastel-colored "multis" expand beyond the eye's reach. Since 2012, when the first 240 families were relocated to the project, new stores, more cars, and pedestrians have increased the traffic on the single-lane road that leads to Portobelo. I imagine that those packed in the bus alongside me must include members of the 154 families displaced from their Sixteenth Street homes in the city's center, which were demolished to expand the Colón Free Trade Zone. The same city center is written in big, bold, brightly colored letters across the bus's front window, indicating the final destination of the city's mainstay mode of transportation, *el diablo rojo*.

Diablo rojo, which translates literally as "red devil," is the colloquial name given to the old US school buses shipped to Panama and modified to reflect the style and sociopolitical history of each of their individual owners. These buses are more than just brightly colored former US school buses. They tell the story of an urban Panama that is multilayered, colorful, and resistant. The buses serve as a moving visual contestation to ideas of a homogeneous Panamanian identity. The neon-colored lines painted on nearly every inch of the bus accompany painted landscapes and portraits of social commentary and protest. They forcefully insert a Black identity (Szok 2012), which mirrors the majority of people tightly packed within.

This is no silent ride through the *carretera*, as we are driving through the sprawl of neighborhoods, small businesses, restaurants, factories, and *chinitos*—bodegas owned by Chinese Panamanian families—that makes up the urban district of Colón. Besides the visual stimulation, our ears also process the uncensored lyrics of Panama's philosophers *del ghetto*—like Colón's own Kafu Banton—booming from the bus's speakers. Nodding my head in sync with the *riddim* and looking out the open window, I am engulfed in Kafu's straightforward lyrics, laden with political messages:

¿De qué me estás hablando? [What are you talking to me about?]
Estás mintiendo [You are lying]
Tu solo te estás engañando [You're just fooling yourself]
Lo que dices no es cierto [What you are saying isn't true]

FIGURE 2.1. A *diablo rojo* bus, a principal vehicle for public transportation in Panama, decorated with colorful artwork. This one's route is from Colón City to Arco Iris. Photo by the author.

Te estoy diciendo [I am telling you]
Yo no te estoy preguntando [I am not asking you]. (Banton 2000)

Peeking out the *diablo rojo*'s window, I see young bodies running along the patch of dirt, trying to make it to the next stop. Where I step off the bus at Cable and Wireless on Thirteenth Street, dirt pitches give way to concrete lots where stately buildings once stood, now surrounded by crumbling structures and makeshift pitches. Mostly boys. Mostly Black. They beat down the pavement where wooden planks, fashioned into goals, mark the boundaries. This is Colón. It's hard to fathom that it is home to the second-largest duty-free zone in the world, much less the place that has produced so many athletic champions.

People scatter through *el Town* (the Town), the colloquial name for the sixteen streets of the city's center. They create traffic on the busy sidewalks, selling lottery tickets, fruits, vegetables, knockoff Panamanian soccer jerseys, purses, and countless other knickknacks. There are no streetlights in Colón, requiring drivers to be extra-cautious as they crowd the narrow avenues.

Construction sites, both active and abandoned, reroute vehicle traffic, lives, and the aspirations of residents, who wait on the arrival of a new city. Emptiness fills the razed lots where entire blocks once thrived. Former residents, some displaced, others now living in the single-family residences along the *carretera*, go about their daily affairs in what remains of the newly rebranded "Casco" de Colón (lit. helmet; the historic Old Quarter of Colón).

In 2014 former President Juan Carlos Varela promised a new Colón to its citizens. Since construction began that same year, and with a new presidency in place with a different set of priorities, the dream of a revitalized Colón has devolved into a nightmare. Scandals related to money mismanagement, poor planning, and shifts in presidential administration have left entire city blocks nearly vacant, with many longtime residents wondering if the "new" Colón is meant to include them—or if it was simply a ploy to displace them.

But daily business must continue. The days of US occupation in the Panamanian republic are gone, but the remnants are never too distant. The scene is picturesque. Older people give "sessions," a Caribbean English Panamanian word for gossip, by moving effortlessly between Spanish and Caribbean-accented English on Avenida Central's park benches. "¡Icing glass! ¡Icing glass! ¡Sí hay icing glass!" (Icing glass! Icing glass! Yes, there's icing glass!) is the singsong chant from the gold-toothed woman dragging her cooler full of the sea moss milk drink that costs *un dólar*. The *patties de carne* (ground beef–filled pastries) and plantain tarts sold at the Panadería de Colón (Bakery of Colón) invoke the spirits of the hundreds of thousands of Black West Indians who arrived in this port city over a century ago to construct the Panama Canal. The cracking sounds of whips, whistles, and onlookers screaming "¡Juega, diablo, juega!" (play, devil, play!), part of the Congos and Diablos traditions of some of Panama's earliest Afrodescendants, echo the historic meeting of the African diaspora in this city. Today their descendants may not be fully Afro-colonial or Afro-Antillean, but in Colón the Afro is visible. This city is forever marked, and it is evident in the speech, music, food, and athletics, as well as the crumbling state that elucidates the historical anti-Black violence forced on its residents, which meets the eye in this city.

Tucked away in the corner of the city stands the city's municipal gym, barely touched by time in a literal sense, marking the contradiction laden in the idea that Colón is the *cuna de los campeones* (the cradle of champions). Sixty years have passed without the construction of a new athletic facility in this city. As one draws nearer to the gym, the screech of basketball sneakers on the hardwood floor becomes louder. The dominance of soccer in the country cannot be felt within the confines of this gym, which bears the name of Colón's own Alfonso Teofilo "Panama Al" Brown. Panama Al Brown was a boxer who became known as the world's first "Hispanic" boxing champion. However, the irony in his "Hispanic" title was that Panama Al was also part *chombo*. His father was a formerly enslaved man from Tennessee in the United States, and his mother a Black woman from the British Caribbean. They met in Colón during the construction of the Panama Canal. Panama Al Brown's hero status was short-lived in Panama, and he found himself destitute, similar to the gym that now bears his name. This is where basketball lives in Colón. Players of all ages hustle day and night, going up and down the court practicing, shooting, and competing. The breezes off the Atlantic Ocean, which surrounds the city, tame the heat of the natural-air gym. Onlookers and fans seated in the concrete stands remain emotionally invested in every second of the quarters. Dunks on the court elicit loud "ooooohhhs," which are nothing compared to the sounds of the *barra* (cheering section). They show their support through orchestrated chants and loud drumming throughout the match. This is the world of basketball, here, on the country's Atlantic coast, tucked away in the corner of a changing city where uncertainty is the only thing guaranteed. Whole city blocks have been resettled in housing projects like Irving Saladino further down the *carretera*. Unemployment rates for youth ages nineteen to twenty-four are over 50 percent, and people have to take to the streets in protest for the ability to work. The screeching of rubber soles on hardwood floors tells this story, but only when the young people who have laced up their sneakers can speak. I took this ride to see Tito play in one of his local games before he headed to *el norte*.

Bus Ride to the US Embassy

Tito and his parents, Ruperto and Katia, rose early one morning to catch the three buses they would need to make it to the US embassy in Panama City for Tito's 8 a.m. F-1 student visa adjudication appointment in 2017. Katia was at Tito's side en route to Panama City for what they hoped would be the newest chapter in Tito's life. She had played an instrumental role in Tito getting seen as a basketball player. She created the pamphlet filled with her son's stats and photos that placed him on the radar of various recruiters. However, a splintered history in the Panamanian isthmus had predetermined the results of the day. Maybe his refusal to take his father's English lessons crossed his mind on that hot early morning, as he stood inside one of

FIGURE 2.2. Arena Panama Al Brown in Colón, Panama.

the last remaining pieces of the United States in Panama: the US embassy and consulate. Or maybe the results of the interview would have been different if West Indians, or *chombos*, as they are pejoratively called in Panama, had not been forced to stop speaking English. Or maybe the US consular officer would not have had to question Tito's proficiency in English. Even though his I-20 form, which had been rushed overnight from his school in La Frontera, Texas, stated he was proficient in the language, it was a lie. Tito was not proficient in English. But English proficiency was a requirement for applicants applying for the F-1 student visa to study in the United States.

Chombo

"My father speaks English. He tells me that his parents didn't speak Spanish well. They spoke more English than Spanish," Tito said. Tito and Katia were talking about Tito's father's heritage and his English surname, Brown. Or as Katia jokingly exclaimed, "His *chombo* name!" Ruperto Brown Ellis Sr., Tito's father and namesake, was approaching his sixtieth year of life. He had grown up in Colón on Seventh Street and Balboa, and as his wife explained, he, like all of his family and friends, was English: "All of them were English. All of them were *chombos*."

He, like Tito, which is what he calls his junior, a shortened version of Rupertito, is a quiet man. His face is stoic. His skin is Black. His hair is now gray. His son has not only his name but also his near six-foot muscular build and frame. Ruperto is a basketball player too. On his off days from Panama's shipping ports, he competes in Colón's older-adult leagues. Ruperto is Tito's father, and Tito is Ruperto's son. They were made in the same image.

Tito smiled, and I laughed, because Katia was imitating how the English they spoke sounded to her monolingual Spanish ears: "'Wachi wachi wuchu!' I didn't understand anything they were saying. Not even half of it."

And I had to ask, even though I knew the answer, "Señora Katia, is your family *chombo*?"

"No, Javier, my family isn't *chombo*. My last name is Hurtado. My father's family is from Colombia and Greece. On my mother's side, they were like *cholos* [peasant farmers], they lived by Gatun Lake. We aren't from the upper nor the lower coast. We are from the lake," she responded.

"Have you ever been there?" I asked.

"Yes, it's like a little island. Now it is in the Embera Indigenous territory. There's a cemetery, but when they flooded the lake, it erased it. My grandparents lived in that area," she responded.

Katia's family is from the center portion of Panama, which has been deeply populated by Black people. Before the construction of the Panama Canal, and more specifically, the US iteration of the project and creation of the US Panama Canal Zone, there were many Black settlements in the area. They are descendants of enslaved Africans forcibly brought to the Panamanian isthmus centuries before. *Cimarronaje* (marronage) was very common on the Panamanian isthmus and reached legendary proportions during the Spanish colonial period.

Although the lake area seems sparsely populated, before the US construction of the canal, there were a number of settlements in the "transit zone." Afrodescendants constituted a significant part of the population. For this reason, contemporarily in Panama, Black people with histories tied to the isthmus's role in the colonial slave trade are labeled *Afrocoloniales* to differentiate their histories from those of *Afroantillanos*, which has been a contentious history at times. I've always known Katia was not of West Indian descent. My assumptions about her ethnic heritage were not deceived by her skin color and physical features; she is indisputably a Black woman.

Her son's deep brown complexion is just one shade darker than hers. It is her name that denotes her ancestors' experiences of enslavement and exploitation orchestrated by the Spanish, which is labeled as *Afro-colonial*, or colloquially is described as Black Spanish, Spaniard, or *paña* in Panama: Katia Rosario Hurtado Garcia de Brown. Of course, de Brown was added once she and Ruperto married. She began to recollect when Tito's father started courting her:

"They would start speaking in English, and I didn't know what was going on," Katia said about Ruperto's family and friends. "That's how Colón was. Everyone spoke English, all of the neighbors, *cholos*, everybody! But it's lost now."

"Yeah, my family is like that," I responded. "My father told me that [Omar] Torrijos [Panamanian military leader and de facto ruler] changed that. He made everyone speak Spanish. Even the Chinese in their stores wouldn't attend to them if they didn't speak in Spanish," I added.

My father would relate the history to the very popular song "Chombo Pa'la Tienda" (Chombo goes to the store), by Fredrick Clarke, which narrates the story of a young boy named Chombo whose English-speaking mother sends him to the store to buy food for dinner. When he gets there, he must speak in Spanish, and when he returns home, he tells his mother that the Chinese store owners were making disparaging comments about her.

I related to the song. I have routinely been called *chombo* in Panama. It is not totally surprising since my last name is Wallace, and just like Brown, it means *chombo* to many people.

"*Chombo* isn't a word just to call a Black person. *Chombo* is a word to call Black people who speak English. It's the English," Katia explained.

"When someone has a *chombo* name, people think they speak English. But, imagine this, Tito, he looks *chombo* with a *chombo* name and doesn't speak English!" Katia explained about her son's inability to speak English and the confusion he caused because of his last name.

Tito interjected and exclaimed, "I am a *chombito*!," suggesting that it should be a term to describe someone like him who has an English surname but does not speak English.

I laughed, and Tito just sat there quietly with a small grin on his face because he was aware of his connection to the language, a language he had always heard and understood very well although he rarely spoke it, at least not around me. Delaying her morning errands, his mother continued to talk about Tito and English: "His father used to try and teach him English, and he would just laugh and make fun of him."

Chombo is a derogatory term historically associated with Black people of West Indian descent, currently popularly referred to as *Afroantillanos*, Afro-Antilleans, or West Indians; they are Black Panamanians with heritage from either the anglophone or francophone Caribbean. This ethnic identity is used to differentiate them from Black Panamanians who are Afro-colonial, which denotes those trafficked to the Panamanian isthmus during the transatlantic slave trade and their relationship to Spanish colonialism and Hispanic American traditions (Lowe de Goodin 2014). There's also the term *come coco* (coconut eater), which is a derogatory term to refer to Black people from the country's Caribbean coast. To truly understand the differences between and complexities of *chombo* and *come coco*, one has to understand that this difference is rooted in Afrodescendant groups with distinct colonial legacies encountering each other on the Panamanian isthmus.

Since 2010 Panama has created space for people with these various histories to identify with certain traditions and cultural expressions via the national census. However, the categorization at times runs the risk of placing Black people in a divisive binary: Afro-colonial or Afro-Antillean. Melva Lowe de Goodin (2014) warns about the danger of locating Afro-Panamanians within the binary because it feeds into the inherent racism within Panamanian *mestizaje*, which claims to exclude on the basis not of race but rather of cultural incompatibility. For instance, the historical tensions between *chombo* and *come coco* highlight the cultural differences that exist among these populations. However, the reality, as Lowe de Goodin (2014) asserts, is that whether Afro-Antillean or Afro-colonial, they are both racialized groups that have been pitted against each other to compete for limited resources in a racist space. One of the most evident spaces in Panama that illustrates this point is residential segregation. Historical Black communities in Panama's urban areas have mostly been created through a history of racist power structures. Both the Panamanian and US governments created racially segregated spaces to contain Black people. Places like Santa Ana or El Arrabal and Silver City in the US Panama Canal Zone were created as segregated enclaves that were excluded from certain services. Over time, because of disinvestment, neglect, and long-standing anti-Black racist attitudes, these communities have become known as *barrios populares*, or hoods. Today many of these areas still have large concentrations of Black people of both ethnic backgrounds living in poverty.

Further, a strict colonial-Antillean binary also obscures the historical relationships and entanglements between the two groups on the isthmus. Their fusions and the encounter of cultures on the Panamanian isthmus created a new consciousness of hybridized national and cultural identity (Mosby 2001, 179). Starting in the mid-nineteenth century, the arrival of enslaved and nonenslaved people of African descent from the British West Indies and elsewhere helped to form this hybrid culture and consciousness alongside Black people who, for centuries, had their own experiences with different forms of coloniality, imperialism, and resistance movements. Tito is situated between both. His mother is Afro-colonial, and his father is Afro-Antillean. However, they are still Black. There are cultural differences that he has experienced because of his cultural diversity, such as his father's Caribbean-accented at-home English lessons. However, there is little difference in the way Black boys, regardless of their ancestry, have been treated by the Panamanian system. Black Panamanians, and Black males in particular, are stereotyped as criminals. Even before he left Panama for the first time, when he was sixteen years old, Tito had been detained, placed in custody, and jailed for breaking curfew. The same cannot be said for many white Panamanian youth, who likely have not experienced the same consequences for doing the same things.

Ruperto Sr., my father, and the thousands of Panamanian-born descendants of Black West Indians were constantly creating their unique identities in a nation that largely believed them to be pariahs. Once General Omar Torrijos rose to power in 1968, he mobilized the long-seated sentiments of US imperialism through its control of the Panama Canal and Panama Canal Zone. One of his essential tools for mass mobilization was fostering a specific Panamanian nationalism that moved beyond the traditional race, class, and ethnic lines. Spanish took precedence. The state's emphasis on Spanish proved unfavorable for historically English-speaking Panamanian communities. For example, as Michael Aceto (2002) points out, public school instruction in Afro-Panamanian communities could be held in Panamanian Creole English before Torrijos's rise to power. However, Torrijos mandated that Spanish be the primary language of instruction in Panamanian schools, which is still the case today. Historically, English language use among Black Panamanians has been a source of discriminatory othering. The Panamanian government actively worked to eliminate the English language among Black speakers. Although English is not spoken in Panama as widely as it was in the past, historical West Indian enclaves are still associated with crime and violence. It was never about language. It was always about anti-Blackness. English was used as a smoke screen to obscure the country's commitment to anti-Black racism. Black Panamanians, regardless of their ethnic backgrounds, have been denied access to English-language education even though the white-mestize elite population, without historical connections to English, have been able to access the language. The white-mestize oligarchy benefited from the neocolonial relationship between the United States and Panama. Spanish surnames connected to the country's most prominent families are dotted throughout the yearbooks of the segregated American schools of the former Panama Canal Zone.

As my father and many others like him understood it, they were being pushed to *ser panameño*, or be Panamanian, which meant speaking Spanish. Kaysha Corinealdi (2022, 147) asserts that earlier iterations of *ser panameño* pressed for the assimilation of Afro-Caribbean Panamanians and called for collective amnesia and a presumption that *ser panameño* could subsume all past transgressions and all future problems. For Torrijos, *ser panameño* meant taking an ambivalent stance toward Panamanians of West Indian descent during the late 1960s as long as they served his interests (Steinitz 2022). George Priestley (2004) makes it clear that even though the Torrijos administration provided opportunities for Black Panamanians that were previously unavailable, the regime actively repressed Afro-Antillean political and cultural assertions and symbols of Black identity. One such measure, Priestley (2004) notes, which is still a point of tension in today's Panama, was the police arresting and cutting the Afros of young Afro-Antillean Panamanian men, especially those who had traveled to Panama from the United States.

The regime's repression of specific manifestations continued until General Torrijos saw they could benefit from the large predominantly Black Panamanian community living in the United States and take advantage of the relationship they fostered with African American activists and political leaders. Famed Panamanian athlete of West Indian descent Cirilo McSween played a crucial role in Torrijos's success in negotiating a new treaty with the United States. McSween was part of the generations of Black Panamanian athletes, preceding both my father and Tito, who sojourned to the United States on an athletic scholarship to create a life that would otherwise have been challenging to obtain for a Black Panamanian who stayed in Panama.

Language, Racism, and Visas (Applying for a Visa While Black)

"It was the same guy that gave me the three-month visa when I went to Washington. He didn't believe the scholarship was real," said Tito. "He said I didn't speak English either."

Following the denial of his visa, after the three-bus journey he had taken with his parents, Tito shared with me what the US visa consular officer told him during his visa adjudication appointment. It was the same officer who had processed a temporary visa Tito had requested and received the previous summer to travel to Washington, DC, for a basketball camp.

After Tito was recruited by Coach Barrigon and offered an athletic scholarship, he applied for an F-1 student visa to come to the United States. He was denied because he did not substantiate well enough to the consular officer that he would leave the United States when he was supposed to. The consulate issued him a 214(b) slip stating that he had not proved his intent not to remain in the United States. Tito, his parents, the coaches, and the school rushed to understand why Tito was denied the student visa.

The US Department of State's Bureau of Consular Affairs states if an applicant is refused a visa under section 214(b), it means that you

- Did not sufficiently demonstrate to the consular officer that you qualify for the nonimmigrant visa category you applied for; and/or
- Did not overcome the presumption of immigrant intent, required by law, by sufficiently demonstrating that you have strong ties to your home country that will compel you to leave the United States at the end of your temporary stay. (H-1B and L visa applicants, along with their spouse and any minor children, are excluded from this requirement.) (US Department of State, Bureau of Consular Affairs, n.d.)

In our conversation Tito mentioned that he did not have a chance to respond to the consular officer's quick assessment of him. It was just no, and he pushed the 214(b) slip through the interview window. Jackal Tanelorn and April Anderson (2019, 278) describe the 214(b) as "Because I Said So: As an apparatus of the state, the US Embassy—and specifically the US Visa Office—operates as a transnational expression of political power which disciplines not its own citizens but foreign nationals." While English is a very important part of the visa process, it is not the only factor that was used to determine Tito's intent in traveling to the United States. They wanted to know if he would be a "risk," remaining in the United States unlawfully once admitted. It was assumed that he might break the law and overstay his visa. He needed to demonstrate he had strong ties at home, which would encourage him to return when his visa expired. Racial profiling for many Black visa seekers begins in the home country. Tanelorn and Anderson (2019) suggest the irrefutable decision of the vice consul is not only steeped in but reinforced by US conceptions of the racialized immigrant, especially those from the Global South. Differently classed, raced, and gendered bodies do not have the same right to move across borders (Tanelorn and Anderson 2019). US embassies abroad are places where those differences are policed. From the moment Tito and his family walked into the US embassy, they were being racially profiled. Their entire histories on the isthmus were being read through their bodies as well as the type of clothes on their bodies and the way they wore them. Their hairstyle; his mother's long, colored nails and red hair; their mannerisms; and the accents of the Spanish they spoke were all racialized. The consular officer decided instantly who Tito was and what he was about.

US consular officers are oftentimes entry-level US Foreign Service officers who have been trained to profile visa applicants (Tanelorn and Anderson 2019). They are usually under time pressure to conduct quick interviews for a line of individuals. Looking at an applicant, a form of profiling, is used to assist officers in rendering quick decisions. Before entering the US consulate, Tito had already been raced, classed, and gendered by his own society, where poor Black boys from Colón are seen as problems. Then, when he went into the US visa office, he was still seen through those frames but with the addition of his Panamanian nationality being read as well. The US embassy's visa office in Panama City is a specific space that disciplines global movement (Neumayer 2006, 2010). A notable case, which appeared in the US courts, demonstrated how visa consular officers in Brazil were encouraged to profile applicants based on their appearance. They were to write "LP" on applications if the applicant "looked poor" (Hersch 2011). This case shows that the nonimmigrant visa adjudication process is not meritocratic. It is complex. Tito's case demonstrates that when the officer "just looked at [Tito] and said no," something additional was transpiring in that space, which impacted the visa adjudication process.

Depending on the number of people in line, visa consular officers must make quick decisions, which are often judgment calls, usually within two minutes or less. Had this officer already made his decision whether Tito would go or not? It was a judgment call. It was him and Tito. What did he see or understand about this young Black man from Colón as he approached the window? Did he see him as a person? What did this young Black man from Colón evoke within him that day? It is a strong possibility that US visa officers rely on implicit biases during the adjudication process. In turn, proving intent becomes much harder for youth like Tito, a Black male from Colón, a part of the country where US embassy personnel are often restricted from traveling due to "protests and criminal elements" (US Embassy in Panama 2020, 1). With all these mediated images and what you see daily living and working in Panama, it is possible that young Black men like Tito are not given the benefit of the doubt about returning to Panama, which is a requirement when applying for nonimmigrant visas. He was young, he was male, and he fit the profile of the "illegal immigrant."

The lack of English proficiency could have been part of the reason Tito was initially denied the F-1 student visa, but his denial and supposed failure to demonstrate strong ties to Panama were a direct result of how Black Panamanians and particularly Black Panamanians of West Indian descent have been intentionally marginalized. His inability to engage academically with English and the subsequent denial because of the lack of English proficiency cannot be disconnected from the historical racial violence that English-speaking West Indians and their Panamanian-born descendants experienced.

Of course, Tito expressed immense disappointment, frustration, and sadness. Just the three bus rides of the day could evoke such sentiments. Tito's disappointment and confusion were the culmination of many long journeys like this one that he and his family had taken over the years for him to even get to this position. During the bus rides from his home in Colón to Colegio Bolivariano, he beat the sun up every morning, but it would somehow set and rest before him every night during his cross-country journey back home. Still, he did it day in and day out. It was his ticket to go to the United States to achieve upward social mobility for himself and his family. It was also his ticket to be further melded into the basketball machine where Black boys' labor, dreams, realities, and sometimes fantasies are added to the Conveyor Belt. According to William Rhoden (2007), "The Conveyor Belt transports young athletes from innocent fun and games to clubs and specialized leagues—where they find increasingly rigorous competition and better training and coaching—and finally to colleges and pro leagues. The well-trained athletes paying fans to watch every weekend represent the finished product."

Basketball has grown and is becoming a more globalized sport. It is part of a giant athletic industrial complex (AIC) corporate machine that is not just confined to the United States. Instead, its tentacles are spread throughout the globe. The fact that Tito could not remain in Panama to achieve a basketball career is evidence of the North American and US-specific basketball industry's neocolonial relationship with the world. Through economic, political, cultural, and other pressures to control or influence other countries, especially former dependencies, the NBA and its recognized feeder systems dictate the movement of talent to the United States to increase their bottom lines. One of Tito's basketball clubs, Fade Away, created by the Mendoza brothers, has altruistic values that provide access to the sport and spoils for a select and lucky few. Yet even it is still a part of the Conveyor Belt, or AIC. Once they recognized Tito's potential, they offered him a scholarship to power-load their team. His talent, better than that of most paying youth, was his monthly contribution.

Fade Away was how Tito ended up in Colegio Bolivariano since the school's coach was one of the Mendoza brothers. He gave Tito the scholarship to attend the Panama City school, where his quick left step could shake a defender and quickly go up as he faded away from the basket in the air, which was enough to cover his tuition. His perfect execution of a defensive stance, hips dropped and knees squared, recapturing his opponent's stolen ball and pushing it coast to coast for the quick layup—just like his coast-to-coast bus rides every morning, jammed in the city's gridlock—brought him closer.

Every step, every point, and every basket he made for Fade Away and Colegio Bolivariano got him closer to adorning himself in a white Nike uniform embroidered with PANAMA on his chest at Centrobasket. It got him closer, literally and figuratively, to the core of the industry in *el norte*, so long as he could defeat or check the US visa consular officer through the small slot in the plexiglass.

Receiving an athletic scholarship was familiar to Tito. He was already on scholarship based on his athletic performances at Colegio Bolivariano in Panama City. Tech's athletic scholarship offer was part of the North American basketball industrial complex, including the NBA, the National Collegiate Athletic Association (NCAA), Nike and other athletic apparel brands, US high schools, and others' efforts to maintain their global supremacy through replenishing the supply of global talent migrating to and dreaming about coming to the United States. I argue that these predominantly North American entities are part of this complex that maintains neocolonial relationships with other parts of the world.

Once Katia informed Miss Rosalia, Tech's admissions coordinator and designated school official (DSO) in La Frontera, via voice note, about Tito's denial and the rationale he communicated from the US embassy in Panama, Rosalia immediately drafted a letter. The new letter, on Tech's letterhead, detailed Tech's interest in Tito's athletic abilities and their commitment to helping him learn English. "At this moment, Tito is not fluent in English, thus we will assign a personal tutor that will help Tito with his mastery of the English language (plus another foreign language that is mandatory). He will also have ESL classes that will help in the transition to a new academic setting. We are very interested in helping Ruperto Brown Hurtado become a responsible, educated young man that will be a productive member of his community" (Tech's letter to US embassy, personal communication, 2017).

Tech wanted Tito. They took the necessary steps to ensure they could have him in La Frontera as quickly as possible, even if that meant being deceitful, as we would later find out. There was an upcoming tournament in La Frontera, and Coach Barrigon desperately wanted Tito to compete to increase their odds of winning.

Tito was at the US embassy in Panama because Tech had offered him institutional aid through an athletic scholarship. They did not shy away from using athletics as their principal qualification to grant him admission and a scholarship offer, giving him partial institutional aid. Many US high schools, like Tech, have offered international players scholarships, often framed as aid.

Although it might not seem like it, Tech's athletic scholarship, or athletic grant-in-aid, representative of a more extensive intercollegiate athletic system in the United States, is also rooted in imperialism and neocolonialism. Kwame Nkrumah (1968, 4) argues that "'aid to a neo-colonial state is merely a revolving credit, paid by the neo-colonial master, passing through the neo-colonial state and returning to the neo-colonial master in the form of increased profits," and athletic scholarships are similar. Tech offered Tito a partial athletic scholarship that would bring him to the United States, the center of the basketball industry, which ultimately expanded Tech's chances of winning and increasing their enrollment. Recruiting young athletes and offering aid ultimately provides a larger recruiting pool of more "developed talent" for US-based intercollegiate basketball and the professional ranks.

However, what does Panama get? As Joseph Maguire and John Bale (1994) stated, while players gain personally from education and employment opportunities in the Global North, the benefits for the nations donating these talented players are limited. Billy Hawkins (2010), although referencing African American athletes, fleshes out the neocolonial relationship that NCAA athletics has with Black athletes. He compares them to oscillating migrants, explaining, "To use these skills and talents, Black athletes and oscillating migrant laborers must relocate to different locations and contract their talents out to these institutions" (128). They must move far from the home community that invested the resources to develop their talent, including spending their limited monetary resources to pay the US visa appointment fees without any guarantee of success. They receive the least in the end. In Tito's case, they paid the bus fares, as well as the costs of missing work and school, for a short appointment with lasting consequences.

Avitus Agbor (2021) argues that a lack of reciprocity makes migration to the Western world a drainage pipe through which Western nations collect African financial resources through exorbitant fees and processes. The same was true for Tito in Panama. When the consular officer denied his application, the monetary resources invested in the application fees went to the United States. Combined with the uncertainty and multiple attempts it often takes to obtain a visa, all of which costs money, it is part of the neocolonial relationships the US basketball industry (AIC) maintains with the Global South.

The United States consumed a lot of Tito's family's resources, and also mine, as I committed to paying the new application fee so that Tito could gather more evidence and try again. The US consular officer held power over Tito's future without the responsibility of everything that went into him being offered a scholarship to Tech, which harks back to Nkrumah's (1968) position on neocolonialism being the worst form of imperialism. He said that for those who practice it, it means power without responsibility, and for those who suffer from it, it means exploitation without redress.

It is hard to make Panama, as a nation, a complete victim within these neocolonial relationships, as historical and contemporary relationships and situations have placed Tito and his young, primarily Black peers in this situation. Tito and his peers were acting in accordance with what Robert Millington (2010) eloquently argues about international youths' decisions to migrate from the Global South to play basketball in the United States. They use "their agency to make individual decisions about if and where to move, but they do so within a political, economic, and historical context that actively shapes the choices available" (Millington 2010, 99). Tito's decision to further embed himself in the AIC on the Conveyor Belt by leaving includes Panama's long history of anti-Blackness and the ways Black people used sport and migration on the isthmus to combat anti-Blackness and forge opportunities for themselves.

Basketball players are not born. They are made. With his talent Tito learned the sport and progressed through different levels of the game. In addition to fueling the AIC, Tito learned about basketball culture. He learned about the synergy between basketball and Black culture, specifically African American urban culture. When his father introduced him to basketball, he introduced him to the world of their Panamanian ancestors, primarily those of West Indian origins, and the ties they had forged with African Americans to create pathways to achieve upward social mobility through sport (J. Wallace 2023). Black basketball culture in the United States resonates with Black youth worldwide (James 2003; Ralph 2007; Aladejebi et al. 2022). Basketball is powerful because it allows Black youth to be seen, feel heard, and talk back. In its origins and early development, I argue that basketball provides "something" to Black people as the Other, not just fuel for or pieces in the Global North's AIC Conveyor Belt. As Janice Brace-Govan and Hélène de Burgh-Woodman (2008) argue, a postcolonial theoretical oeuvre offers a nuanced stance that gives voice to the history of the Other and recognition to their stories where we can shift from the dominating view of imperialism, even as we know it is actively working.

Racism at a Private School in Panama City

The visit to the US embassy was not the first time Tito had been racially profiled and judged while traversing boundaries in search of his hoop dreams. The distance separating the district of Colón from Panama City is roughly fifty miles. However, this short distance between the two terminal cities of the country cannot account for the large cultural differences and racialized experiences that Tito and the other youth from Colón, who traveled round trip daily, faced in their new private school in Panama City.

The long journeys and the new, predominantly mestize school were a physically and emotionally draining experience for Tito. He offered only "tired" when talking about his experiences in Colegio Bolivariano. It was not difficult to understand how beginning the day at 4 a.m. in order to take a series of buses between two provinces through extreme traffic could lead to exhaustion. Every morning, at least in his first year, he would make this journey with four other Black teenagers from Colón.

"Los niños eran diferentes de aquí en Colón" (The kids there were different than those here in Colón), Tito said. Colegio Bolivariano is a private school tucked between hospitals and restaurants filled with nurses in scrubs on lunch breaks in the heart of Panama City's medical district. It lets families with resources avoid the Panamanian public schools, which many believe offer a lower-quality education. It's definitely not among the city's most elite institutions, but they invest in their athletic programs and recruit talented athletes like Tito. At Bolivariano, Tito and his teammates were mainly the only Black students among the majority-mestize middle-class students. Bolivariano's student body was very racially different from his high school in Colón.

Being physically tired was only one part of being at Colegio Bolivariano. Tito was tired of the othering treatment he and his other Black teammates from Colón experienced daily there. He was experiencing the racial battle fatigue that William Smith and colleagues (2016) describe happens when hypervisible Black males experience hypersurveillance in predominantly white educational spaces in the United States. But in Panama City, where the majority are mestize individuals, Tito's hypervisibility as a Black bas-ketball player from Colón, and their hypersurveillance of him, caused his fatigue. Becoming the Other in their Panama City school meant being subjected to racialized discriminatory treatment, or what I label as racial-ized violence, at the hands of teachers and fellow schoolmates. Tito strug-gled to accurately describe his thoughts on the treatment he and the other students from Colón (all of whom played basketball) received in their new private school in downtown Panama City: "Los profesores son como más . . . no sé, no sé cómo decirlo. Como que a nosotros de Colón nos mira-ban diferentes" (The teachers are more . . . I don't know, I don't know how to say it. It's like us from Colón, they would look at us differently").

Once Tito was able to find the words to best reflect his thoughts on being "looked at differently" by his new teachers, he went on to explain, "Como si tuvieran miedo de que nosotros le íbamos a hacer algo" (It was like they were scared that we were going to do something to them).

Immediately, Tito and the rest of the young men from Colón who had enacted their agency, become spatially mobile, and enrolled in a new school far away from their Atlantic coast homes for basketball purposes became the criminalized Others. Their mere presence invoked fear for per-sonal safety among the adults charged with providing them with a sup-posedly better-quality education than they would otherwise have had in Colón. Also, this fear that the Black boys from Colón would react violently in some form against their classmates weighed negatively on Tito's experi-ence in this new educational space.

The only rationale Tito had as to why they were treated this way by the teachers and classmates was "porque ellos piensan que todas personas de Colón son problemáticos, pandilleros" (because they think that all people from Colón are problem-prone, gangsters). These are the stereotypes that have historically constructed Colón City as a deficient place where crime and deviance run rampant (Amen Strayhorn 2014).

The stereotypical perception in the Republic of Panama is that both the Province of Colón and its urban district, the City of Colón, are the Black space in the country. In fact, the most recent census numbers in 2010 confirm the commonsensical notion that Colón is a largely Black space in the country where residents descend from *Afrocoloniales* who mostly arrived as enslaved laborers through the transatlantic slave trade orchestrated by the Spanish Crown as well as from *Afroantillanos* who arrived as non-enslaved laborers to aid in the construction of large projects such as the Panama Canal.

Being from Colón renders them a threat in the eyes of their Panama City teachers and classmates. More so, Tito and the other basketball-playing youth from Colón had to make sense of themselves in a foreign space as they were seen and treated as a concern for the personal safety of the teachers and students in the building. What Tito remembers from his time at Colegio Bolivariano in Panama City reflects the double consciousness that *Colónites* (individuals from Colón) must navigate in their everyday lives in the Panamanian republic.

Being *Colónese*: (In)visibility Is Both a Noun and a Verb

To be *Colónese*, a person from Colón, is to locate oneself within a paradigm of (in)visibility where what makes you hypervisible also renders you invisible. It is the constant engagement to shred the cloak of invisibility that your Blackness produces—whether you are a Black person or not. Blackness becomes a domain, both a verb and a noun (Cox 2015). It is a person, place, or thing, and it is an action. Colón, in this sense, becomes interchangeable with the word *negro*. Therefore, when people proclaim "no todo en Colón es malo" (not everything in Colón is bad), what is to be understood is the claim that not all Black people are bad. It is an attempt to dispel stereotypes and force recognition of historical and systemic racism, which has denied countless generations the opportunity to be seen and treated as fully human. This is the duality of being *Colónese*. You cannot just be; you also must do to preserve your humanity. You are forced to take to the streets to protest injustices. You must proclaim your spirit as a warrior, chain yourself to the gates of the Colón Free Trade Zone, and demand employment. You must burn tires, police cars, and abandoned buildings to exclaim that your resistance cannot be defined. You must excel in sport to be recognized. And sometimes, to be seen, you must migrate, but you never stop being *Colónese*.

This double consciousness that Tito was made to employ and navigate daily as a teenage Black boy from Colón who was in Panama City pursuing basketball opportunities is emblematic of the issues Black urban boys in Panama must contend with. In particular, this relates to the criminalization of Black males and their interactions with the country's law enforcement, which is probably the most tense relationship that young Black men must navigate in their daily lives. Their entire existence is surrounded by law enforcement officials. Their neighborhoods are overpoliced. They experience and witness institutionalized violence daily. Their bodies are always subject to be detained and exhibited publicly. In a report highlighting the racialized policing of youth in Panama, the United Nations International Children's Emergency Fund (2018, 48) found that predominantly Black areas experience much higher rates of militaristic policing, and Black youth are often detained.

These public forms of racialized violence become normalized in the Panamanian psyche. When Black Panamanians mention or highlight this type of racial discrimination, this generally brings little to no recourse. In the name of *panameñidad*, we are forced to think of the nation before ourselves, and mentioning racism is segregating/separating ourselves from a unified Panamanian people. Many parts of the white-mestize Panamanian majority have normalized this type of racial violence. They have been socialized to believe in a meritocratic society where Black and other impoverished and marginalized people have violent encounters with law enforcement and the larger society because *son flojos* (they are lazy). There are beliefs that Black and marginalized people are looking for handouts, seeking to have the government maintain them. The racialization of crime tied to *barrios populares* (urban ghettos), and the dehumanizing language often employed by the media when referring to barrio dwellers, serves to justify their treatment and dehumanization. Principally, the non-Black public does not view the violence waged on Black youth in the country as wrong. It is believed that law enforcement must *proteger y servir*, or "protect and serve," the local populace, shielding them from these parasitic monsters within the society. Barrio dwellers and Black men in general must accept the abuse at all levels. They have not been constructed as full humans worthy of having feelings or obtaining justice, as their lack of participation in society does not give them the right to complain.

Conclusion

The intersection of language and racism contributes to the challenges Tito and other youth like him encounter in their journeys to playing high school basketball in the United States. Unequal relations and their historical development in the current world are at the core of the issue (Amen Strayhorn 2014). This chapter demonstrates that the English language, while required for basketball migration and used to determine intent within the F-1 student visa process, cannot be disconnected from the history of Panama and the United States and the large Black West Indian workforce. During the construction of the Panama Canal and afterward, those who remained continued to face widespread racial hostility and discrimination. The English language was often employed to mask a deeply rooted anti-Black rhetoric that has been in existence on the isthmus since race-based slavery was introduced in the sixteenth century.

The systematic erasure of English and promotion of Hispanic American ideals through a very particular type of populism and nationalism that emerged during the Torrijos era, particularly the use of Spanish as a pseudo-assimilation tool, as my father recalled, fundamentally shaped the Black Panamanian experience from then until the present. These historical occurrences, which still linger in the present, interact negatively with the hegemonic dominance of the United States in the current basketball industry. The negative interaction manifests itself as a push factor in the US basketball industry's inextricable connection with the United States' English-medium education system. A less developed basketball infrastructure in the region and lack of exposure pushes capable youth toward the United States. However, this migration must be facilitated by the F-1 student visa system because of the NCAA's hold over the basketball industry.

The US education system has been the most secure pathway to a professional basketball career in the world. As such, those who would encounter more difficulty in becoming eligible for the NCAA must attempt an earlier entry in the system at the high school level. Earlier entry provides aspiring basketball hopefuls with the opportunity of getting known and, more important, obtaining US English credentials to meet NCAA eligibility standards.

As demonstrated in this chapter, obtaining an F-1 student visa and being approved by the US consular officers is a subjective and often unsure process. The burden of proof remains with the applicant, which is challenging for the racialized and marginalized youth of the sending country.

There are multiple levels for their approval. The biases, stereotypes, and structural inequalities of their home country complicate this process and must be read alongside the perceptions and biases of the interviewing officer and the country they represent. At its core, this chapter highlights the fluidity of anti-Blackness and the historical interactions between different European colonial powers and later American republics and how they manifest themselves through the international interscholastic athletic migration process.

3

LOS BECADOS

The Dangers of Racialized Colonial Discourse

"¡Vamos Lions!" emitted from her tiny frame, dressed in a schoolgirl uniform complete with black knee-high socks. She was one of many student spectators in the stands. It reverberated in unison with the louder "!Vamos muchachos!" (Let's go, guys!) coming from Tech's student and fan section. The students' Spanish chants didn't match the English posters plastered on the wall saying the same thing: "Go Lions!"

Warmed up in their all-gray uniforms, except for the blue right leg of their shorts, all twelve of Tech's players ran to the free throw line, placing their hands behind their backs and standing with full attention. As the student singer ended her rendition of "The Star-Spangled Banner," "For the land of the free and the home of the brave," they rushed back to the bench, huddled up, locked arms behind each other's backs, and began to sway side to side, chanting "aye, aye" and increasing the volume until one player shouted, "Lions on three. One, two, three!" "Lions!" the warriors of the evening responded.

Those were among the last English words Tech's sideline used during the rest of the game, except during a break from the on-court action. "They're playing basketball. / We love that basketball. / They're playing basketball," the multilingual students sang in unison, electrified, repeating every word of Kurtis Blow's 1984 hit "Basketball."

Tech Prep Lions was the visiting team, as usual, since they did not have their own gym. According to Tito, they barely had a real school building. It was a collection of former offices and storefronts in a strip mall pieced into a school. But the student body, parents, and fans crowded into Hope Academy's (a pseudonym) gym in La Frontera, Texas, were more excited than usual this evening. The game was intense, and the score remained close until the final buzzer sounded. Fans from both schools were present and making a lot of noise. As the game drew closer in score and Hope Academy took the lead, each basket made or missed evoked strong reactions from the crowd and the benches.

The Lions' number 4 led the charge down the court, giving a quick fake step, causing Hope's defender to lose his balance, and jumped up with a fadeaway action as the ball left his hands. It went in.

"Josue 'El Pana [The Panamanian]'!" screamed the announcer. Josue, wearing number 4 on his jersey in La Frontera, was the same number 4 who tightly embraced Tito after securing the third-place victory at Centrobasket in the Dominican Republic; looking toward his peers in the stands, he threw his arms up and let out a loud roar, confirming that his shot had once again tied the game. The rest of the Lions screamed and cleared the bench to celebrate as if Josue's shot had won the game. Three minutes and forty-one seconds still remained in the game. "¡Vamos Lions! ¡Bien muchachos!" (Let's go, Lions! Good job, guys!) roared from the visitors' section of the stands.

The Lions did eventually win the match. While I was happy to see Tito and his new teammates leave the court victorious, there were some uncomfortable moments that reminded me how much race was a part of their presence on the team and within the school.

"¡Vamos, Sexual Chocolate!" emitted from the stands whenever Jamal Clark and his six-foot dark-skinned frame, which the students equated to the color of dark brown chocolate, came down with a powering rebound. Jamal "Sexual Chocolate" Clark, as he was routinely called by not only the students but also the game announcers, was one of *los becados* (scholarship student-athletes) from the Caribbean coastal city of Puerto Limón, Costa Rica. Limón is very similar to Colón. Just as being *Colónese* is both a noun and a verb that brings about hyper(in)visibility, so is being *Limónese* in the Costa Rican context. Being *Limónese* is synonymous with being Black due to the country's fixation on the large number of Black West Indians who answered the country's call for labor, migrating to the Caribbean port in the nineteenth century. Costa Rica, too, has a history of Black people's presence predating the arrival of Black West Indians, but that has been largely suppressed. Blackness in Costa Rica has mainly been constructed as foreign, and its epicenter is Limón. For student-athletes like Tito and Jamal, their athletic scholarships lent to their nickname of *los becados*. *Los becados* were the only Black students in the school. Jamal Clark's last name, in the Costa Rican context, was a marker of his Blackness, just like that of his new Panamanian teammate, Tito Brown; both their surnames located them as descendants of Black West Indian migrants to the Central American isthmus. But they also distanced them from the hyped-up white and mestize cheering section in the stands.

Jamal and Tito, however, were not the only Spanish speakers with Anglo surnames plastered on their backs running up and down the court. They looked indistinguishable from what I can only assume to be the African American players on Hope Academy's team, who hustled up and down the same court with similar Anglo surnames plastered on their backs but communicated in English instead of Spanish like Tito and his teammates.

After applying a second time and finally being approved for an F-1 student visa, Tito made his way to La Frontera and immediately began playing basketball and attending school. Within a month of being at Tech, Tito had also acquired a racialized nickname like Jamal. With every quick-assist pass or shot Tito made, the announcer, in a voice more reminiscent of a soccer announcer on Spanish-language media than North American basketball, would shout "Titooooooo," elongating the *o* sound, then continuing with "'La Pantera Negra' [The Black Panther] Brown Hurtado, the pride of Panama City, Panama."

The Depth of Racialized Nicknames

Besides the announcer's error of labeling Tito as coming from Panama City instead of Colón City, where he is actually from, the racialized nicknames announcers and students attached to them invoked five hundred years of racialized power dynamics within the Americas (Mosby 2018). No other player's race was invoked or named by the announcers or the student body except that of the Black scholarship players. Hope Academy's gym in La Frontera, where the US flag stood prominently next to the scorers' table, reveals the racial hypocrisy and anti-Blackness laden within Latinidad.

The very apparent racial and class differences between the majority of the starting five on the court and their cheering classmates in the stands make it clear that race is at work within the mythical Latinx demographic. Everyone from Latin America is not the same, nor do they have the same lived experiences. The youths' uncontested Blackness and the English surnames of some of them clashed against a monolithic idea of Latinidad. The game that night at Hope Academy's gym was like so many other athletic competitions where these racialized dynamics are on display. Baseball and soccer in Latin America are other examples where mostly Black Latin American athletes labor in front of a predominantly white and mestize Latinx crowd. The racialized performance of labor and leisure reveals Latin America's racially stratified societies in which persons of color are actively participating in the naturalization and reproduction of the racial order (Warren and Twine 2008, 541). These ideas cross national borders via the crossing of individuals and mediated content. They do not belong to any one group. Latinxs harbor anti-Black thoughts, rhetoric, and ideas, the same as Anglo North Americans.

These beliefs and stereotypes are well embedded within Latin America. In a news article published in the Panamanian media outlet *La Prensa* (2012), entitled "Panamá, un crisol de fibras" (Panama: A melting pot of fibers), the trainer of Irving Saladino, Panama's first Olympic gold medalist, explained, "Nosotros estamos en la raza de velocidad. Es una mezcla, pero tenemos muchos descendientes del Caribe, y los negros tienen una contextura de fibras rápidas" (We are part of a fast race. It's a mix, but we have a lot of descendants from the Caribbean [British], and Black people have a physique of fast-twitch muscle fibers).

A 2020 Ecuadorian news article claimed that Afro-Ecuadorian athletes possess an advantage in sports that demand strength and discipline compared to mestizo and white athletes:

> "Es un tema genético. El negro tiene fibras blancas o de contracción rápida, que ayudan a un mayor desarrollo de la musculatura, contrario a los mestizos o los blancos, que poseen fibras rojas, esenciales en actividades de coordinación y resistencia. Por eso vemos que el

afrodescendiente tiene más éxito en actividades como el atletismo (en distancias cortas), boxeo, baloncesto, levantamiento de pesas, fisicoculturismo, etc. Sin embargo, no desarrolla tanto en: gimnasia, tenis, natación o ciclismo de ruta, donde se necesita mayor coordinación y resistencia," explica el preparador físico César Benalcázar. (García Diaz 2020)

"It is a genetic issue. Blacks have white or fast-twitch fibers, which help further muscle development, unlike mestizos or whites, who have red fibers, essential in coordination and resistance activities. That is why we see that Afrodescendants are more successful in activities such as athletics (in short distances), boxing, basketball, weightlifting, bodybuilding, etc. However, they do not do as well in gymnastics, tennis, swimming, or road cycling, where greater coordination and resistance are needed," explains the physical trainer César Benalcázar.

The sounds of the white and mestize students' voices screaming these nicknames echoed the previous trainer's comments and made audible what Frantz Fanon argued was central to colonial logic, which reduced Black men to their bodies and made them animalistic; they have been "turned into a phallus or penis" (2008, 88). Although the students might use the nicknames in jest, they still force us to see Jamal as a sexual being and Tito as animalistic, characteristics that historically have been attributed to Black masculinity throughout the Americas. Additionally, it cannot be missed that they were calling him "sexual chocolate," which derives from the Black American popular culture movie *Coming to America*, with Eddie Murphy, remade with the US Olympian-turned-wrestler Mark Henry's Sexual Chocolate persona in WWF wrestling. "Sexual Chocolate, everybody!" Abby Ferber (2007) argued that the narrative that defines Black males as hypersexual, animalistic, and savage is central to white American identity. However, it is not just in white American (read: US) identity that this narrative has taken root. Dominant white/mestize-imposed views of Black masculinity within Latin American countries have framed Black men in similar veins, as irresponsible fathers, criminals, hypersexual beings, and good athletes (La Furcia 2016). In a study of Black Ecuadorian athletes, Jean Muteba Rahier (2008) found that it was rare for their Black skin not to be mentioned as a reason for their alleged "superior physical disposition" for certain sports. Walter Thompson-Hernández (2016) observed and felt that non-Black Mexican basketball coaches and fans valued his Blackness because they believed in its supposed physical superiority.

Clearly, the dynamics and tensions are present at Tech in La Frontera even if the majority of the school's student body, administrators, and owners are Latinx, or "brown," as they are termed in current popular discourse in the United States. The racialized and classed nicknames assigned to Tito and Jamal, including *los becados*, as it was reserved only for the Black students in the school, serve to highlight the normative embodiment of whiteness and its privileges, which mestizes are afforded. Mónica Moreno Figueroa (2010, 399) asserted that historically in Mexico, "when mestizaje became 'the national,' its characterization as historically racialized and national became blurred and the national prevailed, dominated, pervaded and consolidated a shift towards racelessness." As such, mestize Mexicans do not have to name themselves racially and were not named in this way in the gym. Moreno Figueroa's (2010, 388) argument highlights how the homogenizing racial logic of *mestizaje* played a significant role in concealing the racist framing and treatment of Tito and the other *becados*, as Coach Barrigon was Mexican and they were all positioned as part of a unified mythical Latinx family.

This dangerous and fluid ideology is historically based and was present and important within Tito's and the other *becados'* lives before and during their time in La Frontera. In the United States, many mestize-identifying individuals are within a minority with a unique racialized and violent past, especially in the US-Mexico borderlands of Texas where La Frontera is situated. There is a history of state-sanctioned violence, such as lynchings, that intentionally targeted mestize Mexicans in the area. There is also a history of mestize individuals being legally white in the US context and advocating for civil rights on that ground. However, Blackness does not shift in the same way. As Fanon wrote, "Wherever he goes, a Black man remains a Black man" (2008, 150). Tito "La Pantera Negra," Jamal "Sexual Chocolate," and the other Black scholarship players remained Black at home and in La Frontera. Most people in the United States would assume that Jamal and Tito are African American, as their "street race" reads Black, which they are and which is synonymous with African American. Nancy Lopez (2019) coined the term *street race*, defined as social meanings assigned to the conglomeration of a person's skin color, hair texture, and facial features. In Tito's daily interactions in the United States, such as small encounters with store clerks, he noticed that they would speak to his mestize friends in Spanish and him in English. In some cases he was more fluent in Spanish than his friends, but the store clerk's interpretation of his Blackness made the difference. They believed him to be African American.

However, the question is, What does the presentation of a Black person of any ethnicity, but in this case one from Latin America, being called racialized nicknames mean to Latinidad in the United States? It means the social relation to power goes unquestioned. It's assumed, at best, that the racialized nicknames mestize fans hurl at Black Costa Rican and Panamanian players at high school basketball games are an intraracial issue, and racism is not at play. The unequal racial and power dynamic goes unquestioned because pervasive ideas claim that Latinxs in the United States do not fit within the traditional Black-white binary. In response, I argue that Latinx, constructed as a racial/social identity, serves to erase through *morenizar*, or "browning," the racialized experiences of Black people from the region, like Tito. If you are not brown, you are pushed to the margins or become hyphenated with terms such as Afro-Latinx. The Latinx or brown (mestize) subject becomes dominant. Current discourse on Latinidad can be read only through a brown aesthetic lens, which privileges the experiences, epistemologies, and racialized treatment of mestizes in the United States with little regard for or critical examination of the anti-Black ideology and violence that has long been a part of this group's identity making and maintenance.

Racist ideas about these basketball players' Blackness remained attached to their persons and bodies. In similar ways as within their home countries, they were confronting the hegemony of a brown-centric/mestize Latinidad of the United States, relegating Blackness to the margins. The brown-majority school and coach employed their Blackness and maleness in ways no different from white (read: Anglo) Americans' treatment of young Black males as the preferred laborers of the basketball industry. They were recruited to Tech to help the school win games. Their Blackness was there to provide an economic benefit and service—entertainment for the white and mestize majorities screaming racialized nicknames from the stands. Whereas scholars have long studied and been critical of the overrepresentation of Black men in US college hoops and the relationship between Black players and white coaches, staffs, and universities, the dynamic that played out on Tech's basketball court among white-mestize coaches, the school, fans, and Black players goes unquestioned. The Tech student fans' cheers, jeers, and screams are their indictments and convictions that people in Latin America and non-Black Latinxs not only see color but can scream it out in excitement during a basketball game.

The Black Latin American Pipeline

Tech Prep strove to have its own successful high school basketball team. Like many predominantly white elite private schools in the country, including the evening's opponent, Hope Academy, Tech also had a predominantly Black basketball team that did not match the racial composition of their supporters in the stands. It is well known that US private schools recruit Black youth who are geographically and culturally distant to the majority-white student bodies for athletic purposes (Brooks 2009; Thomas et al. 2020). In Tech's case, they recruited Black players from Black spaces in Central America. Panama and Costa Rica were the preferred sources.

Private schools recruit athletes to increase their chances of winning. They recruit Black players of varying socioeconomic backgrounds because they are the preferred laborers of the basketball industry. All things being equal, it should be a mutually beneficial relationship. The school should increase its chances of winning, which comes with notoriety and opportunities, while the players increase their chances of obtaining a "better" education and the next basketball opportunity. The next opportunity could be a scholarship to play at the collegiate level or other pathways to professional ball. Yet that is not always the case from a basketball, education, or socioemotional standpoint. As Daniel Thomas and colleagues (2020) have pointed out, many of these predicaments are taxing and emotionally draining for Black boy student-athletes as they frequently encounter anti-Black structural and cultural assaults that can make their daily school attendance difficult.

Tech intentionally recruited Black players from Black regions of Latin America. Spanish fluency and relationships with local coaches provided Coach Barrigon and Tech with a competitive advantage to recruit and create a pipeline of talent from the region. In the sport of basketball, there is a clear global interdependence involving labor migration following movement patterns often called *talent pipelines* (Falcous and Maguire 2005). Relying on the pipelines that Coach Barrigon had forged, the school was able to recruit and provide percentage-based scholarships, which never totaled 100 percent, to Spanish-speaking youth from Latin America who would otherwise have had challenges obtaining opportunities at similar institutions. In Tito's case, Tech offered him an 80 percent scholarship, with his parents paying the remaining 20 percent. Tech positioned itself to host international players because it was certified by the Student and Exchange Visitor Information System (SEVIS), which authorizes the F-1 student visa for international students. Also, they found ways to offset some of the costs of having scholarship players, such as holding community-wide fundraisers that would supposedly go toward supporting the scholarship student-athletes. Coach Barrigon also found exploitative and illegal ways for *los becados* to work for their room and board.

Tito and *los becados* lived in a far different reality than their more affluent Mexican and Mexican American classmates. Every morning in La Frontera, Tito and the seven other young men crowded into an old van that headed across the border city to get to school. All eight had large, athletic frames, while their complexions varied but were still marked by their *negritud*. They were all crowded into a van grappling with this new space, new opportunities, and shifting identities. Some days they would arrive at school with ample time to get settled before the first bell rang. The majority of the days, however, tardiness was the norm.

"He smelled like alcohol," Tito said. "He would talk about drinking in the bars with the coach the night before." Tito jokingly reminisced about the assistant coach's late morning arrivals. A drunk and tardy assistant coach must have been very entertaining for the eight teenagers. All of them were taller than the average adult male and were dressed in gray slacks, light blue polo shirts, and dark blue blazers, waiting to be shuffled to school in an old, raggedy van driven by a sobering-up coach.

There was plenty of time for stories and laughter en route to school. Their one-bedroom, one-bathroom annex to a house was over thirteen miles from Tech, and La Frontera's morning traffic did not make the journey any shorter. It was not a school dormitory. It was a rented place in a lower-income area of the city without any association with the school. In addition to battling morning rush hour, they picked up a female student from Mexico, one of the thousands of Mexican students and US students of Mexican heritage who trek across the border daily to attend US schools (Center for US-Mexican Studies 2017, 5). Some attend public schools, and some attend elite private schools like Tech. The thirteen miles they traced each way from their annexed apartment to the school moved them across geographic and social boundaries that situated their world far from that of their new classmates.

"It was the *ghetto* ghetto," Tito said, repeating *ghetto* to emphasize the marginality and stark difference of his new neighborhood in La Frontera. Tito never expected to be living in a marginalized neighborhood within the United States, much less sharing beds with people he had never met before. However, emerging from economically and racially marginalized areas was not new for Tito. He was from Colón, and the historical anti-Blackness and colonial rhetoric that framed his hometown as maladaptive were also part of the reason he was thought to be a good basketball player. His origin in Colón, and the stereotypical perception of its people, probably influenced Coach Barrigon's belief that Tito and the other youth would accept their subpar US living conditions.

It is not accidental that Tito and his other Panamanian teammates emerged from Colón City, and the Costa Ricans from the province of Limón. These are two very similar places in Latin America where race, ethnicity, labor, empire, imperialism, and sport all collided (Hutchinson Miller 2012). Both of the cities are located on their respective country's Caribbean coast and have large seaports; both are strongly associated with Blackness, poverty, criminality, and athletic prowess. *Un semillero de grandes deportistas* (a hotbed of great athletes) is a phrase attached to the Costa Rican port city and province. But it's not just Blackness that is inscribed in Limón and connects Jamal Clark and Tito Brown; it is specifically Blackness that derives from mostly English-speaking Afro-Caribbean individuals who began migrating to the region at the end of the nineteenth century in search of economic opportunities.

Coach Barrigon created a talent pipeline from Panama and Costa Rica fueled by youth who are marginal to their societies (Ralph 2007; Brooks and McKail 2008). Historical racism toward Black West Indians has created an environment where such youth have few options other than sport for upward social mobility. The youth of West Indian ancestry are descendants of individuals who were more dispensable than white workers and relegated to the most dangerous jobs in these imperialist projects. Their forebears dynamited the land, clearing the ditch to create the Panama Canal. They dug into the earth, laying train tracks across the Isthmus of Panama and the Costa Rican valleys. They suffered many casualties because of yellow fever, malaria, and other diseases' unrelenting hold.

Youth basketball recruiting is a business that has a racial aspect that works best when it has an ever-replenishing pool of highly motivated, even desperate, youths without access to quality education and with diminishing job prospects (Runstedtler 2018). When coaches come to better understand the types of players that fit their programs, they can recruit from the specific regions that supply these players or return to an area that previously supplied a player to their program (Chepyator-Thomson et al. 2016, 581). In many ways, training their bodies to perform optimally and honing their basketball talents to ultimately become spatially mobile allowed Tito and the other *becados* to forge an opportunity to find respectable adulthoods (Esson 2013) that their countries either cannot provide or refuse to provide.

Tech Prep and Coach Barrigon relied on pervasive stereotypes (which do not relate only to physical characteristics) steeped in anti-Black racism to recruit young men. "¿Tito tiene un papá?" read the text message Katia forwarded me from Coach Barrigon, inquiring if Tito had a father. Katia was surprised that her son's coach would ask such a question. Contrary to Coach Barrigon's assumptions, Tito's parents were married and have lived in the same household since his birth. Coach Barrigon's text stemmed from his analysis of Tito's quietness on his arrival in La Frontera. He believed his reserved nature must have something to do with not having a father in his life, let alone his own biological father. The coach's beliefs were informed by the same racist ideas that led Tech's fans and announcers to give Tech's Black players racialized nicknames. Coach Barrigon's four-word text was loaded with pervasive social stereotypes suggesting Black men and women are sexually promiscuous single mothers and irresponsible fathers.

Tito and the other scholarship basketball players were the only Black students in the school. It becomes difficult to differentiate between African American players and Black players of different nationalities. Basketball has been racialized as a Black sport largely through the principle of labor in some of the sport's most visible arenas, like the NBA. Scott Brooks and Michael McKail (2008) argued that African American males became the preferred laborers of the basketball industry because of their perceived athletic abilities and marginal status within the US labor economy. Michael Ralph (2007) extended the presence of these players to the TVs of Senegalese basketball hopefuls who saw racial kinships and shared economic marginalization as their motivation to play basketball. The connection continues across nation-states, continental divides, and languages and includes Central America.

Tito and his Black Costa Rican teammates could have understood their Blackness as making them better basketball players than non-Black people. They had already encountered ideas about Black athletic superiority at home. And, of course, they could find kinship with the NBA's majority-Black players hustling up and down courts, transmitted through their TV and cell phone screens before they arrived in the United States.

In Need of Being Saved

The school year before Tito had arrived at Tech, the mostly Central American team had won the State of Texas championship in their division. Additionally, Coach Barrigon had been voted the best coach in the state by the same league. The Tech Lions had a strong fan base and following. The players were high school superstars. They were plastered on the school's promotional material. They packed out the school's gym whenever they played. Their athletic talents and labor provided Tech with a valuable recruiting tool for nonathlete students who would pay the school's full tuition. Each win provided Tech with school pride and the ability to boast of having a successful athletic program. Because Tito and his teammates were Black, they were assumed to be *becados* and were synonymous with the basketball team. This also affected how the city of La Frontera mediated the Central American youth. When four Costa Rican students arrived at La Frontera a year before Tito, the local newspaper wrote, "Los cuatro ticos llegaron a [Tech Prep en La Frontera], EEUU y esto le dio un vuelco enorme a sus vidas, ya que las condiciones en las que estaban acostumbrados a estudiar, practicar deporte y hasta vivir totalmente diferentes a las de un país de primer mundo" (The four Ticos arrived at Tech Prep in La Frontera, USA, and this turned their lives upside down, since the conditions in which they were used to studying, practicing sports, and even living were totally different from those of a First World country).

Being in the United States was indeed beneficial to their athletic careers. It is why they decided to come. Playing basketball in the United States potentially offered more exposure, as well as access to a more developed basketball infrastructure than in their home countries. However, as Tito and the other *becados* would learn, being in the United States did not guarantee any of the supposed benefits. The troubling and dangerous component is the supposed US exceptionalism within the quotation from the newspaper. First, the reader is supposed to conclude that being in the United States is an inherent improvement in the lives and basketball careers of the Costa Rican youth. Second, the reader should conclude that the recruitment of youth from the Global South to the "First World" is a humanitarian and charitable act.

Tito entered this ideological and hypocritical world before he arrived at Tech Prep. He was not a stranger to being a scholarship student-athlete and traversing physical, cultural, racial, and ideological borders. He did it years before, making the long journeys from his predominantly Black school, neighborhood, and city to a private high school in the country's capital, where he became a minority. La Frontera was no different.

The articulation of the logic of his presence changed given the regional nuances, but the core of the logic remained. Because he was Black and presumably poor, his presence in this coveted/elite space was contingent solely on his athletic ability. Tech Prep and Colegio Bolivariano were two different types of educational institutions in two different countries. However, they both recruited youth from spaces inherently tied to Blackness, poverty, deviance, and athletic superiority to justify their blazingly transactional recruiting practices (Runstedtler 2018).

These student-athletes' physical presence on campus was an indicator of their financial need and exemplified the notion of Black people coming from impoverished backgrounds. With the exception of two non-Black Mexican *becados*, they were all of African descent and mostly tall. Tito and Josue, the point guards, were the only relatively short ones of the group. Anytime they appeared in school photos with their new classmates, it was reminiscent of the clashes of the third-place game in Santo Domingo against the Mexicans.

Tech's nonscholarship student body looked like the white-mestizo Mexican team that the Panamanians had defeated at Centrobasket the summer before. Their dark brown skins collided against the whiteness and light brownness of their non-Black US Latinx and Latin American peers. The Costa Rican *becados*, who were all Afrodescendant, were also familiar with these types of racial differences as they also represented their country in national competitions. They all shared the same migratory status: noncitizen F-1 student visa holders with "athletic scholarship" written on their I-20 forms from their schools. They were all in a similar predicament. They were all very talented basketball players and primarily spoke Spanish. Collectively, even with their historical ties to the English language, Spanish was their challenge to overcome. They all needed to travel to *el norte* to circumvent the language barriers to entering US college basketball.

Tito saw the opportunity to travel to the United States as a way of chasing his American hoop dream that came with an American education. Tito was invested in and excited by the educational opportunities he felt basketball could provide him. For him, basketball and the way he trained his body to play the sport well could afford him a plethora of opportunities. He saw that for himself. However, the opportunity to travel, play, and foster additional opportunities through basketball was a two-way street that included the individuals who would ensure it would happen. How his teachers, classmates, and coaches perceived him and his presence in these new spaces would determine how he would navigate these spaces and perceived opportunities.

Tech Prep is the preparatory academy for the very prestigious and elite Mexican Universidad Autónoma de Vicente Guerrero (pseudonym). This is their US setup. It is a way of providing a US education to Mexican nationals who live on the US side of the border, those who cross it daily, and any other students who could afford the tuition. The very American pageantry of the school and its athletic programs are elements parents are willing to pay large sums of money for, over $12,000 annually to be exact. Tech Prep boasted itself as an advanced placement (AP) and science, technology, engineering, and math (STEM) school, where the vast majority of the students went on to college. Tito and the other *becados* were placed in an academically rigorous and English-medium school without the necessary preparation or support to be successful, even though Tech's letter to the US embassy in Panama promised that Tito would receive English as a Second Language (ESL) courses and English tutors. Their reality was that they were in Tech to play basketball, and there was no governance that could guarantee they would benefit academically in the same way as non-athletic-scholarship-receiving students.

When Coach Barrigon saw Tito in Santo Domingo, he was attracted to his three-point shots, not his grade point average. Tito's effortless assists and ball-handling skills secured his entrance to the AP school, not his academic profile. His educational attainment was an afterthought. It is almost certain that Tito would not have gone to the United States and enrolled in an academic institution if it was not for his basketball talents. Tech Prep and Coach Barrigon relied on pervasive stereotypes steeped in anti-Black racism to recruit young men to the school's program. Tech's relationship to and treatment of Tito and the other scholarship athletes was very similar to the issues in intercollegiate athletics.

"Discovering" and Height-Mining *los Becados*

Tito stands at exactly six feet with his basketball shoes on. He's short in the world of basketball, but as a guard with a quick first step, he could overcome some height challenges. Height is one of the most prized attributes in the game. The article written about the Costa Rican players at Tech references their height and body stature: "[Barrigon] quien fuera entrenador asistente de la Selección Mexicana de Baloncesto en categorías menores descubrió el talento de cuatro jóvenes ticos que brillaban en la duela y no solo por su habilidad, sino también por su estatura" (Barrigon, who was an assistant coach of the Mexican Basketball Team in minor categories, discovered the talent of four young Costa Ricans who shone on the court and not only for their ability but also for their stature).

Providing these descriptive references forces the readers to mentally paint pictures of towering youth capable of making spectacular dunks and aggressive blocks, which are not-uncommon parts of the game. Especially for international players coming into the United States, "big men" are primarily valued, as it is believed that the United States doesn't produce enough big men for all of the programs that exist (Turcott and Pifer 2018). Just like the four Costa Rican teenagers at Tech Prep—routinely called "las Torres de Limón" (the Limón Towers) by the announcers at the games—were sought for their height.

Michael Ralph in his scholarly article "Prototype: In Search of the Perfect Senegalese Basketball Physique" (2007) illustrates how agents, scouts, coaches, and trainers obsess over the physical characteristics of Senegalese youth basketball players. He argues that these actors seek to recruit these players because they believe certain physical characteristics will translate into athletic success. Furthermore, Ralph argues that these stereotypes are rooted in anti-Black colonial discourse and are circulated around the globe with profound implications for the possibilities of the youth athletes. James Esson (2015b) points out that racial stereotyping is embedded in the recruitment of Black West Africans to the European soccer markets. He argues not only that ideas of Black athletic superiority make Black African youth believe that they are better athletes but also that soccer clubs seek them out for this reason as well. In fact, Ryan Turcott and N. David Pifer (2018) found that the overwhelming majority of African players in the NBA were tall and played mostly center or a power forward position. Due to pipelines sourcing tall Black youth from certain locales, a naturalized discourse begins to take form. Being tall becomes an inherent characteristic of being African or part of the Black race. Scholars such as Stuart Hall (2019) have argued against the essentialization of physical characteristics as part of race because this reinforces the hegemonic white colonial logic that was employed to justify exploitation on the basis of race.

Although Ralph (2007) and Esson (2015a) focused on West African nations, similar discourse and stereotypes were employed in the case of Black Panamanian and Costa Rican youth in La Frontera. Online news stories and school-wide fundraising efforts often framed the *becados* as destitute and in danger of never reaching their full potential because of the lack of basketball infrastructure and opportunities in their home countries. It is important that we read deeper into the centrality of height in basketball trafficking cases. What is absent from the images engineered by journalists is the racist logic tied to colonialism that informs athletic recruiting practices among youth in the Global South (Ralph 2007). There is a paucity of research that focuses on how Black athletes from Latin America have been mediated, but research conducted on migrant Black African athletes provides strong connecting points. Munene Franjo Mwaniki (2017, 251) notes that "varied narratives of African basketball players all stress (1) the dire political circumstances from which they are alleged to have arisen; (2) the diligence through which they transcended these circumstances; and (3) the humanitarianism they promote as evidence of their 'gratefulness'—perhaps even, their inherent nobility."

With the exception of point 3, Tito and other *becados* were framed within a discourse of fleeing and overcoming near-insurmountable circumstances in Panama and Costa Rica. However, what is omitted from these narratives is how non-Black Latin Americans and Latinxs can create stories about these Black players to serve their own interests. Coach Barrigon was framed as the "mestizo savior" who ventured to Costa Rica and saved these supposedly poor Black boys from themselves and their inherently lacking and impoverished communities. Stories like these are not unique to Costa Rica or Panama. They are cast throughout the globe and are paramount to the transactional nature of the athletic industrial complex (AIC). They serve to erase the agency of prospective youth athletes looking for a means of transitioning into respectable adulthood (Esson 2013).

At nearly six feet tall, Tito was relatively short compared to the Costa Rican *becados*, who were at least six feet four, but he was still a great player. He played guard, a position that does not require height like others, but his talent, especially at the high school level, compensated for his lack of basketball tallness. Coach Barrigon knew Tito's size could limit his recruitment options for college hoops, but he also knew Tito could help them win now. Even with their height difference, Tito and his Costa Rican teammates were similar. They shared Blackness, which meant they shared a supposed physical superiority, and Coach Barrigon thought they should share a similar disposition of gratitude and humility for the opportunity to be in the United States. On Tito's arrival, he was placed under the same ideological framing as his new teammates and friends in La Frontera. However, that was not his home life in Colón, Panama.

Is Recruitment Passive or Active?

What does it mean to be found? Neither Tito nor the Costa Ricans were just walking around in their respective homes waiting to be found in the shadows, as the article on the four Costa Ricans in La Frontera describes. They had been hustling for years, traveling, and playing in club basketball tournaments around the country and the broader Central American region. The years they spent investing in their athletic talents demonstrate the agency that Craig Jeffrey (2012) identifies as "orchestrated" strategies aimed at long-term change. He argues that this type of agency differs from the scholarly literature, which often depicts immediate responses to the vagaries of fluid events. Tito, Josue, Jamal, and the Costa Rican players spent years competing for their countries on the national youth teams. Tito alone, before arriving in La Frontera, had played in basketball tournaments in the Dominican Republic, Costa Rica, El Salvador, Honduras, and the United States and had a pending trip to Canada for the 2018 FIBA AmeriCup. Their actions contradict ideas that they were just found. They had been hustling to be seen, intentionally putting themselves where that could happen, which is essential to achieve some kind of success in a career.

The language employed in the news article on the Costa Rican youth is part of a larger discourse that commonly frames international players as "hungrier" than their US counterparts. Also, claims that they are "better off in the United States," which are commonly utilized within basketball recruitment, discount agency and fail to recognize how marginalized international youth seek and find ways to strategically circumvent barriers, become spatially mobile, and achieve their dreams. For many youth of the Global South, the "outside," particularly migration to nations of the Global North, has become a "metaphor for liberation" (Jua 2003). *Los becados* employed their bodies to be active participants in deciding their lives' trajectories, just as Esson (2013) found in the Ghanaian context among young adult men soccer players. However, it must be noted that their agency had limits. Without falling into tropes of Black passivity, it must be stated that individual human agency alone cannot stand up to the US immigration system. I contend these youth are constantly responding to and speaking from their subaltern stations, but within an unbalanced power dynamic, there are extreme limits on how their agency can protect them from the AIC that justifies their exploitation based on age-old tropes and is backed up by the US government.

Conclusion

Tito was recruited to Tech Prep for his athletic abilities. His presence in La Frontera had less to do with his academic abilities. Although Tito and the other *becados* might not have been assessed equally to their nonscholarship classmates, they nonetheless are deserving of the same quality of care and academic investment. However, that was not what they received. This lack of investment into who they were outside of their athletic talents was primarily based on how they were constructed, which was revealed through the racialized nicknames they were given. In popular media and general discourse, Tito and the other *becados* are often constructed as the recipients of a private school's benevolence in the United States, which saved them from a life of plunder through basketball.

Every time the youth were referred to as *los becados*, it not only invoked racialized and classed ideas but also subjected them to a premature adultification that erased even their right to childhood and their status as still children (Dumas and Nelson 2016). By imagining these Black boys as "underserved" scholarship student-athletes (*becados*) who all came from poverty-stricken backgrounds and never received much formal education, let alone proper training and coaching until they arrived at Tech, we are forced to convince ourselves that basketball migration cannot become a form of child labor exploitation and trafficking but rather is a necessary evil to "develop talent" and "give opportunity" to young players (Mwaniki 2017, 25). Peter Donnelly and Leanne Petherick (2004) argue that any conditions in professional or preprofessional sports in which individual athletes under eighteen years of age are treated as a commodity involve young athletes moving from their homes. That, unregulated, might be considered as trafficking of children.

Although the public may be led to believe that Tech and other similar basketball-centered prep schools are necessary evils that give opportunity to youth, there are still very uncomfortable points to contend with. One of the most troubling is the seemingly increasing number of Black children who are displaced from their childhoods and adultified as scholarship student-athletes. We must consider this point deeply because children are developing and materially vulnerable. They have limited access to resources that allow them to influence how they are imagined in society and what is done to and with their bodies (Dumas and Nelson 2016, 32).

Unfortunately, some of these situations can transform into exploitation and, specifically, basketball trafficking. Additionally, there is a high prevalence of Black teenagers and young adults from the Global South, "lured by the promise of a college scholarship and professional sports career, being brought to the United States on F-1 student visas to attend school" (US Department of Homeland Security 2016), who end up caught in precarious situations. As such, it's urgent that we consider further if and/or how basketball-centered prep schools in cooperation with private high schools place international noncitizen minors of color in vulnerable positions to be exploited, mistreated, abused, and trafficked to the United States for their labor, while simultaneously socializing these children into silence as part of mastering the role of a *becado*.

4

UNREGULATED RELATIONSHIPS

The Use and Abuse of the F-1 Student Visa
in US High School Basketball

"Good morning. Please speak with Tito," Coach Barrigon texted me. "He is failing classes. And he doesn't have the right attitude. He doesn't like to be corrected and doesn't want anyone to tell him nothing."

I felt increasingly upset as I attempted to mask my feelings in my reply: "Thanks for the information coach. I'll talk to him and look in the portal to check his homework."

Since meeting Tito through his mother and donating the initial funds for his first basketball trip to Washington, DC, I had always made myself available to assist Tito and his family with his new endeavors stateside. Katia asked me to look out for Tito and help him when possible, and I did it out of the tradition of fictive kinship or "otherparentage" among many Afrodescendants, in which I was raised (Collins 2000). As such, I accepted my feelings of anger on receiving Coach Barrigon's text. I understood reprimanding Tito about his lackluster academic performance as part of my responsibility in caring for him.

In addition, as a former National Collegiate Athletic Association (NCAA) student-athlete and current scholar of race and sports, I knew very well the exploitation that happens to Black student-athletes at the expense of their education. I also had intimate knowledge of the doors that acquiring a US English education could open for Tito over the course of his life, even if he returned to live in Panama. Before he left Panama, I constantly reminded him that this opportunity was a business deal, not one of benevolence. I knew he needed to take advantage of the opportunity in the same way as the school was taking advantage of his athletic talents and labor. I was complicit in his new predicament within the athletic industrial complex (AIC).

However, culpability is a challenging reality for someone like myself who wanted to see a young Black man from Colón, Panama, win. I know my father saw himself in Tito, but I saw myself in Tito too. I often wondered, "If my father hadn't left Colón, would I have been in a similar position to Tito?" I saw what a sport scholarship had done for my father.

When I asked him, "Would you have been able to have the life you have now if you stayed in Panama?" my father replied, "No."

He made it very plain that his life would not have been the same without going to Huston-Tillotson University on a tennis scholarship. There was no stretched-out sermon. Just no.

I saw what my athletic talent, which afforded me a football scholarship to Florida Agricultural and Mechanical (A&M) University, was doing in my life. A torn ACL, a torn meniscus, and a broken finger later, my athletic talents and labor had afforded me two college degrees as well as paid for me to get a doctorate from one of the highest-ranked universities in the world, the same university where my paternal grandfather worked as a janitor. He dreamed of having one of his children attend the University of Texas at Austin because he never could: The university's racist policies barred Black undergraduates until 1956. All of this was on my mind after speaking with Coach Barrigon.

I knew it was nearly impossible for Tito to play in the NBA like he desired. However, I believed he could play college basketball. He was not an average player. From the first video Katia showed me on her phone of Tito playing in that humid gym in the former US Panama Canal Zone, I could see he had talent. He stepped through the air with such force, the loose-fitting black jersey pressed against his chest with sweat, and he dunked the

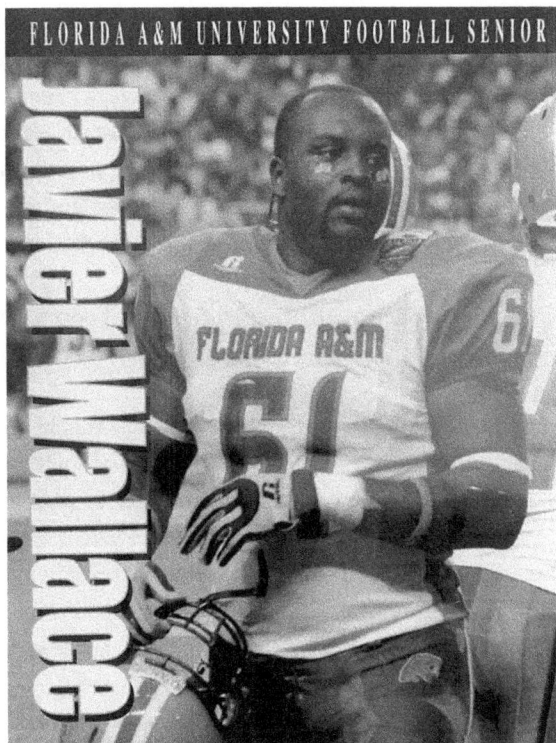

FIGURE 4.1. Javier Wallace's senior football picture from his days at Florida A&M University.

FLORIDA A&M UNIVERSITY FOOTBALL SENIOR

ball over the crouched person under the hoop. By my third year as athletic director at the elite private school in Panama City, I had seen many basketball games in Panama, and I had not seen a kid in Panama do that.

I knew I was part of the "dirty trick" that Reuben A. Buford May (2007) defines as the often-affirmed notion that athletics is a viable means of social mobility. He goes on to say that dirty tricks are part and parcel of a social system predicated on the real human need for hope. Even though I knew the odds of Tito becoming an NBA all-star were not in his favor, I still hoped that basketball could give him *something*, that this basketball scholarship at Tech could provide him with something similar to what I had experienced and what had made me who I am, leading us to eventually meet in Panama. Our aspirational capital fueled the AIC, and in the middle of that was his education. Tara Yosso (2005) asserts that aspirational capital is the ability to hold on to hope in the face of structured inequality, often without the means to make such dreams a reality.

So I became invested in the idea that Tito would at least attempt to get more than what Tech expected of him, which was his basketball talents.

Basketball was his currency to afford upward social mobility. Walking down the main part of campus, trying to avoid the mass rush of students packed tightly on the yellow brick pathway between classes, I began to text Tito. I calmed myself down enough to type, "What time can we talk tonight?"

When Tito answered my call about 7:30 p.m. that evening, he barely finished saying hello before my frustrations got the better of me. I immediately began to scold him about the message I had received from Coach Barrigon.

"We are paying all this money. So many people are making a sacrifice for you to get up there and start failing classes!" I was screaming into my cell phone at Tito.

I truly felt like my parents back when I was in high school and they received phone calls about our behavior at school. For them, there was never any excuse for me or my siblings to misbehave in class. They—but in particular my mother—would constantly repeat, "They already have what you are trying to get," referring to the fact that teachers had already completed their education. Or in cases when we felt the teacher was not being completely honest about us, she would say, "That teacher doesn't have time to be lying on you."

I believed and reacted the same way. Why would Coach Barrigon waste his time sending me messages about Tito during the workday unless Tito was truly in the wrong? I was convinced, as my parents were, that he did not have time to lie about Tito. Following my rant, in which I reminded Tito of all the things he already knew about the sacrifices everyone had made to get him there, I calmed down a bit. I finally allowed him a chance to respond.

"What is going on?" I said.

"I don't understand anything," he said, speaking in a faint voice as if he was preventing people around him from listening to the conversation. "Everything is in English."

"Okay, but you have tutors," I quickly replied to cut out the excuse I believed he was trying to make. "They said you have ESL classes!" I added, referring to the letter Tech had sent to the US embassy in Panama when Tito was first refused the student visa on the grounds that he was not proficient in English as his I-20 stated. Tech wrote that they would provide him with tutors and ESL classes to remedy the linguistic barrier.

"I don't have any of those things," he replied while raising his voice to defend himself. "They haven't given me any of those things."

Concerned, I pressed him for more information. "So, what do you do in classes?"

"Sometimes some of the other *becados* [scholarship students] who understand a little English or other students translate what the teacher is saying."

Still confused and upset, no longer with Tito but instead with Coach Barrigon and the school, I simply told Tito, "I am going to call you back. Have a good night."

I immediately began to draft an email to Coach Barrigon and the school's staff requesting information about Tito's academic setup. However, this was the first time I communicated with the school in English. Previously, I had spoken, texted, and emailed Coach Barrigon, school officials, Tito, and his family in Spanish because that was everyone's common language. However, I drafted my email in English to use the power and position that English affords to get a response from Tech. I did not believe that they treated the Panamanian students and their support systems equally, and they honestly thought they were doing Tito a favor by bringing him to play at Tech. By writing in English, I felt I was pushing through their stereotypes and letting them know that Tito had an American-educated advocate. My earlier emails and other communication written in Spanish about Tito's academic arrangements had gone unanswered. I wrote:

1   Could you please provide me with Tito's weekly practice schedule and a calendar of upcoming events. I need to be able to assist Tito in organizing his schedule to ensure he has the proper time allocated to study and complete academic assignments. This includes weekends too.

2   Also, in reference to the tutors assigned to Tito to assist in his academic development and acquisition of the English language on an academic level, what is his schedule for meeting with these tutors?

Thanks for your time and support. It is in our efforts that Tito is able to benefit holistically from this arrangement and exchange of athletic talent for a quality bilingual education at an emerging institution that stands to gain much attention and pedigree as it excels athletically. (email communication, October 2017)

As I expected, I received a written response. Coach Barrigon replied with one sentence: "Please feel free to call me anytime." Once we began to communicate in English, things started to change for the worse. I think Coach Barrigon felt that I was challenging his authority by asserting myself that way in the email and copying the school's administration. Later I would discover that my use of English revealed parts of my identity that challenged

Coach Barrigon's treatment of *los becados*. It would take *tía* Sonia (Aunt Sonia) to flesh out the complexities of the unregulated relationships in Tito's life since he had arrived in La Frontera. Additionally, his relationships with individuals were deeply intertwined with the relationship his athletic body and labor had with the US basketball industry, which involved more than just people. These relationships also encompassed federal, state, and athletic governance policies that collectively work to police and surveil the lives of noncitizen F-1 student visa holders, all while benefiting from their labor in the multibillion-dollar, education-based US basketball industry.

Sonia, the Unexpected *Tía*

Tito's mother described Sonia as one of her good friends from Panama and a *tía* (aunt) for Tito. Sonia was not a blood relation, but in Panama it's common to refer to an elder as an uncle or aunt. Sonia and Katia developed a relationship in their youth growing up in Panama. By coincidence, after Tito arrived in La Frontera, they realized they were in the same city. Sonia provided many critical insights into how Tito and the other *becados* were living in La Frontera. When it was decided Tito must leave Tech and La Frontera for his safety, Sonia and her family played a very instrumental role in his escape and safe arrival in Austin.

"I talked to her at 11 a.m. in the morning, and at 1 p.m. she was there." Katia told me in a voice note. "She didn't tell me she couldn't. She said that she's going to be Jessica Fletcher."

Jessica Fletcher is the character from the famous murder investigation TV series *Murder, She Wrote*. Sonia was committed to finding out all of the information she could about Tito's new situation in La Frontera. Her husband was in the US military, and over the years, he was assigned to a post in La Frontera and they began a life there. She was excited to be able to look after Tito while he was away from his family and home country. She texted me via WhatsApp:

> Don't worry, you don't have to thank me for everything I do for Tito. I do it with the best of intentions and because Katia is like a very good sister-friend. It is the least I can do for her, to take care of her son in what they allow me because I am a mother and I know how difficult it must be for her to be away from Tito. Even if you see how big Tito looks, he's only a little man. He is only 16 years old, he is still a baby who emotionally lacks the warmth of his family and his country

that is irremediable even if he makes the sacrifice and believes that strength of being here for his studies and sports, it is good to take care of his emotional state so that he can perform in all that his future awaits him. I will always be here for everything that is in my power and I can help. (October 2017)

Sonia took it on herself to provide food and clothes for Tito and the other teenagers. She acted like some Panamanians living in Austin who cared for my father and the host of other Panamanian athletes when they arrived to pursue their studies and play sports decades before. Additionally, she was not lying about acting like Jessica Fletcher. She became the additional set of eyes that we needed to gain more insight into how things actually were in La Frontera. Tito's usual "bien" (good) responses provided little insight into how things were actually progressing. Katia wanted me and Sonia to maintain communication as well since we were both in Texas and were vested in Tito's future.

After a little over a month after arriving in La Frontera, connecting with Sonia's family set Tito apart from many of his new teammates. Some had been there for two years and rarely left the house beyond attending school, practicing, playing basketball in their free time, or generally spending time with Coach Barrigon. However, Sonia's presence began to flip the dynamic. She began to form a relationship with Tito and the other youth. It got to the point that all of the *becados* would refer to her as *tía* (aunt) whenever she came around.

Sonia's relationship with Tito and the other *becados* began when Sonia and her husband picked up Tito to show him around his new host city. Unexpectedly, Josue also joined the outing after, in Sonia's words, "begging" to get out of the house. She secured Coach Barrigon's permission, and Josue joined Tito as they toured some of La Frontera's most popular sites and attractions. They went out to eat with Sonia's entire family, including her teenage son and daughter. Sonia said she wanted them "to have a family day because they were so far from their families." Following Tito's day enjoying his new city, Katia sent me all of the pictures Sonia had taken. More than just showing the sights, she wanted Katia to know that she was there to support Tito while he was away from her.

The good times did not last very long, though. After a while Tito started to become uncomfortable and resistant to the idea of going to church and spending time with Sonia and her family. He reached out to his mother and told her that he did not want to go with Sonia anymore. His concerns were mostly due to Coach Barrigon's insistence that he did not want the teenagers leaving the premises.

Tito explained that they did not have a set schedule either during the week or on the weekends. He wanted to be ready anytime the coach called. "Whenever the coach comes and says, Let's go work out, we have to leave and go work out," he said.

The Centrality of Relationships in International Interscholastic Athletic Recruitment

Having a connection with Sonia, someone not involved with athletics, was important for Tito. Relationships that are separate from the coach-player relationship can prove to be very beneficial in the experiences of minors who are international noncitizen athletes in the United States. A study conducted by Mariah Sullivan and colleagues (2020) found that many intercollegiate student-athletes reported the emotional support received from nonathletic and personal connections to be the most beneficial in managing stress. They also highlighted that social support could be a coping mechanism to combat stress and depression among college athletes. Akilah Carter-Francique and colleagues (2015) employed critical race theory (CRT) and explored the significance of social networks and social connections for Black intercollegiate student-athletes. They found that Black student-athletes indicated that parents and family served as the predominant source of off-campus support and provided emotional, informational, and appraisal support. Additionally, Holly Heard Hinderlie and Maureen Kenny (2002) argued that higher education administrators and staff should recognize the significance of family support of Black students and not attempt to compete with or challenge it. They argue that these nonacademic relationships are instrumental to Black students' cultural adjustment and social well-being. But the F-1 student visa program when used for athletic purposes does not take these types of relationships into account.

The Texas Christian Athletic League (TCAL), the athletic governing body of which Tech Prep was a member, does not regulate, monitor, or account for the time recruited players like Tito and *los becados* spend with their coach or other persons. The majority of the league's bylaws regarding international noncitizen athletes on F-1 student visas deal with recruitment.

A smaller, newer league, TCAL allows for the recruitment of athletes and distribution of scholarships by its member schools. The league's official position is that "all schools recruit, however TCAL enforces a standard that bars our member schools from purposely recruiting athletes. We instead encourage our members to build their programs from within and through the process developing student-athletes currently enrolled" (2016, 31).

The league is part of the shifting landscape of interscholastic basketball in the United States. In 2017, as Tito entered Tech in La Frontera, TCAL admitted a new member school in San Antonio that had abruptly left the Texas Association of Private and Parochial Schools, which was aligned with the University Interscholastic League (UIL). St. Anthony Catholic High School joined TCAL after the association ruled Charles Bassey and other international teenage basketball players ineligible because it viewed their tuition, room, and board as an inducement to attend St. Anthony (Zuvanich 2016).

Bassey, a six-foot-ten teenager from Nigeria who was compared to Shaquille O'Neal, quickly became ranked as one of the best players in the country in his 2019 graduating class after a breakthrough season at St. Anthony's. When St. Anthony's jumped to TCAL, the conference restored all the school's international players' eligibility because TCAL allowed recruitment and inducements.

Surprisingly, neither Bassey nor his international teammates competed in any TCAL competition. They all left following St. Anthony's elimination of Hennssy Auriantal's athletic coordinator position because of the ensuing scandal surrounding the presence of the international teenage basketballers on campus. According to news reports, Auriantal initially brought Bassey to St. Anthony in 2015–16, when they hired him as the athletic coordinator. The following season, Auriantal also facilitated the enrollment of more international players at St. Anthony's, whom he recruited through his sports nonprofit.

Auriantal, Bassey, and the other teenagers moved to Aspire Academy in Kentucky, which hired Auriantal as an assistant coach. After playing one season there, Bassey reclassified and signed to play at Western Kentucky University. The university also hired Auriantal as an assistant coach, compensating him $200,000 after Bassey signed to play at the NCAA Division I program (Sayers 2018).

Bassey emerged as one of Auriantal's more successful recruits, as the Philadelphia 76ers drafted him in the 2021 NBA draft. Auriantal still appears in mediated content with the now-NBA-playing multimillionaire. While Bassey was in high school, Auriantal was granted Bassey's legal guardianship by a San Antonio judge, who signed an order stating that Bassey's father in Nigeria had "voluntarily relinquished possession" of his son to

Auriantal and his wife. However, in an ensuing messy custody battle, another Nigerian man claimed that Bassey's father in Nigeria had signed a document granting Auriantal guardianship over his son under false pretenses (Zuvanich 2017). This other person was vying for the guardianship of Bassey, now a blue-chip recruit. By the summer of 2017, Auriantal won the custody battle and remained Bassey's guardian. Auriantal was also the legal guardian of another teenage basketball standout from Senegal, Moustapha Diagne (K. Maguire 2017).

I am not in a position to speculate on the nature of Auriantal's relationships with any of the international players he recruited. However, Emerita Denis Doyle, the provost of the University of the Incarnate Word, who manages St. Anthony Catholic School in San Antonio, stated, "Their comings and goings are not up to them," implying that other parties dictated their movements. "Everyone knows that if Charles Bassey signed into the NBA, he could make millions in his first year," Doyle continued (McNeel 2017).

What is evident is that Auriantal used Bassey and other international hopefuls to elevate his coaching career, and other parties were interested in doing the same. We must pay special attention to these relationships, which blur the lines among platonic relationships, quasi-parental roles, and straight-up business deals. As these arrangements become more prominent and permissible in conferences such as TCAL, what is troubling is the lack of regulation, oversight, and safeguards to monitor these relationships to ensure they are protective and beneficial to the children.

Tito was recruited to Tech Prep solely for basketball purposes. There was no secret about it. "Athletic scholarship" was written on the I-20 form the school issued for him to take to his visa interview at the US embassy in Panama City. In 2017, when Tito was recruited to play at Tech, a member of TCAL, the governing entity defined how member schools could allocate inducements. The bylaws are stated below:

d **Financial Assistance:** A school shall produce accurate records of financial assistance provided to students. All students should be afforded the same privileges or opportunity to qualify for scholarship type programs, whether those programs are athletic or nonathletic related. It is illegal for a school to give such aid or gifts considered outside of normal operations to those students who participate in athletics solely. This is a violation, including but not limited to forfeitures of games, ineligibility of the athlete(s) in question, school probation, or school expulsion from TCAL.

e Provided Residence: If a school is in the common practice of providing residence to certain students by housing them with families associated with the school or organization, then accurate records and legitimate reasons shall be given for said practices. Housing may not be given to only those students who participate in athletics. U.I.L. Rules shall be applied in these circumstances or the Rules Committee may issue a ruling on athlete(s) eligibility. (TCAL 2016, 31)

These rules stand in stark contrast to the rules on recruitment in Section 5 (cc) of the constitution of the UIL, Texas's principal state athletic association, governed by the University of Texas at Austin; those rules defined *recruiting* as "to encourage a student in any way to change schools for the purpose of participating in UIL activities at any grade level. It could include offering a student or the student's parents cash, waiver of tuition, promise of better conditions at the participant school or on its team, a job or other valuable consideration to induce the student to enroll in a participant school" (UIL 2016, 20).

Additionally, TCAL's ruling on the participation of international noncitizen athletes differs starkly from that of the UIL. The former allowed "foreign (Non-U.S.) transfer students to participate as long as they followed normal school transfer guidelines and have not been a 'professional'" (TCAL 2016, 33). In contrast, the UIL limits the participation of international visa-holding students. According to the UIL (2016 sec. 403[5]), foreign exchange students are ineligible for varsity athletic contests for the first year they attend a member school unless they are granted a waiver. Additionally, foreign exchange students who are granted a waiver may participate in only one year of varsity athletics in the same sport (UIL 2016).

Within the youth basketball world, it is well known that recruiting happens even if it is covert (Dalton 2016). The marked difference between the two conferences and many independent basketball-centered prep schools is the recruitment for and participation in athletics of F-1 student visa holders. The UIL and most other US state-sponsored athletic bodies have barred the participation of F-1 student visa holders due to the system's "ripeness" to be abused and allow coaches and boosters to power-load teams (Kentucky High School Athletic Association 2013). However, relationships between coaches and recruited noncitizen international youth athletes are far greater than just the regulations of inducements. For international athletes we must also consider the amount of time these athletes spend with their coaches within and outside of their athletic pursuits. Also, as was the case with Tito, relationships with persons not involved in athletics can be central to these youth having a positive experience in the United States.

Los Becados Share Their Truths at Sonia's Barbeque Away from the Coach

The Sunday barbeque that Sonia planned for Tito and his other scholarship teammates was a pivotal moment in Tito's experience in La Frontera. Sonia's intentions were primarily to provide the youth with family time away from their coach. This Sunday, unlike previous ones, five of the eight scholarship players attended church with her instead of only Tito.

However, Sonia also wanted to find out more about the youths' living situation and experiences in La Frontera. More important, she wanted to hear their thoughts away from the coach. Her suspicions had already been raised after she visited their house and saw they did not have furniture, winter clothes, or large amounts of food. She ended up donating all of these items to them. Coach Barrigon spoke with her in front of the players, mostly complaining that the parents did not send money for their children and that he had to bear the burden of providing them with everything. It did not sit right with her because when she was leaving, Tito accompanied her to the car and told her that they had been listening to everything the coach was telling her and that it was a lie.

"He's a liar," Sonia sent me in a voice note, directly quoting Tito. In a flustered tone, she ended the message saying, "I don't know, I don't know, Javier, you understand me? I am going to wait for the boys on Sunday to see what they tell me." She paused one more time and repeated, "In reality, I just don't know. Have a good night."

Many truths were revealed during that Sunday's barbeque. Sonia discovered that the boys' life differed from what Coach Barrigon had described to her that night at the house.

"He scolds, scolds, scolds. The boys say that he tells a lot of lies, that he is a horrible liar, he has no humility, he is always saying what he does for them, throwing in their faces, 'I do this, I pay this, I do this, I do the other one,' then he puts the boys down. They say that he lies so much that he believes them himself. He lies to other people about the boys in front of the boys too. Tito is not accustomed to this. I imagine he expected something better," Sonia explained in a voice note after dropping the boys back at their house.

Sonia made more informed assessments about Tito's life in La Frontera and provided them to both Tito's mother and me. Tito and the other *becados* saw Sonia as their fictive aunt who cared. She provided them with the type of care they lacked in La Frontera. Perhaps most important, she was not connected to the school, which likely allowed them to be honest about their situations. Sonia is also a nurse trained to observe behaviors in patients to capture unsaid issues. Only five of the eight players were able to attend Sunday's outing because the other three needed to stay home and work on their school projects. Sonia received conflicting information from the boys and the coach about the reasons some of the boys could not attend. The coach sent Sonia a text message saying, "Last night I talked with Tito until about 1:30 a.m. I told him I am going to send him back to Panama. I don't agree with him not smiling, his teacher says his body language is bad, and he's not being grateful for ANYTHING. This isn't Panama. Here, people like good attitudes and good disposition."

Coach Barrigon requested that Sonia speak to Tito about his attitude at the barbeque. In addition to speaking with Tito, Sonia allowed the boys to share their perspectives. They told her Coach Barrigon went on "talking and talking" past 2:30 a.m. He finished only a couple of hours before Sonia came and picked them up for church. They told her these late-night-turned-early-morning tirades were normal and would often lead to even earlier practices as punishment the next day. Then they expressed the real reason only five of them could attend. After Coach Barrigon's tirade, the other three did not believe they would have enough time to spend the day relaxing with Sonia's family and still finish their school assignments in time to turn them in on Monday morning.

Problems were arising for Tito, and they began to become more pronounced. Sonia and Katia started receiving more text messages from Coach Barrigon complaining about Tito and inquiring about his relationship with me. Monday morning, following the previous day's barbeque, Sonia sent me a voice note: "You will have to excuse me, but I'm thinking about it. I am thinking how you are writing and he is very angry because you are writing emails, sending emails wanting to know a lot of stuff. Now, suddenly he has a problem with Tito. He is trying to hide something or he wants to have full power. Maybe he doesn't like that anybody is questioning him. He's telling Tito that he's going to send him back to Panama, and he doesn't want him to come to him with that attitude, and that the teachers have problems with Tito." She continued, beginning to imitate Coach

Barrigon's voice, "He also told Tito, 'That cell phone that I bought you, I can see all your texts, all of your calls, I can see everything you write.'"

Then, feeling confused, she asked herself, and maybe me too, "Why does he [Barrigon] play psychologically with the boys? Why is he doing those things? I do not understand very well. He [Barrigon] is not well . . . I just don't know, Javier. You know more than me about sports, but this isn't the way to motivate the boys."

What is highlighted in this story is that Tito did not believe he had anyone else to confide in except his mother's friend. The power differential in the coach-player relationship is evident in the way the players must listen to the coach's lies without the power to counter them. This hierarchy could be a factor preventing athletes from seeking support from coaches. The coach is the person who evaluates an athlete and makes decisions regarding playing time, travel, and other issues impacting performance (Sullivan et al. 2020).

Just as Katia said, Sonia got to the bottom of Tito's situation like Jessica Fletcher, but she also got caught in the hierarchal relationships. Sonia, Katia, Tech's admissions officer and designated school official (DSO) Miss Rosalia, and I went back and forth, meditating on how the coach and player interacted. Whether we knew it or not, we were influencing the entire situation. I could confront Coach Barrigon about Tito's lack of tutoring in ways Tito himself did not feel empowered to do, but doing so placed Tito in a strained situation with Coach Barrigon, who ultimately decided whether to maintain Tito as a team member or not. Sonia also became part of the situation and became complicit in Tito's journey to pursue this elusive American basketball dream. Even though she might not have been as aware of the exploitative nature of the system as I was, she recognized the inconsistencies and abuses upfront. She did blow the whistle but without risking ruining Tito's "opportunity." After all, she was also from Panama and knew the realities that await most youth like Tito in Colón versus the supposed opportunity in the United States.

At any rate, we both reveal here that it is not just coach-player relationships that matter. The players need different types of advocates and people in their lives. Sometimes they need a *tía* like Sonia to give them some semblance of home. Or they may need someone like me who is more knowledgeable about the situation and can advocate on their behalf or broker conversations between them and their coaches. The challenge becomes how athletic governing bodies and schools can better integrate their players, especially international minors' diverse needs, within their programs while protecting them from retribution and the power imbalance that favors the coach's side.

In Tito and the other *becados'* case, the coach made the decisions about their lawful migratory status in the United States, which added additional layers of complexity to coach-player relationships at the interscholastic level. In this case, the *becados'* lower hierarchical position in combination with their delicate immigration status prevented them from confronting the coach. However, when given the opportunity to communicate with someone outside of the program, they were able to share their grievances and experiences. Sonia's relationship with Katia, presence in La Frontera, and interactions with Tito and the other youth were coincidental and not intentional, a type of connection that many other international players across the country do not always have. The basketball players recruited by Coach Barrigon at Tech spent the majority of their time under his direction and surveillance.

Currently, the F-1 student visa program does not contain any provisions about the amount of time visa holders can spend with their sponsors (Pleso 2017). In the case of elite basketball, where the stakes of winning are high, the lack of regulation and governance leaves space for exploitation to happen. This is especially true for international noncitizen youth athletes who are in constant contact with their coaches. The negative consequences of the lack of regulation showed up in the lives of Tito and the other *becados* in the form of berating speeches into the early hours of the morning.

The F-1 student visa is a visa for academic purposes, and there are no provisions that address its use for athletic purposes. However, within the US education-based athletic infrastructure, F-1 student visa holders can engage in the billion-dollar interscholastic athletics industry. In 2017, the year Tito entered the United States, the NCAA reported over twenty thousand international student-athletes enrolled in their member institutions (NCAA 2017). However, no uniform data exist at the high school level. I was able to source data from the US Department of Homeland Security via the Freedom of Information Act, which revealed that in 2017 there were a total of sixty-three international noncitizen F-1 student visa holders in US high schools who had "athletic scholarship" listed on their I-20 forms (US Department of Homeland Security 2020, 17), like Tito. This number is revealing and troubling because the same report states that at the bachelor's degree level, there were 20,959 international student-athletes on F-1 student visas receiving athletic scholarships, which is very close to the NCAA's published numbers. According to Department of Homeland Security data, in 2017 only two Panamanians at the secondary level had athletic scholarships listed as a funding source on their I-20s. It is possible that the two listed were Tito and Josue, but we cannot be sure because the data are not listed by individual sport. However, what is certain is that Tito and Josue were not the only Panamanian basketball players laboring in US high schools. There were three others from Colegio Bolivariano, their Panamanian high school, in the United States at the same time. This reveals the disturbing lack of knowledge of F-1 student visa holders laboring at US high schools. A lack of knowledge leaves the door open for exploitation and trafficking within the multibillion-dollar youth sports industry.

As such, international noncitizen labor is being used within interscholastic athletics, which have been plagued with abuses and contentions about protecting players' labor from exploitation. We do not know how many international F-1 students are actually participating in US interscholastic athletics. For Tito and the other *becados*, their F-1 student visa did not offer any protections for their labor, nor did it prevent their unfavorable living conditions. This is particularly perverse considering that this inequitable exchange of labor for an education and safe living conditions provides more benefits for the coach and school than it does for the actual laboring youth.

"Solo es un Gasto Más": Using Academic Eligibility to Remove Tito from Tech

> Señor Wallace solo para avisarte que le terminaré la beca a Tito debido a sus bajas calificaciones, faltas de tareas y poco interés por estudiar!! Te pido por favor que te comuniques conmigo ya que para enero ya no quiero que el esta aqui!! El esta *reprobando* 5 materias de 7 esto es ridículo y no es posible becar a ningún atleta de esta manera. Espero q lo comprendas.!!! solo es un gasto más.

> Mr. Wallace just to let you know that Tito's scholarship will end due to his low grades, missing homework and little interest in studying!! I ask you to please contact me since by January I no longer want him to be here!! He is FAILING 5 subjects out of 7 this is ridiculous and it is not possible to award a scholarship to any athlete this way. I hope you understand.!!! he's just one more expense. (November 2017)

After receiving this text message from Coach Barrigon, I decided to orchestrate a teleconference to make sure Coach Barrigon, Tito, Katia, and I were all on the same page. The conversation began calmly but soon escalated.

"Y'all sent me a damaged player!" Coach Barrigon screamed over the phone. He was convinced that Tito secretly came to the United States with a knee injury sustained in Panama and was going to make him pay for a surgery in the United States. Katia refuted the accusation and accused Coach Barrigon of lying. The conversation was very intense and quickly departed from his original messages about Tito's academic performance. In an effort to bring the conversation back to his original question, I asked the coach one final question. "Are you taking Tito's scholarship after this semester? Yes or no?"

"Yes!" responded Coach Barrigon.

I asked Tito if he was okay, he responded that he was, and we thanked the coach and ended the call. It was late November 2017, barely two complete months after Tito's arrival at La Frontera, and this was the first time that Katia had spoken to Coach Barrigon about her son in his program. He had never seen her before. He did not develop a relationship with her or Tito's larger family during the recruiting process. Although he complained, he never reached out to the parents of *los becados*, and they did not reach out to him either, at least not in the case of Tito. It was not until his threats of retracting Tito's scholarship and sending him back to Panama reached me that the coach had conversations with Tito's parents. The three-way call connecting Panama, Austin, and La Frontera was supposed to discuss Tito's academic performance and Coach Barrigon's desire to terminate Tito's scholarship.

Throughout the conversation Katia stood up for her son's integrity while trying to protect his basketball opportunity at Tech Prep. She was assertive and believed Coach Barrigon was not being forthcoming with information.

"You are saying that Tito does not like talking and always has an attitude. No," Katia said from her end of the line. "My son has always been quiet and reserved."

It reached the point where Coach Barrigon screamed at Katia, "You should be more appreciative of what I am doing for your son! I brought him to the United States! I have bought him shoes, and I have bought him a cell phone! You need to be more grateful!"

"I think you are making excuses trying to get rid of my son," Katia responded. "You are an adult. You should know each child is different!"

At the core Coach Barrigon believed that he was facilitating this opportunity for Tito. However, he was missing how Tito's talents and labor allowed him to achieve the successes he was having in his career. His logic is no different from the logic, which is dominant throughout the United States, regarding African Americans athletes playing for predominantly white institutions at all levels. This logic is that they should not only feel a sense of gratitude but also express gratitude for this saving grace of an opportunity they are receiving (de B'béri and Hogarth 2009; Frederick et al. 2017).

Neither Tito nor his family had anything to be grateful for to this coach. In his anger Coach Barrigon revealed his true thoughts about Tito. He considered Tito a "damaged good" that was costing Coach Barrigon money. "Solo es un gasto más" (he's just one more expense) was a phrase he would text on more than one occasion. If Barrigon was truly concerned about Tito's academic performance in an all-English environment in the United States, he would have investigated Tito's Panamanian academic records. He was more concerned with what he believed Tito could do physically; the academic parts did not matter. However, because commercialized athletic competition is so closely tied to US institutions of higher education (Clotfelter 2019) and secondary schools, Coach Barrigon had an easy way out of the arrangements he had made with Tito and his family. He blamed Tito for underperforming academically and subsequently revoked his athletic scholarship, which was connected to Tito's lawful right to be in the United States. Eddie Comeaux (2018) points out that the disposability of Black male athletes based on academic underperformance is a common feature of US intercollegiate athletics. He argues that athletic stakeholders tend to blame Black male athletes for their academic failures or choices, believing it is a problem with the athlete rather than a problem with the college or university system (Comeaux 2018), which is highly problematic in the use of the F-1 student visa for athletic purposes. Just as Coach Barrigon offered Tito an athletic scholarship that was academically based, he was able to absolve himself of responsibilities to Tito because of the visa's nature. And, unfortunately, Tito's predicament is not an isolated incident.

In 2018, halfway across the United States in Florida, Marvens Petion, a teenage Haitian basketball player in the United States on an F-1 student visa, secretly recorded the verbal lashing his high school coach, Mike Woodbury, directed at him.

"I don't want to hear shit from you. Bottom line. The next thing I hear, get the fuck out!" Woodbury screamed at Petion. "I don't give a shit. I control transcripts. I control where you go next. It could be back to Haiti, motherfucker. That's how easy it is for me. Listen, I am the one thing you don't want to cross because I am the dirtiest baddest motherfucker on this earth," Woodbury continued (Santucci 2018).

Coach Barrigon's late-night tirades could have resembled Woodbury's in Florida, but what is more revealing is how both high school coaches used the unequal power differential and the academic nature of the F-1 student visa to coerce and control the labor and movement of the international teenagers under their care, which fits the United States' definition of human trafficking.

"I've been dealing with this almost over a year but I was scared to leave this school because he always said he will cancel my I-20," Petion told a local newspaper after his recording went public (Santucci 2018).

Both coaches weaponized the F-1 student visa's academic eligibility requirement to wield power over teenage athletes in unequal exchanges. Coach Barrigon's influence and control over academic transcripts at Tech proved very detrimental to Tito's next move as the coach advanced on his decision to end Tito's scholarship.

Even though Coach Barrigon's text implied he was surprised that Tito was failing classes, he was not. Coach Barrigon knew that Tito and, for that matter, Josue were not proficient English speakers, and it caused them academic problems. He had expressed that sentiment to Tito's coach in Panama in a text message that was forwarded to Katia before Tito departed Panama: "And all conditional on him being able to pass the entrance exam because I doubt that in 2 years, he will be able to learn enough English to go on to graduate and go to university ... Josue is in the same process. If he DOESN'T learn English, it will complicate everything. His size and his lack of offense that this year I want him to produce more. But coach you know they have to focus on English if they want to succeed in this country" (Jesus Barrigon, personal communication, October 2017).

The F-1 student visa provided Coach Barrigon the security to rid himself of specific players or trade them if he proved that they were academically underperforming, as was the case with Tito just two months after he arrived in La Frontera.

It was nearly impossible for Tito to perform well in the academically rigorous environment he was placed in. Not only was he a non-English speaker attempting to learn the basics of the language without the promised support, but he was in advanced academic courses like robotics, physics, and geometry that were taught in English. All this was in addition to the specific challenges that Elaine Allard (2015) describes come with the experience of being 1.25-generation migrant English learners in US secondary schools who arrived in the country during their adolescent years. Unlike 1.5-generation migrant students, who have spent much of their formative years in the United States, teenage migrant students, in addition to acquiring a new language, must deal with the social complexities of being in a geographically and culturally distant place; their social connections and sense of belonging are not rooted in the new locale. Also, because Tito and his teammates were the Black *becados* in a mestize and white Latinx school, they experienced transitional challenges consisting of academic and cultural adjustment, social isolation, and racism due to their minority status (Carter-Francique et al. 2015).

Because Tito had been in La Frontera for only about two months when his relationship with Coach Barrigon began to fall apart, he was still connected to Panama. His peer group was Panamanian. Josue was the only Panamanian peer of a similar socioeconomic background that Tito had in La Frontera. They had been in this boat before. The small piece of family life that Tito would have in La Frontera was Sonia, but Coach Barrigon's tight controls and manipulative behaviors ensured Tito would not have a sense of security. It was time for Tito to leave.

A couple of days after our phone conference, I spoke with Ruperto Sr. over the phone. "Mi hijo no está bien" (My son isn't okay), Tito's father told me. "I know my son, and something isn't right. That coach isn't right. Something isn't right," he continued to repeat. I, too, believed that. Tito's parents decided their son could no longer remain under the care of Coach Barrigon.

As Tito was getting ready for his departure, he became concerned about his visa and sent me a text message: "Hola señor Javier, una pregunta" (Hello, Mr. Javier, one question). Following my reply, he inquired about the visa: "Is the visa going to be fine?" He was concerned that his migratory status in the country would be jeopardized by leaving. The school's DSO was inquiring about his future plans once he left Tech. I assured him that all would be fine. I did not know if everything would be fine, but I pretended that I did.

Tito was ready to go but would have considered remaining so as not to jeopardize his F-1 student visa. He was grappling with remaining and accepting the label of a "cancer," as he was often called by Coach Barrigon. He had no one to turn to. His whole support network other than some of his teammates all were outside of the school and out of his reach. The closest adults within his circle of confidence—Sonia and I—were ostracized by the coach, making it difficult for Tito to maintain communication. Ridiculed and embarrassed in front of his peers, Tito no longer desired to attend church with Sonia because he feared Coach Barrigon would call him "pastor" during team practices. Coach Barrigon instructed Tito not to speak with me and sent texts to Katia telling her I was calling Tito throughout the day, attempting to cause dissent among us. Also, Coach Barrigon did not like the *becados* talking to Tech's DSO and academic dean, Miss Rosalia, about anything outside of basketball.

Tito was first introduced to Miss Rosalia when Tech offered him the scholarship. Through mostly WhatsApp voice messages, she worked with Tito's family, including me, on his transition from Panama to La Frontera. As the DSO, she was tasked with providing all of the legal documents, such as the I-20 form and the supporting forms for the F-1 student visa adjudication process at the US embassy in Panama. Miss Rosalia's signature appeared on the letter of support that falsely guaranteed Tito English as a Second Language (ESL) classes and English tutors. She had intimate knowledge of Tito's academic situation and knew that the lack of the promised English support services was the cause of his underperformance, which became Coach Barrigon's basis to revoke his scholarship. Also, as the school's academic dean, Miss Rosalia was in a position to intervene through more than just questioning Tito about his plans once he left Tech. How could Miss Rosalia not recognize that a nonfluent English speaker, as she attested in her letter to the US embassy, with less than two months in an English academic environment would be struggling without any support?

Maybe Miss Rosalia was not privy to Coach Barrigon's true reason for wanting to kick Tito out. He forbade *los becados* from speaking with her about anything other than basketball. Tito said she did not even know where they lived in La Frontera. Coach Barrigon had more control than Miss Rosalia over admitting and dismissing students, at least international scholarship basketball players, without having to sign any official documents. That was Miss Rosalia's job and commitment with the Student and Exchange Visitor Program (SEVP) as Tech's DSO. Although she might have been in a position to help Tito in La Frontera, he did not see her as a person of confidence because she was a representative of the school's infrastructure. Nor did he feel he could confide in any other adult within the school because of Coach Barrigon's preferential treatment by the school and its owner. Tito and Miss Rosalia's relationship was very transactional. She offered him tangible support only on issues related to the F-1 student visa. Sullivan and colleagues (2020) suggest tangible support focuses only on the problem itself rather than the emotional aspects that accompany the problem. Tito did not feel comfortable engaging with Miss Rosalia about the emotional aspects of attempting to maintain an F-1 student visa issued for athletic purposes.

Tito's person, body, and legal status were attached to his F-1 student visa. It was clear that his body was no longer needed by Coach Barrigon or Tech Prep, and his person had to leave. On November 29, 2017, Coach Barrigon texted me:

> Él no pone interés en su escuela y ya hoy tuvimos la junta administrativa donde van a cortarle la beca él va a ser un jugador inelegible durante los dos primeros meses de temporada entonces para que me traje a este chico si no estudia y no podrá jugar tampoco Solo es un gasto más.

> He is not interested in his school and today we had the administrative meeting where they are going to cut his scholarship, he is going to be an ineligible player during the first two months of the season. So why did I bring this boy if he does not study and will not be able to play either? He's just another expense.

Although the F-1 student visa program is based on academics, performance in the classroom had little influence on why Tito went to La Frontera and why he was now leaving. Coach Barrigon believed that Tito was used and damaged goods and an additional financial burden not only because he was perceived to have a knee injury but also because he had too many people advocating for him.

These behaviors were not observed during Coach Barrigon's interactions with the white and mestize parents who were presumably paying tuition. Coach Barrigon said and did whatever he wanted to Tito and his mother because of his racist and classist ideas about how they should behave in "his" space. He believed he was doing them a favor by allowing Tito to be at Tech on a basketball scholarship. And no recipient of his benevolence should ever question or challenge his authority. My emails questioning Tito's academic situation, Katia's defense of her son, Sonia's involvement, and Tito's refusal to comport himself as desired all challenged Barrigon's ideas about how he thought we should behave. Coach Barrigon's actions further highlight that African-descended youth, not just African Americans, are constructed and employed as preferred laborers of the basketball industry. The coach's utilitarian power (Comeaux 2018) can employ academics as a ploy to remove noncitizen student-athletes from their programs for athletic or other reasons. There is little recourse for the F-1 student visa holder. Tito was accosted by Coach Barrigon and subsequently had his scholarship revoked because of his perceived knee injury, which meant a lack of productivity, a bad attitude, and poor body language. These issues and also, as Sonia stated, my intrusion within his business were the real reasons Tito was targeted and removed from the school. However, Coach Barrigon was able to justify Tito's removal from Tech's athletic program and school not because of the aforementioned reasons but rather because of Tito's supposedly poor academic performance, used to legitimate the canceling of his athletic scholarship. What is shown here is that international noncitizen athletes on F-1 student visas can be exploited, abused, and removed from programs and have their lawful migratory status within the United States revoked for nonacademic reasons. Currently, due to the lack of regulations within the interscholastic departments that allow F-1 student visa holders to be recruited for and participate in athletic programs, the youth's labor is not protected and can ultimately be used to decide their fate within the United States.

Conclusion: The Importance of Coach-Player
Relationships and the Lack of Regulation

Coach-player relationships are important. If there is a bad relationship and it is continuous, with no break from it, it could possibly impact players' lives in many ways. Tito was constantly surrounded by Coach Barrigon and the basketball program. Coach Barrigon, or one of his assistant coaches, transported Tito and the other youth to school each way. The coach was in the school building. They practiced and trained with the coach daily. He provided their food and supposedly emotional support. Within its regulations the TCAL did not offer any protections through monitoring these relationships. Even if they did offer some type of guidance in their bylaws, there is no certainty of enforcement.

There was no break from Coach Barrigon. Unlike in Panama, where he traveled cross-country, in La Frontera Tito could not end his day at home with his family. In Panama, he knew he at least had some type of distance from the sport and its business. Infrequent communication with his parents and friend group was his new norm in La Frontera. Although major athletic apparel companies market the phrase that "ball is life," it is not, and it is a dangerous concept.

Tito balled himself beyond his borders to La Frontera. The arc on his three-point shot swooshing through the net guaranteed him a shot at Tech. But it all came at a cost, more than the one he and his family had assumed when they decided he would leave Panama. Who was Ruperto "Tito" Brown Hurtado Jr.? And who was invested in his holistic development and well-being? The same thing that got him to La Frontera became his life.

He lived, ate, traveled, and was demeaned and ridiculed in basketball. *Tía* Sonia, the unexpected aunt, was the only person in La Frontera who took Tito out to see, explore, and meet people not associated with Tech.

Tech Prep, the advanced placement school, was not invested in exploring other parts of his identity, let alone his academic identity. They never gave him the educational support they promised him. And when he performed poorly in the classroom, the only remediation Tech offered was revoking his scholarship. Coach Barrigon brought him to Tech to play basketball and for "ball" to be his life, as it was Coach Barrigon's profession. He capitalized on Tito's labor within the billion-dollar youth sport industry that depended on Tito and the other *becados'* labor and American hoop dreams. There was no regard for who they were off the court.

When Tito did not meet Coach Barrigon's expectations and had a support network that challenged his authority, Coach Barrigon abused him psychologically. He was calling him "a cancer," "pastor," and other names. He suffered through these abuses for the basketball opportunity. His mental and emotional health was impacted because basketball consumed his life. Who was there to check on Tito's mental health as he navigated this opportunity?

One of the implications of "ball is life," and everything that comes with the culture, is that Tito had limited to no time to define himself or explore other aspects of his life or identity beyond basketball. "Ball is life" was leading him on the route of possible "identity foreclosure," defined as a commitment to an identity before one has meaningfully explored other options or engaged in exploratory behavior, such as career exploration, talent development, or social clubs or interest groups (Danish et al. 1993). Scholars such as Krystal Beamon (2012) and Louis Harrison and colleagues (2011) have extensively researched the higher rates of identity foreclosure among Black male athletes. Black males like Tito have higher rates of being socialized as athletes than their nonwhite peers. When young people do not have the ability to disconnect from the sport, they can experience fatigue and burnout (DiFiori et al. 2018).

Currently, the F-1 student visa does not account for the psychological, emotional, and physical needs of visa holders outside of their school experience. But more important, there is an absence of these considerations in the visa's use within the multibillion-dollar amateur basketball industry. The visa does not include any provisions for the number of hours student-athletes can spend on school-related athletic activities, such as practice time. The other education visa that is managed through the US Department of State is the J-1 student visa. The J-1 student visa addresses many of these issues (Pleso 2017), but the limits of this exchange visitor visa do not allow for student-athletes to be placed in private schools on athletic scholarships. As such, with their F-1 visas attaching them to Tech, Coach Barrigon was the students' coach, guardian, and sponsor—almost their everything. At least that is how he would describe the things he was doing for them. The stakes of winning and attaining advanced opportunities for the schools, coaches, and players can make it difficult for people to do the right thing.

Also, we must consider that many of these youth are in the United States by themselves, without the support of trustworthy adults. They have limited options of persons whom they can trust and who can legitimately help them if they find themselves in a precarious situation.

5

The inbound pass went straight into player 00's hands during the full-court press. The defender was tightly pressed against him, but a quick behind-the-back fake-out caught the defender off guard. Tito drove down the sideline, carefully maneuvering between the losing defender and the out-of-bounds line. The crowd erupted as Tito, now wearing his new jersey number, began his ascent in the air from the free throw line. He planted his left foot, faking out the remaining four defenders, then pivoted back onto his right foot and went up for the point. He missed, the ball bouncing off the rim, but he drew the foul.

It was eerily reminiscent of the third-place victory he had secured for Panama in Centrobasket nearly a year before. Tito walked up to the free throw line and looked down to make sure his Nikes were positioned closely behind the line. He bent his knees, and with careful precision, he drove up and released the ball. It soared to its highest point and, with a soft swoosh, passed through the net.

The crowd screamed! A very audible "Sit yo ass down, white boy" rang out from one of Tito's new classmates in the student section of Dorothy Turner High School's gym in Austin. It was a good game, but the competition was below Tito's level. Tonight he was playing on the junior varsity basketball squad because, according to University Interscholastic League (UIL) eligibility standards, he could have changed schools for athletic purposes. In the UIL's constitution the section "Changing Schools for Athletic Purposes" reads (UIL 2016, sec. 443):

(a) Determination by district executive committee. The District Executive Committee is to determine whether or not a student changed schools for athletic purposes, when considering each student who changed schools and has completed the eighth grade, whether or not the student has represented a school in grades nine through twelve.

(b) Common Indicators. District Executive Committees should look closely to determine if a student is changing schools for any athletic purpose. Some common indicators committees should include in their considerations include, but are not limited to: checking to see if a student was recruited; ascertaining whether a student was in good standing in the previous school, either academically or in a sports program; determining if a student was unhappy with a coach in the previous school; determining if a student played on a non-school team and is transferring to the school where members of the non-school team attend; determining if a student played on a non-school team and is transferring to the school where the non-school team coach or a relative of the non-school team coach, is the school coach; and determining if a student received individual or team instruction from a school coach and is transferring to the school of that coach.

(c) INELIGIBLE. A student who changes schools for athletic purposes is not eligible to compete in varsity UIL athletic contest(s) at the school to which he or she moves for at least one calendar year, even if both parents move to the new school district attendance zone.

Without a waiver Tito would remain ineligible for varsity competition for at least one calendar year because he had competed in official games at

FIGURE 5.1. Tito in action during a game in Texas when at Turner High School, 2018. Photo by the author.

Tech Prep in La Frontera. According to UIL policy, Tito was indeed "unhappy with a coach at the previous school," but Coach Barrigon was also "unhappy" with him. Tito didn't transfer to Turner for athletic reasons, but under UIL rules, the burden of proof rests with the transferring athlete, not the previous coach.

The crosstown school Turner played that night was peppered with a couple of Black players, but it drew a largely white and engaged crowd. The other school mostly dominated the night, but once again Tito's free throw shots secured Turner's victory. Not only did his performance silence his on-court opponents, but his new Black classmates also silenced those in the stands, basking in the triumph of their school's victory.

As I stood there with my father, both of us elated to see Tito doing well in *el norte*, albeit not in the way any of us had imagined, I could not help but wonder if Tito's new classmates knew that he was not African American but a Black Panamanian from Panama. The night of the game was during Tito's second week in his new public school in Austin. There were nearly three thousand students in the school building. Maybe it did not matter that Tito was *not* African American to the boy in the stands screaming for the white boy to sit his ass down.

Tito's barely six-foot, muscular frame and medium dark brown skin blended in well with the other young men battling it out on the court. There would have been no way of telling from the stands, as a spectator, that he was a monolingual Spanish speaker from the Central American country of Panama. How would the fans know that he did not have a stable migratory status in the United States and that he was navigating a public high school as an unaccompanied child? From the stands, the only thing visible was his Blackness, the same Blackness that he shared with other young men in search of "making it" in the world of US basketball.

Turner High was a place where his Black body would not automatically mark his *becado* status or foreignness, because nearly 10 percent of the over three thousand students were racially Black, mostly African American. However, Turner did demographically mirror Tech with respect to its non-Black Hispanic/Latinx population. About 80 percent of the student body identified as Hispanic/Latinx, but this was far different from Tech's Latinx population. Advanced placement courses, economic affluence, whiteness, and a 100 percent college placement were not the norm at Turner, unlike Tech. Turner was a public high school where over 60 percent of the student body has been framed as economically disadvantaged according to district statistics. Tito was around more students like himself, from working-class backgrounds and with varied migration backgrounds and statuses. Many of his new peers at Turner balanced school and other responsibilities, like caring for family members and working.

While the term *economically disadvantaged* is a loaded term, much like *at risk*, which carries deficit views of students—particularly when applied to Black and non-Black Hispanic students (Brown 2016)—it nonetheless highlights the racial and class-based segregation within Austin's schools, which can significantly impact students' futures. In Austin students labeled as economically disadvantaged are predominantly concentrated in schools attended by Black and Hispanic students, such as Turner.

In contrast, in Austin's Travis County, white students attend schools where only 25 percent of the population is labeled economically disadvantaged. Meanwhile, economically disadvantaged students make up 67 percent of the student population at schools attended by Black students and

71 percent at schools attended by Hispanic students (Sterne 2020). These disparities have long-term consequences, as students attending these schools are less likely to enroll in and graduate from college and often earn less over their lifetimes.

Black Panamanian Immigrant Connections: Coming to Austin

"He can come here. He can enroll in school here," my father told me after learning about Tito's situation in La Frontera. His decades of experience working in the local school district along with his own personal experience as an international student-athlete in his youth informed his recommendation. We knew Tito could not remain in La Frontera, nor did he have the money to return to Panama right away.

"He can't go back until he gets what he came here for," my father would often repeat when talking about Tito, a young man he had met only once and had no blood relation to. However, he knew that the local public school in Austin could offer Tito not only protections guaranteed by *Plyler v. Doe* but also an opportunity to fulfill the dream that had brought him to *el norte*. My father had arrived in Austin through a network of diasporic conversations that connected his mostly Black West Indian enclave in Panama to an African American community in Austin.

Austin was a place my father initially knew nothing about. New York City had been his preferred destination, as it was for many of his peers and the generations of Black Panamanians of West Indian descent (Corinealdi 2022). However, Austin was the place that presented him an opportunity to use sport to create a life for himself that he did not believe would have been possible had he remained in Panama. There were also other Panamanians in Austin. He built a life there. He became an educator in Austin's public schools. He began as a physical education teacher and ended his career as an assistant principal at Turner High School, the same place where he recommended that Tito enroll. In reality, my father saw himself in Tito. He expressed that his younger self had yearned to transcend his borders, and many people in his community had supported his dreams.

My family and I decided to welcome Tito to Austin so he could continue pursuing his American hoop dream. It wasn't just a matter of coincidence or immigrant connections, which Vilna Francine Bashi (2007) describes as the "spoke and wheel" of transnational Black migration. Tito found refuge in a community that could offer him safer living conditions, as well as emotional and financial support. This was, in part, a result of the decades-long nurturing of Black Panamanian athletes within the sporting congregations at historically Black colleges and universities (HBCUs). After all, it was a member of Alpha Kappa Alpha who helped push my father's application through at the local school district, just a couple of years after he had pledged Alpha Phi Alpha, placing him within the network of the Divine Nine, a group of nine historically African American fraternities and sororities.

When my father graduated from Huston-Tillotson in 1978, his Panamanian American high school in the US Panama Canal Zone, Escuela Secundaria de Rainbow City, had been shut down the previous academic year. The majority-Black school, under US control, just like schools throughout the contiguous United States, was closed, and students were either bused to the "American" schools or subsidized to attend Panamanian schools in the republic. Many teachers were phased out. This all disrupted the athletic pipelines teachers and coaches had forged with HBCUs, which had offered youth like my father opportunities to employ their athletic skills for an education in the United States. It all virtually came to a crashing halt. Derrick White (2019) details how school desegregation ravaged the connections Black coaches had with HBCU athletic programs. All of these historical factors were important in my moving to Panama, meeting Tito, and now attempting to help him while living together in the home my father and mother had created in Austin.

However, I believe Tito was one of the few international noncitizen youth athletes who have a supportive external community outside of their athletic program and recruitment. I got on the phone and informed Katia of my parents' decision. "That would be great if he came to stay with you. He already knows your parents, and he asked if he could come to your house," Katia explained.

Her biggest concern during this ordeal was not relying too much on her friend Sonia's generosity. She did not want to involve Sonia any more than she already had, even though Sonia was an integral part of Tito's time in La Frontera. Moreover, Katia did not want to place Sonia in an awkward situation where her teenage daughter would be living with a new teenage boy. She believed that Tito would not overstep any boundaries, but as a mother of teenage daughters herself, she understood the concern. Moreover, I was young and had maintained an active relationship with Tito since he and I lived in Panama less than a year before.

"He Can't Remove Your Visa": The Absence
of a Legal Coach-Player Relationship

On January 4, 2018, after leaving Tech, Tito arrived in Austin and registered
as a student at Turner High School. Per my father's instructions, he registered
as a homeless youth and English language learner (ELL), both of which he
was. According to the McKinney-Vento Homeless Assistance Act (sec. 725),
a federal law, school-age youth are classified as homeless if they are sheltered;
live doubled up; live in a hotel/motel, car, park, and so on; or are unaccompanied youth. Even though we provided Tito with a stable residence in our
home, he still qualified as homeless due to his departure from Tech. Additionally, the label made Tito eligible for certain protections and benefits. For instance, homeless students have the right to receive a free, appropriate public
education and to enroll in school immediately, even if they lack documents
normally required for enrollment, and they receive educational services comparable to those provided to other students, according to the child's needs.

Tito was now settling into his new residence in Austin, but he had never
intended to be removed from Tech in La Frontera. It became his responsibility to fend for himself. His F-1 student visa laid all of the responsibility
on him—that is the nature of the visa. The irony of the situation was that
for Tito to be safe, he had to make a decision that went against the stipula-
tions of his student visa. When he left La Frontera, he violated the terms
of the F-1 student visa, effectively violating US immigration law. We did
not go through the official process to have his Student and Exchange Visitor Information System (SEVIS) number transferred to an eligible school.
We didn't have enough time or money to find an eligible school that could
transfer the number. The few private schools where Tito's SEVIS could have
been transferred within reach all required a couple of thousand dollars
for entrance. Turner High School didn't qualify. We had to make a choice
within our circumstances. Also, to intentionally make it difficult for Tito,
Tech refused to release any of Tito's grades. They said he owed tuition for
the year. It was a choice that Coach Barrigon knew would have significant
detrimental impacts on Tito's life. Still, it was one he could wield over him
because of the power differential between him and Tito, the basketball recruit he had brought from Panama. Sonia later forwarded me the messages
the coach had sent her regarding the way Tito left the school and how he
would be considered "illegal in the country," in the coach's words.

In good faith, Tito had made a contract with the US government when
he accepted the conditions of his F-1 student visa, believing that Coach

Barrigon and Tech Prep would provide him with the basketball and educational opportunities he sought. However, Coach Barrigon's name did not appear on any of the official documents during the process. Despite being the one who "discovered" Tito at the Centrobasket tournament and brokered the deal with Tito's basketball coach in Panama, Coach Barrigon was not the school's designated school official (DSO) nor an academic administrator involved in the Student and Exchange Visitor Program (SEVP). That role belonged to Miss Rosalia.

Coach Barrigon was fundamentally responsible for Tito's housing and physical well-being. Most important, Tito would spend the majority of his time under Coach Barrigon's guidance, participating in team practices, travel, and games. While Coach Barrigon had the authority to revoke Tito's scholarship, he had no legal authority or responsibility for Tito's student visa status.

The absence of Coach Barrigon's name from the legal migration paperwork was a fact Tito discovered in Austin during a phone call with the SEVP customer service line. I was not exactly sure how to handle the situation, but I thought it would be a good idea to call SEVP, at the very least because they oversee schools and students in the F-1 visa program. As Tito sat in the dining room of his new residence in Austin, alongside my father and me, we discussed his situation with the young woman on the other end of the line. I translated most of the conversation between Spanish and English. Tito explained his situation and the fact that the coach had revoked his scholarship. She quickly asked what his name was.

"Juan Barrigon, and the school's name is Tech Prep Academy," Tito replied.

Computer keys clicked away in the background as the young representative searched the system with Tito's information. "I don't see his name in any of our official documents," she said after a few moments of silence. "He can't remove your visa. His name isn't listed as the designated school officer [DSO]. Only they have the power to remove your visa." Beyond that very important piece of information, there was little else the young woman could do to help us.

We all sat there, stunned and confused. How does someone with so much power have so little responsibility for the young people they recruit to come and play basketball? In the "International Student Athlete Q&A" from the March 2017 issue of the SEVP *Spotlight*, SEVP field representative Meghan Lane explained that given the nature of competitive sports and the inconsistent timing of sports seasons across the globe, as well as the busy schedules, it is common for F-1 student-athletes to be unclear about the rules for maintaining their status once they arrive in the country.

"International student athletes may not proactively seek out their DSOs because they presume their coach will take care of everything for them or proactively pursue their DSO," Lane said. She suggested that DSOs should take extra time to do special orientations to verify that the new international F-1 student-athletes understand what actions they need to take to maintain legal status.

Back in late August, Tito had rushed from Panama to La Frontera, as Coach Barrigon wanted him to participate in a tournament Tech was hosting. As he arrived late and jumped straight into school and athletic life, we naively presumed that Coach Barrigon was taking care of everything Tito needed. Miss Rosalia, Tech Prep's DSO, never oriented Tito on how to maintain his legal status. She questioned him only once he could no longer safely remain at Tech.

At that moment we realized that we did not have any of Coach Barrigon's information beyond his cell phone number. We did not know where he lived. We were left to wonder what Tito would do now. What became clear was that individuals like Coach Barrigon who have the most contact with and power over international students' lives and their lawful presence in the United States could be legally absent from the entire process. The coach did not appear in SEVIS, which monitors student visa holders but does not track information on coaches.

This is what happened in the Evelyn Mack case. In November 2019 Evelyn Mack, the owner of Evelyn Mack Academy, a private school in Charlotte, North Carolina, was sentenced to eighteen months in federal prison for concealing, harboring, and shielding "unlawful aliens." A federal indictment stated that throughout the school's operation, Mack received approximately $1,000 per student from athletic recruiters to falsely represent about seventy-five international teenagers as students in Evelyn Mack Academy, which was authorized to enroll high school students through the F-1 student visa program (US Department of Justice 2019). Coaches placed international noncitizen teenagers on basketball rosters across the United States but not at the F-1 "authorized" Evelyn Mack Academy. Many of these youths have yet to be located.

"Certainly, it starts in a certain sense with Mrs. Mack, but the real culprit are the coaches, and they are still out there, and they are free, and they are still doing the same thing all over the country," James Exum, Mack's attorney, said in a news interview following her sentencing (Tolison 2019).

Mack must be held accountable for participating in this human trafficking scheme. Additionally, as her attorney stated, the coaches who participated equally in the scheme remain free and could potentially do it again. Mack was caught because the official paper trail ultimately led back to her. The coaches' signatures, like Coach Barrigon's, were nowhere to be found on the legally binding documents. That is a problem that needs to be addressed. Coaches and recruiters also need to be held responsible during all phases of the process, primarily because of their power to determine a student's eligibility while at the school.

In an effort to protect himself, Tito left Tech and went to Austin. The decision was made from a place of fear and uncertainty but was necessary. The alternative would have been to stay and endure the abuse and negligence of Coach Barrigon. Tito could not call any authorities to help him. He believed that any knock on the door could be immigration wanting to send him and the other international youth back home. He did not even know the address where he was living. All we had was a picture of a stop sign and a street sign attached to a metal post that Sonia sent me as a text message. It was not until later, while using Google Maps in Austin, that Tito was able to identify the house where he had lived. Using the street name from the photo, he reached back into his memory and traced the exact route from the school to the place where he had lived. Pressing the arrow key and seeing all the places he remembered, he also pointed out the coach's auto body shop, where the boys would sometimes labor if "they needed something," as Tito described Coach Barrigon's priming of him.

Within His Rights: *Plyler v. Doe*

Public schools in the United States are not permitted to deny education to any young person based on their immigration status. In states like Texas, with a large transnational population, policies like these allow many youth with unstable migratory statuses to attend public schools. These current statutes in US education emerged from a class action suit filed against Texas. In 1975 the Texas legislature revised its education laws to deny enrollment in public schools and to withhold any state funds for the education of children who were not "legally admitted" to the country (US Courts, n.d.). However, the *Plyler* court held that undocumented children are entitled to a state-funded primary and secondary education (M. Lopez 2004).

This landmark case protected Tito's decision to enroll and continue his education. Tito did not come to Austin or enroll at Turner for basketball purposes; his primary motivation was safety. However, he did play basketball at Turner and was a welcome addition to the team. Turner High could not boast that any other student on their squad had represented their country on international stages. However, the UIL would view Tito's status and move from La Frontera differently. Their rules, as outlined in previous chapters, did not account for the complexities of Tito's situation. It seemed as though Tito might have moved for athletic purposes, which would render him ineligible for varsity-level competition. This is a common tactic used by athletic governing bodies to discourage transfers for athletic reasons. There are numerous documented cases of students, including international noncitizen youth on F-1 student visas like Tito, transferring schools for athletic purposes.

Yet the statute protected by the Equal Opportunity Clause of the Fourteenth Amendment has also been exploited by basketball traffickers to take advantage of the labor of noncitizen youth within US public schools. While researching basketball trafficking stories in an attempt to understand what was happening to Tito in La Frontera, I came across stories where the *Plyler v. Doe* Supreme Court decision was being used to facilitate basketball trafficking in US public schools. Although there was no direct mention of *Plyler*, my father's experience in public schools, where youth without stable migratory statuses were welcomed, as he had recommended for Tito, prompted me to explore how other international teenage athletes were entering US public high schools.

One notable case was part of a national basketball trafficking scandal that rocked Paterson Eastside High School in Paterson, New Jersey. Two Nigerian teenagers, Sam and Jackson, enrolled at Paterson Eastside with the assistance of Andre Rickett, a New York City basketball scout (Stanmyre and Politi 2017). The two boys had previously been at Genesis Prep Academy in Post Falls, Idaho, after they first entered the United States on F-1 student visas a year earlier. Genesis Prep was in the business of recruiting international talent and sponsoring their I-20s. Sam and Jackson made national headlines when local journalists uncovered the Paterson Eastside basketball trafficking scandal.

Mediated news sources tell only part of the story. Still, it's highly likely, given what we know, that Sam and Jackson did not follow the proper process for transferring their SEVIS through the SEVP system, which rendered them out of status. According to Genesis Prep School's principal, as quoted in a news story, "We didn't know exactly where they were until the New Jersey story hit" (Clouse 2017).

Perhaps the school did not know their whereabouts because, when they departed, Genesis's DSO did not transfer their SEVIS record through the official government portal. The same situation occurred at Tech. They knew exactly where Tito was only once Turner requested his official transcripts. Tito's silent departure from Tech had intentionally protected him from Coach Barrigon, who knew the legal ramifications of Tito's departure. I could not locate a news article where either Sam's or Jackson's voices were recorded detailing why they left their authorized prep school in Idaho, but some clues left the door open for further questions.

"They left on their own. They just weren't happy, I guess," their basketball coach at Genesis, Marshall Colbert, said, according to the *Spokesman-Review*, a local newspaper in Idaho. "I don't know. That's something you have to ask them," Colbert said regarding why the two Nigerian teenagers left the school.

While I support their agency to leave Genesis for whatever reason, there are still uncomfortable questions, especially when considering the complexity and vulnerability international youth face in these athletic situations. As in Tito's case, for many of these international youth, things within their school or home life can be more complicated or layered than they appear or are reported to be. Tito was not happy at Tech. Coach Barrigon verbally and psychologically abused him daily, constantly threatening to send him back to Panama. He was far from his family and support network and left Tech for Austin, against the rules, out of concern for his safety. All the while, Coach Barrigon, the source of his endangerment and his recruiter to the United States, did not face any consequences. When youth athletes are unhappy, it becomes their burden to bear. The UIL rules deem a transferring student ineligible for competition if a district executive committee determines that "a student was unhappy with a coach in the previous school." Due to the unequal power dynamics between players and coaches, a coach claiming that a child left because they were not happy places the entire responsibility on the student. As Eddie Comeaux (2018) pointed out, at the collegiate level, athletic stakeholders tend to blame Black male athletes for their choices, assuming the problem lies with the athlete rather than with the college or university system itself.

Even though *Plyler v. Doe* protected Sam's and Jackson's enrollment at Paterson Eastside, it did not protect them from the dangers of the athletic industrial complex. Coach Juan Griles, Paterson Eastside's basketball coach, wanted to win, and he used *Plyler*'s protection enabling noncitizen youth to access education in the United States to power-load his team. In an eerily similar predicament to Tito's in La Frontera, as I would later find out, the two Nigerian teens joined seven other international boys living in the home of Eastside's head boys basketball coach. They reported to the newspaper that he was abusive, threatened them, and kicked some of them out of the house; those who stayed were forced to live in deplorable conditions, lacking food.

Eastside's tactic of recruiting international talent could also be seen in the Evelyn Mack Academy basketball trafficking scandal in North Carolina. Blessing Efijor, a Nigerian teenager who entered the United States on an F-1 student visa sponsored by Evelyn Mack, never made it to North Carolina.

"When I asked why I wasn't going to North Carolina, I was told that I didn't have a ready host family . . . I ended up in Jersey," Blessing told a reporter once the basketball trafficking scandal came to light.

Blessing also played on the Paterson Eastside girls basketball team and was among other young international girls moving from home to home, playing basketball at this public school that they were technically not authorized to attend because of their type of visa. They did so because of how their coaches and recruiters abused *Plyler v. Doe* protections.

I am not arguing that the *Plyler v. Doe* decision should be overturned or modified. A modification could further expose these youth to vulnerable situations due to their immigration status. However, the intentional abuse of the protections afforded to any person underscores how US laws and policies can be exploited to facilitate the trafficking of international youth. This also highlights that US public schools and state-sponsored athletic bodies must take basketball trafficking seriously. They cannot treat it as an issue only for private schools processing F-1 students for athletic purposes. Young international athletes like Tito can find themselves in US public schools either seeking refuge or being coerced into performing athletic labor.

Why TCAL and UIL Are Both Complicit in Producing Basketball Trafficking

Whether or not the athlete participates in a Texas Christian Athletic League (TCAL) or UIL school for athletic purposes, schools are responsible for ensuring their care and safety. It is not a matter of whether the student is athletically eligible or not. While athletic eligibility is important, it does not supersede academic eligibility within the rules of the F-1 student visa program. The school, and by extension the athletic governing bodies, decides the student-athlete's athletic eligibility status, which can be a complicated process. However, it is Immigration and Customs Enforcement (ICE) that enforces eligibility. It's not about compliance; it's about what the system produces. The current system does provide opportunities for youth like Tito to access basketball and educational opportunities in the United States. However, it is a highly policed system with contradictory policies that can disrupt children's lives.

Without schools like Tech and governing bodies such as TCAL, which emphasize athletic recruitment, there would be limited opportunities for aspiring international teenage athletes to enhance their exposure in the US interscholastic athletic system—ultimately hindering their pursuit of basketball dreams. However, the issues of exploitation and trafficking of international youth athletes are not exclusive to schools or leagues that sanction their recruitment and participation. Schools that are members of the UIL, which prohibits international visa-holding students from participating in competitions outside of one season in the same varsity sport, are also complicit.

Not all international noncitizen youth enter public schools as a participant in the F or J visa student programs. Through the protections and abuses of the *Plyler v. Doe* decision, some of these youth enter public schools seeking refuge and protection, while others are trafficked into these schools by coaches and other basketball profiteers. State athletic governing bodies must be vigilant about these trends because players' athletic eligibility can also have negative consequences for them within public schools. US interscholastic athletics, including public school basketball, is a high-stakes industry, filled with corporate sponsorships and incentives for winning (Hawkins 2010).

This is particularly true for trafficked youth, who are dependent on the recruiting coaches. When things do not work out, if deemed ineligible, they can become valueless and be discarded by the very individuals who should be providing care. Additionally, attending a public school—even under the protection of federal law—cannot shield undocumented international noncitizen Black athletes from being surveilled, placed into immigration custody, or forcefully removed from the country.

Conclusion

Athletic eligibility cannot be separated from lawful presence in the United States for international Black noncitizen F-1 student visa holders here for athletic purposes. The NCAA, UIL, and TCAL determine eligibility, while

ICE enforces it. Athletic governing bodies, such as the NCAA, become non-state enforcers of immigration policy. Basketball trafficking is dangerous not only because it involves exploitation by individuals but also because it is part of a larger exploitative system. As a host agency for the SEVP and F-1 student visa program, ICE allows athletic governing bodies like TCAL, UIL, and NCAA to recruit athletes using the F-1 student visa to meet their needs. In exchange, these athletic governing bodies become extensions of ICE. They can act as what Jennifer Wolch (1990) has described as *parastate actors*, which are individuals or entities who technically work outside of the state but whose work is intertwined with it. Through rules regarding athletic eligibility, compliance, and enforcement, they work to police noncitizen youth athletes in the country. To continue this mutually beneficial relationship, each entity must do their part. They can use each other as forms of social control (Golash-Boza 2015). To remain in good athletic standing, an athlete must be academically eligible. If they are not academically eligible, they cannot lawfully remain in the country on an F-1 student visa. The opposite is also true: When athletic governing bodies or coaches are done with an athlete's labor, they return them to ICE. While there is supposedly a goal of helping the athlete succeed, if they fail, they are handed over to ICE to fuel its mission of protecting the United States from immigrants who are alleged to be unlawful and dangerous. Historically, Black and Latinx men have been disproportionately forcibly removed from the United States via deportation (Golash-Boza 2015; Goodman 2020), which is significant in the context of basketball. Black male athletes, like Tito, are the preferred laborers of the basketball industry and are highly visible in news stories about basketball trafficking incidents within the United States.

This is important because ICE is not a rehabilitative or an educational task force. It has been tasked to protect the borders of the United States as a law enforcement agency. Black boys often have early encounters with law enforcement compared to their white counterparts (Dumas and Nelson 2016). A dependency on Black male labor within basketball and the larger AIC places these noncitizen international teenage athletes at the mercy of ICE. Both statuses are ideologically constructed from the same racist logic, which is the same logic that law enforcement agencies use to surveil, police, and punish Black and Latinx males in the United States (Rios 2011; Neal 2013). Tito's academic struggles (such as failing classes) are viewed almost as criminal offenses, marking him as out of status or unlawfully present—a violation of the rules that could lead to removal proceedings. This was particularly troubling for Tito, as he felt that his identity as a Black boy from

Colón influenced how others saw him. It's important to note that "the re-moval of aliens, however severe its consequences, has been 'consistently classified as a civil rather than a criminal procedure' by the courts" (Garcia 2006, 1). The stakes are higher for international noncitizen Black F-1 stu-dent visa-holding athletes as their academic eligibility or status as a stu-dent ultimately decides their fate in the United States even though they might not have been recruited, prepared for, or received the necessary sup-port to be in an English-language academic setting.

Moreover, their status as athletes also complicates the matter because their athletic performance can influence how their academic performance is evaluated. However, under the current rules, there are no safeguards to take into account the vagueness of the system. Ultimately, it is the Black males who stand to suffer the worst consequences, becoming out of status, accru-ing unlawful presence, and being placed into removal proceedings if caught.

6

ILLEGAL HOOP DREAMS

*The Il/legibility of the Il/legality of Being a Noncitizen
Black Male Basketball Trafficking Victim*

A couple of months had passed since I had started making active progress on dealing with Tito's immigration status. A friend who was also pursuing her PhD and focusing on Black immigrants in the Americas gave me some recommendations and a list of pro bono legal service providers in the Austin area from her extensive networks. With the screenshots of the providers' contact information, I started making appointments. The first agency, American Pathways Austin, denied Tito services and referred him to Religious Charities, who also stated they did not have the capacity nor the resources to take on a case such as Tito's. It would be "too resource intensive" (Religious Charities representative, personal communication, April 23, 2018). Seemingly, every time Tito or I would mention basketball as what had brought him to their offices, there would be confusion. The use of basketball as a tool of exploitation was a foreign idea to many of the advocates within these agencies. It was difficult and sometimes beyond their means to find support for such a case.

The consistent no's that we encountered were discouraging. Additionally, the everyday trials of living and working as a full-time PhD student and looking after a teenager took precedence. However, I knew that Tito could not remain in the United States with an unstable migratory status.

One Sunday morning, as Tito lay asleep on our living room couch, I found myself unable to sleep. As I tossed in bed, my mind raced with thoughts about Tito remaining in the United States and continuing to create his life without a stable migratory status, but it did not sit well with me. I felt that it was part of my responsibility to assist him. The way he had arrived in Austin kept me tossing and turning in my bed. I felt that Tech and Coach Barrigon had victimized him. For some odd reason, I was thinking of calling the National Human Trafficking Hotline. The idea of calling them had not occurred to me before. First, for a long time I did not know that there was a human trafficking hotline. I had never been in a position to need to make such a call. Second, I was wrestling with labeling what happened to Tito as human trafficking due to shame, stigma, and my limited knowledge, even when my PhD adviser, months before, first mentioned human trafficking when I described Tito's situation in La Frontera and how it had started to take a turn for the worse. Hollywood's depiction of the sex trafficking of young women was stuck in my mind. Like so many people, I blindly believed that human trafficking could be only one thing because of how I learned about it: through media depictions. Jonathan Todres (2015) explains that popular portrayals of human trafficking influence the general understanding of human trafficking, which, in turn, informs policy choices made to address the problem. However, as I continued finding more cases similar to Tito's from around the country and the use of human trafficking kept appearing, I finally rolled over, grabbed my cell phone, searched for the National Human Trafficking Hotline, and called.

After a series of prompts, I was directed to speak with a representative. With the information I had, I told the young woman on the other end of the line what was happening with Tito and that we needed help. She provided me with a list of resources, which included both American Pathways and Religious Charities. However, we were exhausted of dealing with them since they were not helpful. So, when the operator suggested the group Displaced Person Services (DPS) alongside the previous services, there was no excitement. It felt like it would be just another resource to explore in case they could provide any assistance.

This vignette is important because a list of available resources that speak to the complexities of basketball trafficking does not exist. It is clear that basketball trafficking is a phenomenon within US interscholastic athletics. The June 2020 US Department of State's *Trafficking in Persons Report* stated that the United States has an issue with the human trafficking of athletes (US Department of State 2020, 570). In 1994, when the Department of State began to monitor trafficking, they focused exclusively on sex trafficking of women and girls. Since the release of the first *Trafficking in Persons Report* in 2001, as the understanding of human trafficking has expanded, the report has grown in both its breadth and depth of analysis. Additionally, a US Department of Homeland Security (2016) *SEVP Spotlight* article entitled "Trafficking of Student Athletes" highlighted that international noncitizen youth were being trafficked and exploited through the F-1 student visa program: "Homeland Security Investigations (HSI) has recently uncovered an alarming trend of student athletes being trafficked by their coaches and caretakers." However, composite information on where victims can find help does not exist. Nor has the trafficking of athletes caught a lot of national attention or sympathy. What's important to highlight within these trends is the general public's and government officials' lack of care about the predominantly noncitizen Black males who are victims of basketball trafficking. Munene Franjo Mwaniki (2017) asserts that the general public views many of these cases filled with corruption and exploitation as necessary evils to develop players. Additionally, he highlights that there is a general lack of empathy and care in society for Black youth who are portrayed as victims within Western media. In addition to Mwaniki's (2017) arguments, I sustain that the lack of care for Black boys is replicated within human trafficking discourse. Not only do males have a more difficult time being thought of as victims of human trafficking, but with the intersection of race, Black males are less likely to be seen as victims overall (Jones 2010; Esson 2020).

Not being read as a legitimate human trafficking victim can have negative consequences if these youth find themselves seeking relief. The ability to be presented as a victim and invoke empathy is key within pro bono immigration work (Lakhani 2019). Many of these organizations work through grants and often with limited resources, as the Religious Charities representative explained in her email about Tito's case. As such, pro bono legal workers must be very selective about the cases they take on, choosing those with the best probability to be successful (Lakhani 2019). Black boys trafficked through and for basketball might not make a compelling case for expending their limited resources. Tommy Curry (2021) sustains that the history of scapegoating Black men for rape and deviance is a major obstacle to seeing Black boys and men as victims. The pervasive stereotypes that cast Black males as beasts, insatiable sexual savages, and violent animals must be considered when empathy is necessary for obtaining assistance for trafficking relief. Back in Panama, in Colegio Bolivariano, Tito believed the teachers and students thought he was a criminal and, at any moment, would violate them. Once in La Frontera, within less than a month, his mostly mestize peers screamed "La Pantera Negra," "Sexual Chocolate," and other racialized nicknames at him and his Black scholarship peers. Their mestize peers did it in jest, but those nicknames are not disconnected from the ways in which Tito was profiled when he needed relief. These anti-Black, misandric tropes impacted Tito every day. Realities such as these weigh heavier on Black noncitizen youth like Tito, whose maleness and youth subjected him to be surveilled and targeted by law enforcement. However, being denied legal services was not the only way in which Tito was denied relief. The consequences of being a Black male and not being read as a legitimate victim translate into immigration enforcement. Black and Latinx men are subject to racial profiling by law enforcement agencies (Golash-Boza 2015). Trafficking victims are routinely portrayed as white European women or children trafficked for sex and needing rescue by law enforcement (Jones 2010). That has lasting consequences, one of which is the feedback loop that Todres (2015) highlights. He explains how cultural productions such as Hollywood films impact human trafficking policymaking. In response to public outcry, policymakers craft most human trafficking policies to address the situations depicted in media, leaving others, like Black boys victimized through basketball, without relief or awareness. There are few opportunities for the general public to gain awareness of Black boys being trafficked. Instead, the media prefers to show rags-to-riches stories of Black athletes overcoming insurmountable circumstances to make it to the NBA, rather than focusing on those who are not successful.

The same physical and athletic features that Tito was recruited for also rendered him more vulnerable to victimization. There's no definitive way of determining if Tito's inability to secure assistance from American Pathways or Religious Charities had anything to do with race and gender. However, as Sarah Lakhani (2019, 1673) points out, in "low bono" spaces for noncitizens who cannot afford the fees of private immigration attorneys, "legal services routinely face *who to help* when not everyone can be helped. Lawyers must rank potential clients in some order of priority." Therefore, there is a possibility that Tito's race and gender influenced how his case was ranked within this space.

How Race Was Read in Pro Bono Immigration Services

Walking through the door of Displaced Person Services (DPS) was like being transported through a portal. This social service agency describes itself as dedicated to providing assistance to refugees and other displaced persons fleeing persecution based on race, religion, nationality, political opinion, or membership in a particular social group. Many languages were spoken by the different groups of people waiting in the reception lobby. For instance, a woman wearing a hijab directed her children to play with some of the toys available in the waiting room in Arabic as she approached the window with a man who might have been her husband.

I called DPS, and they agreed to have Tito come in for a screening. They wanted to speak with Tito alone. It was the common intake procedure. We had done it numerous times before. I waited in the lobby for about an hour, carefully analyzing the flow of people coming in and out of the building.

Finally, Clarisa, a DPS caseworker, opened the door separating the waiting room from the caseworker offices. She asked me to follow her. I entered the office, which was large enough to fit the small couch where Tito was sitting, facing Clarisa and Tiffany, the principal caseworker, who were sitting in chairs. I sat down beside Tito and listened as the caseworkers probed Tito for more details about his time in La Frontera.

"He bought me a phone and told me that he was monitoring my calls, but I knew he couldn't do that," Tito said in Spanish.

Clarisa quickly replied, "Actually, yes, he could be monitoring your calls." Tito had a look of surprise on his face once he realized it could be true, the coach could have been listening to his calls. Clarisa's quick rebuttal made it clear that whether Coach Barrigon was merely making threats or was actually monitoring Tito's calls, it was further evidence of his abuse of power and manipulative techniques.

Tito recounted that the coach had said, "Who is this guy, Wallace? If he really cared about you, he would be taking care of you. I am the one who buys your food, shoes, and pays for your phone!" Tito was referring to how the coach began to act once he believed I was intruding too much on his basketball program.

"He thought Javier was Latino. He told us not to speak to gringos." Tito continued, "They wouldn't understand how we do things here. He told us not to answer the door if someone knocked. It would be the police, and they would deport us. If anybody asked us where we were living, we were supposed to say with the coach."

While Clarisa translated Tito's every word from Spanish to English for Tiffany, I was processing. I was baffled by how Coach Barrigon had weaponized Latinidad to disguise his abuses and exploitation of Tito and other youth. I knew identity was malleable and largely depends on the context, but I did not estimate its impact on Tito's experience playing basketball in La Frontera.

Finally, Clarisa firmly interjected between Tito's statements and exclaimed, "Fraud!" Collecting herself, she explained to Tito, "That's fraud. You were promised one thing before leaving Panama, and you didn't receive any of those things once you got to La Frontera."

I continued listening to the exchange, learning so much information about Tito's experience in La Frontera. By this time, we had spent months together going about our new lives in Austin, but he never spoke in detail about the extent of his experience in La Frontera. Some of Coach Barrigon's forwarded text messages that Tito's mother, Katia, sent me in addition to her text messages and voice notes had given me some insight. However, none of those distant communications revealed as much as Tito's testimony at DPS.

Tito continued to share more of the conversations he had with Coach Barrigon about me. "'Who is Wallace? Who is Wallace?' he was screaming," Tito said. I was not completely oblivious to the issues the coach had with me, but I was surprised by the degree to which it reached Tito. Sonia and I had been in constant communication, and she had warned me about the coach's concerns about Tito's and my relationship.

This vignette highlights that when abuses happen, they can transform into traumas that youth are forced to live with. Thankfully, in the case of Tito, DPS provided professional support that helped him reveal the traumatic experiences and abuses he faced while in La Frontera. He was also affirmed in what he shared with them. His experiences were not minimized in front of the caseworkers. They explained to him that being promised something, even if it is within the realm of high school basketball, and not receiving it is fraud. The US Department of Homeland Security (2013) defines *human trafficking* as follows: "Human trafficking involves the use of force, fraud, or coercion to obtain some type of labor or commercial sex act. Every year, millions of men, women, and children are trafficked worldwide—including right here in the United States. It can happen in any community and victims can be any age, race, gender, or nationality. Traffickers might use violence, manipulation, or false promises of well-paying jobs or romantic relationships to lure victims into trafficking situations." It is important for victims of basketball trafficking to recognize they have been trafficked and to know their rights. It is also important that athletes' and families' rights are shared with prospective student-athletes before they depart their countries. And it is of the utmost importance that coaches or sponsors of F-1 student visas for athletic purposes are held accountable for their actions toward the youth they recruit to labor at their institutions.

In the F-1 student visa's current state, sponsoring institutions are not required to provide housing or orientation for incoming international students (Pleso 2017). The visa was designed this way so that applicants would bear the financial burden of being a nonimmigrant student in the United States. However, with the visa's use for athletic purposes and the numerous abuses that are happening, we must revisit the visa's structure. Faye Pleso's (2017) in-depth study on the experiences of F-1 student visa holders in the United States revealed that fraud and abuse are rampant within the visa's use outside of athletic purposes too.

"You Have to Give Them Time": Tito Slowly Reveals More
Traumas Experienced in La Frontera

During the appointment Tiffany decided that DPS would be able to provide support for Tito. Tiffany, with the help of Clarisa translating, explained to Tito what type of services they could provide. Finally, these were the first women who seemingly understood how basketball could be used to traffic and exploit young people. Additionally, they were also willing to expend significant time and resources to aid Tito.

He was enrolled in a special program for teenage victims of abuse and refugees where he was able to access some basic services like groceries, a laptop, and Christmas gifts. The support was very helpful. Most important, they provided Tito with access to a pro bono immigration attorney and help filing for federal trafficking relief for children and families.

As we departed DPS and I drove Tito back to Turner High to finish his school day, the ride felt a bit lighter. We talked, and I asked him why he had never shared those stories about La Frontera with us before. He simply stated, while shrugging his shoulders, "I don't know."

However, I was still concerned about the new information I learned from Tito during the interview. Clarisa texted me later to provide some additional information, and I asked her about why Tito had not been forthcoming about his life in La Frontera before. She explained that his behavior was common among trafficking victims. She said, "You have to give them time. Sometimes they remember things at random." Not too long following that conversation, Tito would have another random recollection about the abuses he experienced in La Frontera.

It was a Saturday night, and Tito came to my room and said, "I'm hungry. Can you take me to get something to eat?"

Initially, I blew him off and told him, "Go eat something that's in the kitchen. I am tired." A few moments later, I went into Tito's space in the living room and told him, "Let's go. But this is the thing. The first place that I pass is the first place you're going to eat, I don't care what it is. That's where you're going to go."

Taco Bell was the first open restaurant that I passed after Tito and I left the house. Admittedly, I was hungry as well, and when I got to the drive-through, I placed an order for my food. I then turned to Tito and asked him for his order.

"I don't want anything," he replied.

I immediately became upset and told the cashier to hold on a second as I began my rant: "What do you mean, you don't want anything, I drove way over here tonight." I paused and told him, "Okay. You know what, you ain't gonna get nothing. I'm gonna eat now, and whatever you find at home, you eat."

We pulled up to the second window, and I got my food and decided to calm down. I began to think there must be a reason he did not want to eat there.

As nice as I could, I asked him, "What do you want to eat?"

"I want, I'll go to Wendy's," he replied.

"Cool, I'm gonna drive to Wendy's, but that's it!"

I pulled out of Taco Bell and accelerated past oncoming traffic to reach the other side of the road in Wendy's direction.

"Señor Javier," Tito said.

"What do you want?"

"Well, you know why I didn't want to eat at Taco Bell?" he asked.

"No, I don't."

"Well, you know, when I was in La Frontera, we didn't really have a lot of food, but it's a lot of Mexicans there. So we always had tortillas, like Mexican tortillas. You know, like the flat tortillas. We always had Mexican tortillas, and one night I was in the kitchen, and I wanted to cook some tortillas, and I wanted to heat it up. So I put it on the stove to cook it, and I didn't look in the pan when I was cooking, so I cooked the tortilla and went to take a bite. And when I bit it, I noticed it had rat poop on it. So, when we got to Taco Bell, the smell. It reminded me of that."

There was nothing I could say in response. I was disgusted. I was angry. It was disheartening to know that Tito and the seven other youth were living in such awful conditions. It was more disheartening to think that their pursuit of basketball was the cause of their trauma. Tito's delayed recall of the rat-feces-laced Mexican tortillas in La Frontera may have been a traumatic memory he attempted to suppress. Much research has been conducted to better understand memory concerning traumatic events in individuals' lives. Diana Elliott (1997) stated that the general population might intentionally suppress traumatic events until intrapersonal, interpersonal, or environmental cues that closely match the original trauma trigger them. The Mexican-inspired fast food chain's late-night aromas triggered the recall of the disgusting conditions Tech forced him to endure as they used his talents for their athletic glory.

After combing extensively through media news stories on basketball trafficking, I discovered that Tito's trauma was not exclusive. Deplorable living conditions and, specifically, the lack of food were reoccurring themes in other mediated cases of basketball trafficking.

"No heat. No food," Rostand Ndong Essomba said about his living conditions at a prep school in Georgia. Rostand was recruited from Cameroon to the US prep school and encountered deplorable conditions on his arrival. Youth from different countries and from the United States suffered similar conditions trying to achieve their hoop dreams.

In 2015 an exposé in *Harper's Magazine* by Alexandra Starr entitled "American Hustle: How Elite Youth Basketball Exploits African Athletes" detailed the disturbing conditions that three Nigerian teenagers were subjected to in pursuit of their American hoop dream. While in Mississippi, in addition to sleeping on the floor, they recounted the lack of food. They would escape nightly from their residence to buy food at a nearby convenience store. Their coach sporadically gave them fast food meals, but it was not enough. They were constantly practicing and competing and were hungry.

The Illegibility of Black Boy Basketball Trafficking Victims

Currently, there are no dedicated organizations or efforts toward preventing basketball trafficking or working with trafficked basketball athletes within the United States. Additionally, as Breanne Palmer (2017) notes, in general, there are only a handful of organizations that advocate for Black immigrants' particular needs. The European context has advanced in dealing with trafficked athletes because of the proliferation of Black West African youth exploited through soccer networks. The organization in charge of regulating international soccer, FIFA (Fédération Internationale de Football Association), has even adjusted their transfer policies for minor athletes to work toward eradicating the irregular movement of aspiring youth soccer players (Yilmaz et al. 2020). However, James Esson (2020) asserts that Black West African male soccer trafficking victims do not evoke the same amount of care or action as other human trafficking victims because they do not fit the mainstream constructed image of such victims. I bring attention to this matter to challenge the notion that athletic, strong, and agentic young people of African descent cannot be victims of trafficking. Because they do not fit the constructed image, it is harder for them get relief. This is true even in spaces dedicated to helping noncitizen victims. As highlighted in this analysis, Tito utilized his agency and decided to migrate to the United States, where he found himself in compromised positions, and he decided to violate the terms of his F-1 visa to protect himself.

The strategic placement of mostly women in antitrafficking campaigns creates stereotypes about not only what trafficking is but who can be a victim of trafficking. It also affects the allocation of resources for those who need assistance. When Black boys fail to be considered legitimate victims of human trafficking, they will continue to endure in silence. Black boys' inability to be seen as victims is part of what Mark Anthony Neal (2013) describes as being part of the *illegible* Black male body. They are *illegible* as victims because society is used to seeing Black males as the perpetrators of crimes. As such, when they are victimized, like Tito, their victimhood cannot be read by the larger society. Youth basketball players encounter added layers of complexity or intersections if they are to be included within human trafficking discourse. Mwaniki (2017) has asserted that the general public is less empathetic to human trafficking cases among athletes because they see hard training as a "necessary evil." Esson (2020) continues to strengthen this argument in the case of Black West African males trafficked for soccer. He claims that their maleness and the agency they enacted to become spatially mobile for athletic purposes are used against them within trafficking discourse and relief efforts.

Trump's Memorandum: A Sudden Change
in US Immigration Policy

In the game of basketball, momentum is very important. Teams and coaches want momentum on their side. You can also get caught and allow unexpected momentum shifts in the game, which can rattle your team. It can throw off your rhythm, leads can diminish, and the crowd can get rambunctious. This is especially true on a turnover of a live ball. It can shift the momentum in favor of your opponents. A sudden change in the flow of the game play can disrupt one's game plan. The most common response a coach utilizes to attempt to slow down the momentum once it has shifted is calling a timeout.

August 2018 was the live ball turnover we were not prepared for. "Hola Javier," the usual text from Katia popped up on my cell phone screen, but this time with some screenshots. Following the greeting, she texted, "You know they just told me the school [Tech Prep] closed, and they had to look for a new school for Josue, but he was denied the visa."

"Wow! I didn't know anything about Josue! What a shame for him. What a shame," I kept repeating in my voice note back to Katia. I also pondered what became of the other boys from Costa Rica.

While the news that Tech Prep had closed was surprising, it competed with the headline of the newspaper article that Katia sent as screenshots. It read "Riesgo de deportación a estudiantes que acumulen presencia ilegal" (Risk of deportation for students that accumulate unlawful presence; see also Cancino 2018). A change had arrived. President Donald Trump's administration's adjustment to the student visa unlawful status went into effect. The May 2018 memo, which made national headlines in August, changed how unlawful presence was calculated for student visa holders. It started the clock for unlawful presence in the United States immediately after their status was violated, even if they were unaware or never officially told. Before the memorandum, student visa holders would begin accruing unlawful presence only after US Citizenship and Immigration Services (USCIS) or an immigration judge formally notified them that they were out of status. Katia's message from Panama came minutes after Tito's pro bono lawyer, Sharon, whom DPS helped secure, sent me an email in respect to the unexpected change: "I do need to discuss with Tito the new immigration ruling that came into effect and how it can negatively impact him if a T-Visa application is submitted and denied. The new rule states that if an application, such as the T-Visa application, is denied the applicant [Tito] would immediately be placed into deportation proceedings." The Trump presidential administration is not the cause of restrictive immigration policies in the United States. International noncitizen youth athletes were being abused and exploited via the F-1 student visa before that administration's start. However, the fearmongering and the heightened sense of nativism promoted by Trump (Caty 2019) directly influenced Tito's fear. He was within a "hostile environment" (Wardle and Obermuller 2019), to quote the name of the UK policies designed to make unlawful immigrants' lives difficult and force people to "self-deport" from that country (Goodman 2020). Tito felt the impacts of these rapid anti-immigrant policies, even as a person who was lawfully present in the United States at the time. The whole plan we had devised with Tito's caseworkers went into disarray. Our initial plan would not withstand the change in policies. Before we learned about the change to the statute on the accrual of unlawful presence, the plan was to keep Tito enrolled in Turner High School and have him play an official senior basketball season on varsity, where he would gain more exposure. He would be eligible for varsity at the start of the spring semester of the new academic year; his year of not participating in varsity competition would be complete since his departure from Tech. It became crucial for Tito to compete on Turner's varsity squad because the culminating Amateur Athletic Union (AAU) summer season did not go as expected as a result of the NCAA's residency rules for summer competition. The NCAA deemed Tito ineligible to play in the largest tournaments across the country because he moved from La Frontera to Austin within the same year. As with University Interscholastic League (UIL) rules, the NCAA proclaims it implements residency rules even in summer competition to prevent recruiting abuses and unethical power stacking of teams (NCAA, n.d.). Additionally, with the assistance of Sharon, the pro bono lawyer, Tito learned he was not in the country unlawfully. He was under the age of eighteen, and as a minor he could not accrue unlawful presence in the United States even if he was not attending the SEVIS-designated school listed on his I-20. Officially, "no period of time in which an alien is under 18 years of age shall be taken into account in determining the period of unlawful presence in the United States under clause (i)" (8 U.S.C. § 1182(a)(9)(B)(iii)(I)). The 2018-19 academic year rolled around in August. After long discussions between Tito's coaches at Turner High and his coaches with the Austin Longhorns, his AAU team, it was decided that Tito needed to play his senior season on the varsity squad as soon as possible instead of junior varsity during the first semester until he became eligible according to the UIL. His coach at Turner wanted to submit a waiver to the UIL on Tito's behalf so he could play on the varsity squad. This would prove to be a difficult process because Tito had been at Turner for less than one year and UIL's "Changing Schools for Athletic Purposes" (2020, sec. 443) requires that transferring students not compete in varsity athletics for one academic year. After the previous summer's issues with becoming eligible with the NCAA, Tito realized he would not be academically eligible to play NCAA basketball either. He did not have the grades. He was still trying to recover from the failing transcript that Tech Prep sent to Turner High when he transferred in the previous academic year. Tech Prep issued Tito all failing grades for the semester when he was enrolled for only about three months. They intentionally did this to demonstrate their power to damage and impede Tito's future. Even with the NCAA's sliding scales for GPAs and SAT or ACT scores, it would not be enough for Tito to qualify. Tito's lack of English proficiency would prevent him from scoring high enough on either the SAT or ACT to supersede his low GPA and become eligible for the NCAA. It must be noted that as of 2023 the NCAA permanently eliminated standardized test requirements for Division I and Division II eligibility. The shift derived from the NCAA's plan to advance racial equity in the wake of the social movements of 2020, as a result of the continued murders of Black people in the United States. But there is no recourse for Tito or others like him who were bounded, restricted, and denied opportunities before the NCAA's change.

We believed he surely would have an opportunity to at least gain a scholarship to play junior college basketball. Junior college basketball allows more flexibility than most traditional four-year university intercollegiate governing bodies, namely, the NCAA. It's also a viable way to make it to a four-year university with a couple years of athletic eligibility after transferring from a junior college. The National Junior College Athletic Association (NJCAA), the largest US junior college athletic governing body, defines student-athletes as eligible for competition if they meet the following requirement: "A student-athlete must be a graduate of a high school with a state department of education approved standard academic diploma, state department of education approved general education diploma, or a state department of education approved high school equivalency test" (2019, sec. 2[B.1]). Unlike the NCAA and other four-year athletic governing bodies, all Tito would need to do is graduate from high school to play. By completing his senior year at Turner, he would have time to improve his English proficiency. In an attempt to acquire the language more effectively, he enrolled in additional English language classes in a local church. However, most important, as Sharon mentioned in her email, the plan was to have Tito apply for a US trafficking visa, or T visa, and a special status for child victims of human trafficking. Sharon and the caseworkers at DPS worked with Tito and submitted an application for the initial relief before he turned eighteen. They were hopeful that even though Tito would be turning eighteen soon, if he could get the application submitted before his eighteenth birthday, he could access more benefits and potentially a pathway to a stable migratory status. However, the plan was derailed as the Trump memorandum went into effect on August 8. We wouldn't have time to go through UIL's appeal process. Time would no longer permit Tito to remain at Turner and finish his senior year while playing a season of varsity basketball and gaining more exposure. It was a sudden change.

"I Don't Want to Be Illegal": The Deportability
of Black Male Basketball Trafficking Victims

Sharon did not want to speak with Tito over the phone. She requested he come into the office, which was near downtown Austin. In our normal fashion, whenever Tito had these types of appointments, instead of going to Turner, I drove him to the appointment. When the appointment finished, in a nonchalant but matter-of-fact way, Tito told me, "I don't want to be here illegally," as he was getting in the car.

"That's cool, and I agree," I responded.

Besides the music coming from the radio, we rode back home in near silence. The disappointment hung on Tito's face as he sat in the passenger seat. This was what *el norte* was turning out to be for him: a bureaucratic mess. However, it was his decision to make about running the risks of remaining in the country with the new changes in pursuit of a hoop dream. At the very least, Tito had the proper legal counsel to assist him with his decision-making process. It was a tough decision but one informed by a qualified individual. The Black body is at the core of the issue. Sharon reminded me over the phone, "He's Black. It's not if he'll be stopped. It's a matter of when he'll be stopped by the police."

It didn't matter that Tito's nationality was Panamanian. He was Black. He was Black at home and now in Texas. He did not "look Mexican," which is the stereotypical way people think about illegality in the United States. Andrea Gómez Cervantes (2021) asserts that connecting a stereotypical look with illegality is the product of homogenized and stereotypical images of being "Mexican," "Hispanic," and "Latina/o" that stem from the racialization of illegality in the United States through immigration laws, judiciary hearings, and enforcement strategies. Instead, Tito looked African American, which does not automatically signal unlawful status in the country but other racialized tropes. It did not change for him in the United States. White and mestize individuals from Latin America largely do not have to contend with being imagined to be criminal in both their home countries and the United States. In many countries in Latin America, mestizes and white people are the dominant and normative group. They have not been constructed as outsiders to the nation or criminals.

Tito's intent when departing Panama for the United States was to go play basketball. This was what he pledged to do within the confines of his nonimmigrant visa, to come and do something temporarily. He did not come as an immigrant with the intent to stay. His ability to make good on this bargain was truncated by a coach who washed his hands of the responsibility. In Sharon's experience as an immigration attorney, she thought it would be difficult for Tito to qualify for a trafficking visa; his story was not exceptional enough. As we sat around a gray table, Sharon began asking Tito a series of questions.

"Is there any person in Panama looking to harm you?" Sharon asked him.

"No," he answered.

"Do you have an unstable home life in Panama?"

"No."

"Are you scared to go back home?"

"No."

Sharon explained to Tito that there was no point in him remaining in the United States, potentially accruing unlawful presence, and risking deportation.

"He's different. It's not, like, this is his only option. It would be different if this was all he had," she told me in front of Tito. Her questions were rooted in the US requirement for human trafficking and gang and domestic violence victims in their home countries to establish extreme persecution to qualify for asylum or relief (Congressional Research Service 2021). Tito's responses and reality, which belied stereotypes about victims in her experiences, would not make for a compelling visa application story that would evoke empathy. Given the sudden changes in the United States created by Trump's memorandum, she asked Tito if it would be worth it to stay in the United States and be "illegal."

She was absolutely right. We listened. But it did not make the decision any easier. To remain in the United States would place him in harm's way through the means of deportation. Fear of deportation reigned over Tito's existence and livelihood as it had done before.

During Tito's time in La Frontera, Coach Barrigon would use the threat of being apprehended by immigration officials and deported if Tito and the other *becados* ventured beyond their annexed one-bedroom apartment. It was highly unlikely that would actually happen because, at least in Tito's case, his migratory status was stable. However, it does not lessen the actual threat by the individual who is tapping into the institutionalized use of deportation as a form of social control (Golash-Boza 2015). Tito now found himself having to consider what would be most important in his life, to play basketball while living with the fear of deportation or to go back home.

Being placed in deportation proceedings for an F-1 visa overstay is far riskier for Black male noncitizens like Tito. According to the Black Alliance for Just Immigration, Black immigrants are stopped and searched at higher rates than non-Black immigrants and are overrepresented from sentencing to prison. Seventy-six percent of Black immigrants are deported because of contact with the police and criminal legal system (Morgan-Trostle et al. 2015). We had to consider all of these facts, given the peach fuzz sprouting above Tito's lip, outlining his growing mustache. The tops of his shoulders were rounding up, leaving natural dips for his basketball jersey to sit between his growing neck and shoulder muscles. Daily he was becoming a more beautiful Black man. But the beauty my eyes beheld would not be enough to prevent the larger society from seeing his body, trained for years, as a threat. He was growing into the material consequences of the danger of deportation, which are far greater for Black noncitizens in the United States (Golash-Boza 2015). There was no uncertainty about Tito's future encounters with law enforcement in the United States, as was also the case in Panama. His Blackness, his maleness, and his large frame made this a matter of fact. Looking African American is enough to be victimized by US law enforcement (Warde 2013; Dumas and Nelson 2016). In the article "Racial Naturalization" in the *American Quarterly*, Devon Carbado (2005) reflected on being a Black male immigrant in the United States and his encounter with US law enforcement. He argues that the intelligibility of Blackness is skin deep. It is epidermal. It is inscribed on one's body and prevents one from crossing the phenotypic borders of Blackness. Palmer (2017, 109) highlights that "Black immigrants are forced to 'deal with' the fact that citizenship does not protect them from police brutality, criminalization, and anti-Blackness." Racial profiling by law enforcement was not a new concept for Tito. In Panama, as a minor, he was taken into custody for breaking curfew, which was informed by the Panamanian police's racialized enforcement that imagines Black boys, Blackness, maleness as threats. The perceived threat that Black males pose to society is transnational. Or as Carbado (2005) asserts, Black is a country. He continues to argue that "citizenship is neither a necessary nor sufficient condition for American identity, and American identity is neither a necessary nor sufficient condition for citizenship" (638). Tito would have to contend with the consequences of white supremacy in either country. Tito's encounters with Panamanian law enforcement and his guaranteed encounters with US law enforcement demonstrate a fluid "legibility" of Black masculinity as deviant, criminal, and needing to be punished. Tito's subjectivity reveals that Black masculine "il/legibility" has never been confined to one particular nation-state. Panama is a place where mothers like Katia often fear for the lives of their Black sons (Lowe de Goodin 2014). This was true for Tito in the United States too.

Remaining in the United States while waiting to see if his trafficking visa would be approved and finishing out his senior year at Turner, Tito would still be a Black child transitioning into adulthood, yet he was already adultified. Black children occupy life in a liminal space, where they are denied childhood status and carry adult-like culpability (Gilmore and Bettis 2021). However, he would not have the proper documentation to demonstrate his lawful right to remain in the country. Until this time Tito had used his Turner student ID card to ride Austin's city buses for free, and he had traveled to Orlando by air using only his student ID. However, as time progressed and he turned eighteen and his bodily frame continued to develop, his student ID from Turner High School would be less of a protection. He would be a Black male without any documentation, which would further complicate his future encounters with law enforcement.

Tito might not have been in any physical danger by returning home, but the question was *what* he would be returning to.

"Javier, honestly, there's nothing here," Katia told me over a phone call discussing the next steps for her son. She insisted that we push forward with a new plan. There was nothing to lose. This was his shot to break through the chains his home country had placed on him for just existing. Panama might be more economically stable and suffer less from political instability and everyday violence than other countries in the region. However, income inequality and disparity are real and further exacerbated by race (Szok 2012; Amen Strayhorn 2014).

The New Plan: To Stay or to Go?

Just like in the fourth quarter with no timeouts left and the clock ticking, it was time to adjust. Time was not in Tito's favor. The mad shift began in August. Tito would be turning eighteen in November, and he would automatically be granted a 180-day grace period before he would start accruing unlawful presence. Since Tito had decided he did not want to remain in the United States unlawfully, there were only two options: either depart the country and lose out on the victim of human trafficking status he was pursuing, or find a junior college that would offer him a scholarship and a new I-20. The latter was his last, best hope for staying in the country legally.

Tito and I went to the library and began to make a highlight film from all the video clips we had of him playing basketball. Tito sifted through all of his international games available on YouTube and the videos I had recorded on my cell phone. By the day's end, Tito created a near two-minute highlight reel ready to be sent to junior college coaches around the state of Texas. It did not take long for Tito to get a response and a scholarship offer.

Coach Martin (a pseudonym) of Vessey County Community College (a pseudonym) was impressed with Tito and excited that he was a Panamanian. Coach Martin had experience with Panamanian players in the past. In his over twenty-year coaching career, he had recruited and coached some of Panama's most notable basketball players. He was excited by Tito. Right away, Coach Martin moved Tito's admissions application and athletic scholarship into motion. Finally! Tito got his college basketball scholarship! It's what he had dreamed of. I sent Tito, his parents, and my parents the information Coach Martin sent me. We were all excited. Well, at least it seemed that way.

"Señor Javier, I need to talk to you," Tito told me as I walked through the house door later that evening. He was sitting with his legs wide open on his couch-turned-bed in our family's living room. It stopped me in my tracks. Rarely, if ever, did Tito, the teenager, want to speak with me.

"I am not going. I am going back to Panama," he said in a low, muffled voice. It was as if he had been practicing telling me this, knowing what my reaction would be.

"What?" I roared.

"I am not going. I want to go back home," he repeated.

I could feel my blood boiling on the inside. It was an uncontrolled response.

"No. You are going!"

However, in the moment, I forced myself to remember what I was taught at DPS. I had to revisit the night in the Taco Bell drive-through. How could he want to go home now, after all of this? So I asked him, "Why do you want to go home?"

He sat there. His chest began to puff up but not in anger. It was the puffing action many people notice when younger children attempt to hold in their tears. It was unsuccessful. Tears began running down his face. In a flustered voice, he tried to explain, "I don't speak English. I don't want to go to school anymore. I don't speak English. I just want to go home."

"Why are you crying?"

"Javier!" I turned my attention to my father, slumped on the couch watching TV. He continued, "Leave him alone."

I walked away from Tito and left him there. I tried to reason with my father, but my father, *el abuelo* (the grandfather), as Katia would refer to him, had experience on his side.

"Remember, he's still a child. He is far away from home and his family. He's scared. He'll be all right. He's just scared right now."

It was difficult to tell if Tito's fear emerged from the current situation and not speaking English, as he said. Or maybe he feared encountering another situation like in La Frontera with Coach Barrigon. Yet my father's interjection and ability to sympathize with Tito in ways I never could calmed the tension. He had been Tito at one point in his life. He saw himself sitting somewhere like Tito nearly fifty years before when he wanted to leave Colón. From that same position on the couch, he would tell me about when he left Panama the first time and where he thought he was going.

I always thought my father's first time in the United States was when he traveled to Austin on a student visa to play college tennis. It was not. Before receiving his tennis scholarship to Huston-Tillotson, he entered the United States unlawfully at the US-Mexico border in South Texas. He made the journey from Panama to the US border by bus with a friend when they finished high school.

"Where were y'all going?" I asked.

"Dallas," he said. "We were going to New York, but we knew Dallas, Texas, from the news. That's where John F. Kennedy was killed. We knew if we made it to Dallas, we could catch a bus to New York."

His sister and many other Panamanians he knew were already living in the States. He decided he wanted something different in his life. However, their voyage to Dallas was truncated when they were asked for their immigration papers on a bus when they got on in Texas.

"We walked across the border. They thought we were Black Americans. We got caught because my friend didn't speak English well like me." Sitting there in near amusement, he continued to recount how they were caught. "When the sheriff got on the bus, he asked Juan some questions in English, but Juan couldn't respond and turned around and asked me to translate. That was it. They pulled us off the bus and sent us to Houston. From there, they sent us back to Panama." The irony of the situation was that my father was born and raised in the US Panama Canal Zone (PCZ). Growing up in the US neocolony, he had many interactions with white Americans. The English he spoke from birth was shaped through schooling in the PCZ, allowing him to mold his accent to sound more "American" if needed. Yet, even though he was at least the third and possibly the fourth generation that served the United States in the PCZ, paid US taxes, and lived in US-owned homes, he was not American. He was unlawfully entering the United States, a border he crossed nearly daily, moving between the PCZ and the Republic of Panama. Unlike my father, Juan did not grow up in the US PCZ and was not of West Indian descent, but his Blackness read African American until his English came into question. My father did not leave again until 1974, when he was offered an athletic scholarship to Huston-Tillotson University. He knew what *el norte* was. He knew the hope, the desires, the adventures, and the fear—the fear of leaving home. He knew what it was like to decide to live as an undocumented person in a new country. He repeated, again in reference to Tito, "Leave him alone. He'll be all right."

Clearly Tito was getting good advice from DPS, and they made him aware of the changing nature of the US immigration system and how that would affect him. The lawyer let him know that his race and gender would only heighten the uncertainty and surveillance he would encounter if he remained. He was able to make an informed decision. However, not all exploited youth athletes, coaches, or caregivers will have this information. Tito was able to access the necessary resources because he had individuals like me, his parents, my family, and Sonia who were able to recognize the severity of his situation at Tech and get him out. Although he might have had to confront some hard truths, especially as it pertained to his ability to remain in the country lawfully or unlawfully, he was informed. Since basketball trafficking has not received much attention, many individuals are not aware of their rights and the larger structural issues, like the 2018 May memorandum, that impact their migratory statuses. This vignette also highlights the emotional toll "illegality" takes on the lives of undocumented youth in the United States. Roberto Gonzales (2015) elucidates

FIGURE 6.1. Panamanian tennis players at Huston-Tillotson University in 1975, making their mark in collegiate sports. Ernesto Wallace Sr. is third from left. Huston-Tillotson University.

Tennis Team Members: Carlos Aguilar, Victor Ruiz, Ernesto Wallace, Vernie Miles.

Men's Tennis

Huston-Tillotson College's tennis teams are senior Vernil Miles known as (Joe) from R'bow City, Panama'; Victor Ruiz, sophomore from R'bow City, Panama'; Carlos Aguilar, sophomore known as (Mandi) from R'bow City, Panama'; and a new comer this year Ernesto Wallace a freshman from R'bow City, Panama'. The Rams going to do it this year until they are Satisfied. The teams record is 13-5 (3-11-75).

HOUSTON-TILLOTSON TENNIS SCHEDULE FOR 1975

TIME	DATE	TEAM	
2:00 p.m.	March 12	T.L.C.	Seguin
2:00 p.m.	March 14	Southwestern Univ.	Georgetown
2:00 p.m.	March 18	St. Edwards Univ.	Austin
2:00 p.m.	March 20	St. Mary's	San Antonio
2:00 p.m.	April 4	Le Tourneau	Longview
9:00 a.m.	April 5	E.T.B.C.	Marshall
2:00 p.m.	April 8	T.L.C.	Austin
Conference Tourney, April 11-12			Longview

that adolescence and the transition into adulthood are a period of great stress and anxiety for undocumented youth.

Bartering with Illegality: "You Don't Have to Go Home"

Immediately following Coach Martin's offer from Vessey County Community College, Tito unenrolled from Turner High and began to prepare for testing in a home school program. To take advantage of this new opportunity, Tito needed to graduate from high school. He could no longer wait until May to graduate with his classmates. There would not be enough time with the new policy change. By May he would have accrued more than 180 days of "unlawful presence" within the United States, which would trigger a bar of reentry to the country. Depending on the amount of accrued days, he would be barred from entering the United States for at least three years or even permanently (8 U.S.C. § 1182). The administration at Turner helped Tito find a suitable study program; it was common for students there to need to depart school early to find jobs to provide for themselves and their families. Within a couple of weeks of receiving Coach Martin's offer and completing the necessary paperwork, Tito, my father, and I packed into my mother's Toyota Avalon and made a road trip to Vessey, Texas. My father believed it necessary for Tito to see where he would be going. He believed that if Tito could see the campus and meet the coach and other players, he would become more comfortable with the idea of making another quick change in his life. Coach Martin was excited to have Tito visit on game day.

"What do you think? Can you keep up with these guys?" said Coach Martin.

"Sí," replied Tito.

Coach Martin wasn't a Spanish speaker, but he had enough experience with players from Panama that he understood Tito's confirmation.

"I just want to know if he can hit those threes," Coach Martin continued to tell us as I translated for Tito. After watching the game and seeing how the players from Vessey sank three-pointers from all along the arc of the three-point line, it was not a surprise that Coach Martin was interested in Tito. The majority of Tito's two-minute highlight film showed him sinking three-pointers around the world. His highlight tape consisted of him playing in Panama, in the Dominican Republic, and at different tournaments in the United States. Tito had every right to be confident in his abilities to contribute to his new team. He had earned the right to be in Vessey County Community College's gym deciding if he wanted to attend and play for this school.

This was Tito's new school. It was his only option. Before we drove up, Vessey County Community College had sent Tito a new I-20 via FedEx. They followed the same shipping process as Tech Prep so he could take it to the US embassy. The new I-20 was in his hands. Unlike when he came to Texas in the first place, in this case his family would not have to contribute any funds to the school. Personal insurance would be their only expense. However, the possibility of being denied reentry still loomed.

The conversation continued in the gym for a while as the remaining fans and parents were exiting. My father continued in conversation with Coach Martin about the program and how they would get Tito set up in English language classes. Coach Martin, no taller than any of us, a white man with a shiny bald head, listed all of the Panamanian players he had coached over his career.

"So, when you are coming?" Coach Martin asked Tito.

"Well, Coach, he is going back to Panama to process the new visa, and we hope that all works out well, and he'll be back the Monday following Christmas," I said.

"Well, you know, he doesn't have to go home. He doesn't need the new visa. The scholarship is his. He will have it," Coach Martin said. His assured response highlighted his decades of experience coaching at the collegiate level and working with international student-athletes. Tito would not be his first player having visa issues. "We have a kid right now in Canada having similar issues. Matter of fact, I remember going to Panama and taking the kid to the embassy myself after having some visa issues," the coach said.

It was true; Tito did not have to go home. At this point he had been advised of the risks of not being able to return to the United States. Sharon had been open about the big possibility that he would not be approved for a new visa. There were also new stories I shared with Tito about international youth just like him who had been denied reentry into the United States after getting a legitimate opportunity. Tito knew the possibilities of denial. He had been denied visas at the US embassy in Panama before. He now had to make a decision. What would be better? To risk staying in the United States as an undocumented person to continue chasing a hoop dream? Or to return home, do the process the right way, and risk not being allowed reentry into the United States and ultimately losing his hoop dream?

With his new I-20 in hand, Tito boarded the plane back to Panama, his home, a few days before Christmas. My father and I took his picture in the gray Atlanta hoodie he had bought on his trip to Atlanta for a basketball tournament earlier that year. I shook his hand, and so did my father. Tito's face cringed just a little from my father's (his *abuelo's*) firm grip. I was transported back to when he dropped me off at college fifteen years before and gave me the same handshake. It is probably the same one his father and Tito's father had each given them when they were leaving Panama for *el norte*.

On the surface, it appeared that Tito would have more opportunities to create movement and achieve upward social mobility if he remained in the United States unlawfully. Yet, given the legal realities he faced as an undocumented Black man in the United States, he chose to return to Panama. There he risked denial of reentry, but not the status of illegality. Gonzales (2015, 200) argues that for undocumented youth in the United States, mostly the 1.5-generation DREAMers who have spent most of their formative years in the country, early experiences of inclusion such as protected public education "left them mentally and physically defenseless, unsuspecting of the kinds of experiences that awaited them in adulthood. Adult lives brought experiences of exclusion, stress, stigma, expulsion." Tito's childhood and athletic talents afforded him certain protections, which masked the adult exclusions he would encounter as an undocumented person in the United States. He could legally attend junior college on full scholarship and potentially obtain an associate's degree, transfer to a four-year institution while exhausting his athletic eligibility, and obtain a bachelor's degree but not legally work. Without a driver's license, constantly thinking about his lawful status and its limits, he would never be a full member of society (Gonzales 2015). His exclusion from society and risks would be greater as an undocumented Black man. Black immigrants from Africa, the Caribbean, and Latin America experience a more difficult immigration process and are racially profiled, leading to disproportionate rates of immigration detention and deportation (Palmer 2017).

Doing It the Right Way and American
Hoop Dreams Denied

Tito did not even make it to his family's home before getting back on the Panamanian basketball courts in his Atlantic coast city of Colón. In the many pictures Katia sent me via WhatsApp, Tito was still dressed in the winter clothes he had on when he departed from Dallas's airport. Tito and his family were smiling in the selfies they took together. It had been over a year and a half since they last saw each other. So many people from his neighborhood showed up to welcome him on the concrete court. The local adult basketball league was culminating their season the day Tito arrived home. During the championship game, Tito was the honoree. The local league brought him to the middle of the court for the game's tip-off. They even brought him back to half-court when the game finished. Cameras flashed all around him, and Tito stood among the winners, holding the championship trophy with the players. Katia and Tito's sister stood behind them, smiling and looking on. He was back home.

Tito had a safe community in Panama that supported his basketball dreams. Yes, many believed that being in the United States for basketball and even general employment could be more financially rewarding than being in Colón. However, that does not mean they believed that the United States is inherently better than Panama or their community. It merely presents different opportunities for upward social mobility.

Contrary to the news articles that positioned his former Costa Rican teammates in La Frontera as being saved by Coach Barrigon from deviant, crime-ridden, and impoverished communities and taken to a more developed nation, they did not get saved by any coach from the United States. Tito's community in Colón, for instance, pulled their limited resources together to initially support Tito in his dreams of pursuing basketball in the United States. His mother canvassed the neighborhood soliciting funds to support their neighborhood superstar they had witnessed grow. His father not only taught his children his first athletic passion but also coached neighborhood kids as a means to keep them on the right path. What Coach Barrigon saw in Santo Domingo was the product of years of community support that continued celebrating Tito that afternoon at half-court.

Tito's trip home was one of rejuvenation and one of business too. He had only a couple of weeks to spend the Christmas holidays with his family and friends. Most important, he was home to adjudicate a new F-1 student visa for Vessey County Community College. Since 1996 all US visa adjudications must be made outside of the United States (Gonzales 2015). Tito's parents had collected enough money to get him back to Panama and ready for the visa appointment.

Ruperto Sr. had also promised he would speak to Tito about taking advantage of the new opportunity back in the United States. Over the phone Ruperto told me, "When I was Tito's age, I would have given my right arm to get a scholarship like that. I am going to talk to him. I'll get him ready."

Just maybe, if Tito and his family had been able to show up to their appointment at the US embassy in Panama City together with Coach Martin, the day would have turned out differently. They would have had the power of whiteness on their side.

"Here, what rules is this," the US embassy's security guard told Tito and his parents as he pointed to and began to rub his dark brown skin, which matched theirs. He was telling them that race was the biggest determining factor within the US embassy in Panama. To make such an assertion, he must have borne witness to numerous approvals and denials that matched the racial hierarchies of both countries. He stood between the borders of the two nations. He belonged to one and was employed by the other.

Tito was at the US embassy again after spending over a year laboring in basketball in the United States. He was there to process his immigration papers the right way. Here Tito stood again at the crux of both countries, both of which benefited from his athletic talent and labor. Today it was Tito versus the United States: not the nation but the few individuals charged with determining intent. This was round 2. A week before, he had been denied the new visa on the grounds of 214(b), the same provision that barred him in 2017.

Following the first, failed attempt at getting his new F-1 student visa, before the second appointment we shuffled around talking to different people and obtaining letters of support from Panamanian officials. Ironically, in spite of the homecoming he received at the neighborhood basketball game, Tito needed to prove he had strong ties to Panama and would return to Panama following his studies in the United States. Tito was counseled on multiple occasions to just tell the truth. They should be sympathetic to the truth. They should be able to see that despite everything that happened to him in the United States, he had upheld his side of the bargain and returned to Panama to adjudicate his migratory status within the confines of the law. However, this second day, as he arrived with his manila folder full of documents and support letters in hand, the security guards would not allow his parents into the building. He was forced to enter alone.

"I got in line, and they called me into a room by myself," Tito recounted. "A woman came in with a clipboard and started to ask me questions." Being pulled from the general line waiting to see the consular officer at the window unexpectedly deviated from the other times he had gone to the US embassy for a visa appointment.

"What did they ask you?" I said.

"What exactly happened when I was in Texas."

"What did you tell them?"

"I told them the truth and everything that happened. Then she told me okay and sent me back in the lobby to get back in the regular line. I got to the window, and I tried to give him the papers, but he would not look at them. They denied me the visa." The consular office did not explain the nature of the interview or interrogation by the woman. It is not easy to know what exactly happened because this was the first time his parents were not allowed to enter the lobby with him. The guard at the gate had received instructions not to let them in. They stood outside, and together we listened to Tito recount what happened.

I stayed abreast of the entire situation by phone as I was still in Texas. "Hello, hello," I asked through the phone. Through Tito's complete silence I could hear the sounds of Albrook, Panama's largest mall and transportation center. Like many places in the former US PCZ, Albrook had transformed from a US military installment into a highly economic hub within the reverted area. The hustle of the big city screamed in the background. But the silence still echoed through the phone receiver, as if the day paused.

Then Ruperto Brown Sr. pierced the silence and said, "She's crying."

Katia could not speak. All her efforts, energies, hopes, and desires for her son must have collapsed on her at that moment. After all, she had tirelessly labored throughout this process to ensure Tito would have a chance to use his basketball skills to carve out his life. She had brought this all together. We were defeated. The roars of the souped-up exhaust pipes of *diablos rojos* volleyed in the background.

"¡Colón! ¡Colón! ¡Expreso! ¡Hay puestos! ¡Hay puestos!" ("Colón! Colón! Express! There are seats! There are seats!") broke the defeating silence. It was as if the screams of the *pavos* (bus assistants), mostly Black, mostly young, and exclusively male, made the truth loud and clear. You can do everything right. You can follow the law. You could have given your all to a country, but there are limits to your success.

I will never know exactly what Tito's thoughts were as he and his family mounted the bus and rode alongside the canal, the engineering feat that had brought his paternal side to the isthmus. It connected African people separated by centuries of European colonialism in one place. It was the engineering feat that secured the United States' status as a world power. The "big ditch" with its waters made brown through the blood shed by thousands of Black West Indians to complete it. The same blood that runs through his veins. Before hanging up the phone, Tito told me, "I am going to stay here. I am done."

Conclusion

In the most unfortunate of senses, Tito became the prime example of the possible consequences/risks that await Black players from the Global South who desire to maintain a lawful migration status in the United States after being exploited. Black noncitizen youth who enter the United States on an F-1 student visa are faced with the decision to remain "illegal" or depart the United States and attempt a new visa adjudication. In that case, they must take into account that they may be denied, rendering their hoop dream completely ended.

Tito represents how Black people's, and specifically Black males', bodies are read, surveilled, controlled, and punished in global migrations. As critical race theory (CRT) scholars note, race is endemic to US society, including

US immigration policies. Kevin Johnson (2012) forces recognition of this notion because he argues that the US immigration system operates to keep poor people of color from entering the United States and to severely punish those within the country. Global anti-Blackness dictates the decisions of Black athletes. They contend with these issues in many ways that white migrants do not (Carbado 2005).

I am not suggesting that US high school basketball creates illegality. I am arguing that the historical exploitation of Black bodies in the athletic industrial complex (AIC), global anti-Blackness, and the racist immigration policies of the United States force young people to barter with the idea of illegality in exchange for a hoop dream. It is a decision they are forced to make, and they must live with the consequences. However, the AIC, which ultimately benefits the most from their decisions, deals with the least negative consequences. There has been some recourse in high-profile cases like the Evelyn Mack scandal. However, that is just one case of many that do not get reported or make national headlines. Disturbingly, in the Mack scandal, the whereabouts of many of the children whose visas she processed are still unknown. The ability to benefit from legal or illegal labor without consequence is precisely the function of the AIC, which has reached global proportions (Brooks and McKail 2008). The seemingly unending supply of Black marginalized youth worldwide, including within the United States, willing to pursue a hoop dream make it easy to dismiss all those who are not successful.

CONCLUSION

"Me voy para México" (I am going to Mexico) appeared on my screen sometime in mid-October 2019. It was a text message from Tito. It was not clear if he was seeking my permission or informing me of his decision to go to Mexico. Regardless, I responded, "Great! Where are you going?"

There was no need to question his decision, or, better said, his need, to *leave* Panama again. Ten months after the US embassy had denied Tito's new F-1 visa to attend Vessey County Community College in Texas, his mother's words from that time rang true: "Aquí no hay nada," she had said, referring to the reality that there was nothing Tito believed he could do in Panama to chase his basketball dream. Maybe he was suffering from a case of athletic identity foreclosure; many African American male football and basketball players cannot see themselves beyond their athletic identities (Harrison et al. 2011; Beamon 2012).

I had spent so much time with Tito that I knew how much his identity was informed by athletics and, more specifically, by basketball. He was like many African American student-athletes in the United States, who are more likely than their white counterparts to see themselves only as athletes and more likely to believe that others see them only as athletes (Harrison et al. 2011). Tito believed his athletic ability was his only real currency to create the life he desired.

However, it is important to note that Tito was not delusional in believing his athletic abilities could take him beyond the confines of Colón. He had genuine opportunities for his basketball talent to help him overcome the historical socioeconomic challenges that have systematically marginalized many Black people, limiting their chances for upward social mobility. In Colón, as in the entire country, the youth in Tito's age group are over 50 percent unemployed (Instituto Nacional de Estadística y Censo 2023).

With Tito's talent, basketball could be what tennis was for my father or what football was for me—a way to get a college education and professional career. However, unlike my father's generation, Tito's generation is nearly devoid of Black coaches, teachers, and community members who leveraged sport to access education and mainstream resources (J. Wallace et al. 2022). Much of their fate is in the hands of the mainstream athletic industrial complex (AIC), a by-product of white racist capitalism (Cooper 2019)—or, in this case, white and mestize racist capitalism. They are the objects of the Conveyor Belt, which William Rhoden (2007) argues is controlled by white interests that simultaneously deny Black people access to positions of power, isolating young Black males at impressionable ages. In addition, the conveyor belt exploits Black bodies through the manipulation of the mind.

Tito had to leave Panama again. Mexico's growing intercollegiate basketball system, which mirrors that in the United States but is nowhere near as prominent, recruited Tito to try his luck again by playing college basketball. He would continue in the path of his forebears who were trying their luck (Newton 1984) when they migrated to the Panamanian isthmus in search of opportunities during the construction of the Panama Canal. Basketball leagues in Mexico recruit in ways similar to Coach Barrigon. They look to predominantly Black areas in Latin America, like Colón, Panama; a couple of Tito's peers from there were already playing in Mexico. They also look to the United States for Black talent.

Tito had remained in Panama since returning home to adjudicate his new visa for Vessey County Community College in December 2018. One week after Tito's visa for Vessey was denied, we received an email from Texas's Department of Public Safety approving him for special status as a youth victim of human trafficking. However, Tito lost the status when he departed the United States. To be eligible for a trafficking visa in the United States, the applicant cannot leave the country. Tito, his parents, and the rest of us were shocked, but what could he do? His window of opportunity at Vessey had closed, and they were no longer holding the scholarship for him. He wanted to avoid further dealings with the US embassy, since he did not believe they would help. When they interrogated him, they did not care that he was telling the truth or even believe him.

Tito had continued with his life. With his US high school credentials, he was able to enroll in a local Panamanian university. My father was very proud that Tito had received his high school diploma in the United States. He would often repeat, "He can't go home empty-handed." My father knew better than anyone what shame would await someone from Colón who went to *el norte* and did not have anything to show for it. Although Tito did not walk across the stage at Turner, my father made sure Tito took senior pictures in the standard black tuxedo and bow tie and appeared in the yearbook. My father purchased Turner's yearbook and the graduation photos and asked me to take them to Tito's parents. They were proof that Tito had achieved something in *el norte*.

Back in Panama, Tito started playing basketball in different adult leagues in the country. He even traveled to play internationally in Costa Rica and Mexico over the next year. During a showcase in Mexico, he was offered a scholarship to attend a Mexican university. However, he declined the offer because the university was in the city that Coach Barrigon had moved to from La Frontera. After Tech Prep closed, Coach Barrigon announced on his Facebook page that he had been named head coach of a Mexican professional basketball team. It did not feel right for Tito to be in close proximity to the person who had abused him in La Frontera. Since his interactions with Displaced Person Services and the immigration attorney, Tito was more attuned to analyzing situations critically and more informed about protecting himself against possible forms of retribution. He had matured in his decision-making and decided that it would be better to miss an opportunity than place himself in harm's way again.

Through public records I was able to discover that Tech Prep filed for bankruptcy and closed its doors at the end of the 2017–18 academic year.

That is all of the information I was able to obtain about the school's closure. However, it is very strange, and somewhat telling, that the school closed following the events that transpired with Tito. Initially, Tech had refused to release Tito's transcripts without a back payment for his three-month stay in La Frontera. In response, I sent a detailed email with the information I had available at the time, implicating the school's administration in knowingly mistreating Tito and failing to provide what they had promised him. That email changed their tone, and they released Tito's transcripts, albeit with failing grades, without any further issues. Around that time I also notified Child Protective Services about Tech, with the limited information I had, and I know they went to the school. At the time I did not have a physical address for where Tito had been staying, so they were not able to go there. But I believe that Tech started to feel the increasing pressure. I discovered that after the school closed, Josue went to live with Miss Rosalia, Tech's designated school official (DSO), and transferred to another private school in La Frontera. He continued to labor in basketball at the new school. Another parent told Katia that he was denied a new visa, but I was not able to confirm that. I did learn Josue returned to Panama, but I am not sure if he graduated high school. Through social media I was able to see he continues to participate in Panamanian adult professional basketball leagues. He and Tito reunited a couple of times in Panama.

As far I can tell through his social media accounts, Jamal "Sexual Chocolate" Clark, the Costa Rican youth player, is back in Costa Rica. He appeared on a news special about international student-athletes at a prep school in a West Coast state. Somehow he made it to this school, presumably after Tech closed its doors. On the segment he talked about the difficulties of being away from home laboring at basketball in the United States. As he was speaking, he choked up and cried a bit. Again through what is visible on his social media profile, he seems to be searching for another opportunity to play basketball in the United States. At one point he was constantly uploading his highlight clips and statistics on his social media profiles.

Another Costa Rican player, the oldest of the group while Tito was in La Frontera, is still playing college basketball in the United States. He received a scholarship to attend a junior college in the Midwest and is now on the roster of a four-year college in the United States. He was one of the lucky *becados* (scholarship athletes) who survived the deplorable conditions at Tech and continued achieving his American hoop dreams. I do not have any data on the other *becados*. Tito did not remain in contact with them after his departure from Tech.

Tito and I continue to maintain a relationship and are in constant contact. He is currently waiting for some movement in his life (Esson 2015a). The COVID-19 pandemic interrupted his plans to reenroll in a local university. He did enroll in a different Mexican university on a basketball scholarship once some COVID-19 restrictions were lifted. After his visa to reenter the United States was denied, I began to contact different state agencies and solicit services from several pro bono immigration services. I was able to secure a series of appointments with the attorney general of the State of Texas Human Trafficking and Transnational/Organized Crime Section. They were very interested in Tito's case, but since Tech had closed and Coach Barrigon was no longer in the United States, I was told there was little they could do. After some convincing by different members of my doctoral dissertation committee at the University of Texas at Austin, I decided to take the four years I had spent working with Tito and investing both emotionally and financially in him and dedicate this book to basketball trafficking.

Basketball Trafficking

Basketball trafficking is produced by an inequitable global system that assigns value differently based on an individual's nationality, race, and language abilities. Black populations are affected the most within this global apartheid, whether they hail from the Global North or the Global South. As Chonika Coleman-King (2014) argues, Black people in both zones experience inequality similarly. Within the United States, often thought to be a part of the Global North, African American youth are the preferred workers of the US basketball industry because of their marginalized positions within US society and the economy as well as their perceived innate physical superiority (Brooks and McKail 2008).

Many scholars have studied in depth why African Americans are drawn to sports like basketball (May 2007; Rhoden 2007; Hawkins 2010). However, a population that has yet to receive adequate attention until now is the international Black noncitizen youth navigating the AIC. In many cases, similarly to their African American counterparts, they are marginal to their societies and economies. Sport has been fashioned as one their most salient opportunities to create movement in their lives and achieve a respectable adulthood, which is the manifestation of a broader struggle for survival amid a sense of a less-than-certain future (Esson 2015b).

However, in a world where movement is heavily policed and punished depending on nationality, Black youth from the Global South encounter challenges when attempting to migrate to the United States that their African American counterparts do not contend with. Heidy Sarabia (2015) gives credence to this assertion, as they found that mobile citizens from the Global South are not treated equally to their Global North counterparts. Black athletes from the Global South must contend with racist and class-based US immigration policies that strive to keep poor people of color out of the United States and treat those within the United States harshly (Johnson 2012). The additional layer of immigration constraints that affects Black immigrants from the Global South has to be taken into account when analyzing the AIC. These restrictions also apply to those with exceptional athletic talent. Visas dictate who has the right to be spatially mobile between different nations, and differently classed, raced, and gendered bodies do not have the same right to move across borders (Tanelorn and Anderson 2019). The AIC, and specifically the United States' education-based basketball model, either knowingly or unknowingly participates in the policing and enforcement of racist and classist US immigration policies. It is at this intersection, where the AIC and US immigration system collide, that the model reaps the benefits of exploiting Black youth and produces basketball trafficking. However, within this globalized economy, a larger pool of Black youth all over the world are made available to fuel the system (Runstedtler 2018) instead of just African Americans, as has traditionally been the case.

Movement is crucial within the current system of youth basketball. The need to change geographic locales and teams is seen in the high number of school transfers. However, despite the need to change locales to obtain better opportunities in the current system, free movement is not allowed for athletes. In similar ways to immigration enforcement toward nonimmigrant F-1 student visa holders, athletic governing bodies police and punish unauthorized movement. I agree that governance is necessary within a multibillion-dollar industry where youth, who put in the most work, stand to benefit the least. However, I am pushing us to consider the negative consequences of the enforcement of F-1 student visa rules.

Laura Caty (2019) holds that the increasing uncertainties of the F-1 and J-1 student visa programs in the United States will cause prospective international students to choose other destination nations, which lessens the profits US institutions will garner. However, in the realm of intercollegiate basketball, the United States' athletic conferences still provide one of the best routes for professional basketball aspirants. The globalization of US basketball leagues like the NBA and the creation of NBA-sponsored development leagues like the Basketball Africa League, the Mexico City Capitanes (an NBA G League team and its first-ever franchise in Latin America), the NBA Youth Academies, and the NBA's Basketball Without Borders in every continent only further increase the hegemonic dominance of US basketball. These offshore leagues and academies continue to serve as development grounds for US-based leagues, including operating as feeders for intercollegiate basketball. It is true that a select few will potentially benefit from these NBA-sponsored academies and camps, but there are still many who will not.

The policing and punishment of unauthorized movement, which is a feature of both the AIC and the US immigration system, continues to negatively impact the lives of Black athletes but especially international noncitizen Black athletes. At the core, those who remain in compliance, no matter how precarious their situation can be, do not run the risk of strict punishment. But those who do not will be ruled athletically ineligible and simultaneously in violation of their student visa, subsequently jeopardizing their stable migratory status within the United States.

Throughout this text I have demonstrated, primarily through Tito's experiences but also the experiences of many other youth, that many of them face exploitation that changes their migratory status. There comes a point where they must barter with illegality in exchange for their US hoop dream, which is not just about basketball. It is about the chance to have the life they desire, and their athletic talents may be the only currency they have to achieve it.

However, what is revealed in the decisions these young people are forced to make is where their benefit truly lies. Many schools at both the interscholastic and intercollegiate levels offer protections for undocumented youth to access education. Those with high athletic talent can also tap into these opportunities—if they are made aware of them. Unfortunately, many are unaware, and most who enter the United States on an F-1 student visa are not technically eligible for these protections due to the visa's limitations. One question that emerges among this population is how these institutions engage with youth who lack a stable migratory status. How have intercollegiate athletic departments worked with these young athletes? These are legitimate questions that must be approached urgently. However, focusing solely on helping exploited youth from the Global South who survive and achieve some success misses a crucial point: how the intercollegiate system ultimately benefits. US interscholastic and intercollegiate athletic leagues and governing bodies must locate themselves within the system that places young people in these predicaments. Whether they enter lawfully and maintain proper status at the high school level, are trafficked, or arrive in the first year of college, the AIC ultimately wins. The restrictive barriers to entry and eligibility are most damaging to the most vulnerable populations—Black youth from the Global South. Noncitizen players who do not find success within the system are sent back to their countries or left at the mercy of US Immigration and Customs Enforcement, which will enforce their removal from the United States.

The reasons I have decided to follow basketball trafficking are twofold. First, I aim to influence policies surrounding the use of the F-1 student visa for athletic purposes in US interscholastic basketball, since it is currently being used to exploit and traffic international youth to and within the United States. Second, I have decided to follow basketball trafficking to counter the dominant narrative associated with Black Panamanian youth like Tito. Society has cast them as deviant, criminal pariahs to society. Tito disrupts these false and racist assertions through his history and actions in pursuit of creating his own future. For too long, the labor of youth like Tito has been undervalued, along with their humanity. This project does more than expose the atrocities happening in amateur basketball around the globe. It serves to excavate the humanity of young Black boys in the African diaspora who need to be visible beyond what they can do on a court or field.

APPENDIX

Implications and Recommendations

It is imperative to note that the F-1 student visa, when utilized for athletic purposes, extends beyond academics. It enters into the $19.2 billion US youth sports industry (Wintergreen Research 2020), which is fraught with issues. This research has several practical implications. In what follows, I outline a few of my key recommendations in detail. While this is not an exhaustive list, it aims to initiate the necessary changes to protect noncitizen F-1 student visa applicants and holders who migrate to the United States for athletic purposes at the secondary level.

Athletic Governance for All Secondary
Schools in the United States

The entire F-1 student visa program needs to be updated. In the program's current state, there are no provisions that mandate that sponsoring institutions provide housing, meals, or supervision for K–12 F-1 student visa holders (Pleso 2017). While the US Department of Homeland Security offers some best practices, without proper oversight and enforcement schools have little incentive to ensure that youth are properly educated and cared for. The necessary protections for F-1 student visa athletes are lacking, especially when their labor is being used in a multibillion-dollar industry. Although the F-1 student visa is an educational visa, safeguards must be implemented to protect the labor of these young athletes. Most athletic governing bodies already limit the amount of time student-athletes can spend in extracurricular activities, but similar safeguards are not required for institutions that run athletic programs outside of these governing bodies. A national standard must be established that applies to all institutions using F-1 student visas for athletic purposes.

Data Collection on International Noncitizen
Athletes in the United States

There is an urgent need to collect data and determine how many F-1 student visa holders are in the United States for athletic purposes. Currently, no such data are available. According to the 2018 *SEVIS by the Numbers Report* of the Student and Exchange Visitor Program (SEVP), there were 84,840 nonimmigrant student records in US K–12 schools (US Immigration and Customs Enforcement 2020). However, it is impossible to know how many of these students are in the United States specifically for athletic purposes.

In 2020 I obtained data from the US Department of Homeland Security through a Freedom of Information Act request regarding F-1 student visa holders in the United States who had athletic scholarships listed in the financial section of their I-20 forms. I requested these data after carefully analyzing Tito's I-20 forms from both Tech and Vessey County Community College. In the financial section, both institutions listed "athletic scholarship" as a source of funding. I believe this financial categorization can provide valuable data on the number of F-1 student visa holders in the United States for athletic purposes, as the Department of Homeland Security does not officially maintain these aggregated numbers. The data revealed thousands of F-1 student visa holders at the intercollegiate level who fit this description. For example, in 2017, the academic year Tito entered the United States on an F-1 student visa, there were 24,734 students at the intercollegiate level (associates, bachelor's, master's, and doctoral programs) who received athletic scholarships, according to their I-20 forms. This number closely aligns with the 19,402 international student-athletes reported in the NCAA's 2018 Country of Origin Database for Student-Athletes (NCAA 2018). It is important to note two things: First, some intercollegiate athletes may not receive athletic scholarships; and, second, the NCAA is not the only intercollegiate athletic organization offering scholarships to international student-athletes. However, the congruence between these two sources of data is notable.

In contrast, the 2017 data show only sixty-three secondary students with an athletic scholarship listed in the financial section of their I-20 forms. While I could not obtain definitive evidence that this number is inaccurate, my findings, as discussed in the case of Panama, suggest a discrepancy. Specifically, I demonstrated that at least five students from Tito's Panamanian high school were enrolled in US high schools to play basketball, rather than the two students reported in the Department of Homeland Security's 2017 data.

I recommend that US Immigration and Customs Enforcement and SEVP implement an additional category on the I-20 form that requires institutions to disclose if the prospective student will be attending the institution for athletic purposes. This way we will receive a more accurate number of youth laboring in athletics at US educational institutions. These data-collecting functions should track these students throughout their time in the United States. Obtaining and maintaining these data is crucial for locating students. Currently, there is no reliable system to track noncitizen youth who enter the United States on F-1 student visas for athletic purposes. The Evelyn Mack Academy, which I believe to be the first basketball trafficking case prosecuted in the United States, is one clear example that highlights the necessity and urgency of such recordkeeping. In November 2019 Evelyn Mack, the owner of the academy, was sentenced to eighteen months in federal prison for concealing, harboring, and shielding unlawful aliens (see chapter 5). I believe that linking youth athletes directly to the sponsoring institutions could help prevent trafficking and ensure accountability.

Holding Coaches, Recruiters, and Designated
School Officials Responsible

Many youth athletes are recruited to US schools by athletic coaches and re-cruiters, but these individuals are typically not the institution's designated school official (DSO). Only the DSO has the authority to adjust an F-1 student visa holder's status within the Student and Exchange Visitor Informa-tion System (SEVIS). As a result, recruiters and coaches do not appear on any official paperwork related to the youth athlete, which leaves the door open for exploitation. All parties involved in recruiting an F-1 student visa holder in the United States *must* be part of the visa adjudication process. I recommend that all of the involved individuals must provide their legal information and take legal responsibility for the whereabouts, education, and safety of the noncitizen athletes they recruit.

Additionally, many basketball-centered prep schools that recruit non-citizen minors are not able to issue an I-20, and they have been recorded sites of trafficking, exploitation, and abuse. These schools often partner with an SEVP-authorized school that can issue the I-20 form. These non-SEVP-approved or unlisted partnerships make it challenging for students and parents to "thoroughly research their intended school, looking at both the academic and athletic programs" (US Department of Homeland Secu-rity 2016). There are very limited protections for a child who is contracted by a basketball prep school, which pays their academic tuition but at any point can remove the child from the program and cut their funding for "athletic performance" or other reasons. At this point the child may be ren-dered without support while the basketball-centered prep school is spared any repercussions, as they have no legal responsibility to the visa-holding youth. I recommend that SEVP update the I-20 form to require autho-rized institutions to disclose whether they are housing their own athletic programs or partnering with a third party. Partnerships with third-party athletic businesses should be prohibited in the SEVP. There are too many uncertainties, making it impossible to guarantee the child's protection and hold the proper adults responsible for their safety and educational development.

How Intent Is Gauged in the Nonimmigrant
Visa Adjudication Process

The gauging of intent within the nonimmigrant visa adjudication process must be ended. Jackal Tanelorn and April Anderson (2019) argue that the US nonimmigrant visa adjudication and determination process is arbitrary. This arbitrariness contributes to basketball trafficking. Due to the uncertainty inherent in the process, noncitizen athletes may be reluctant to leave the United States to address their visa statuses because they cannot be guaranteed reentry. Tito was denied reentry into the United States on the basis of 214(b), for not proving nonimmigrant intent. Paschal Chukwu, a former basketball student-athlete from Nigeria on the University of Syracuse's renowned basketball team, was quoted in a news article: "'If I leave, I can't come back. Even if I have an idea of leaving and going to visit any other country, I would need to go back to one of the embassies in Nigeria and get the visa,' Chukwu said. 'The downside of that is there's always a chance they're going to deny you, no matter what. You might have the right documents, but if you come out wrong in some way, the person interviewing you can deny you, even if you're already in school. Then you're stuck there'" (Ditota 2019).

For some noncitizen youth athletes in the United States, the decision to barter with illegality and remain in the country without the proper migratory status is a calculated risk taken in pursuit of upward social mobility through sport. The nonimmigrant visa adjudication process is not only arbitrary but also expensive. The application fee is $160, which must be paid for each adjudication appointment. These fees can be prohibitively high for some youth and their families (Agbor 2021). Recently, it was reported that it took five visa adjudication appointments for Brigham Young University's Nigerian basketball student-athlete Gideon George to be approved for an F-1 student visa (Muh 2020). That's a total of $800 in application fees alone, not including transportation costs or the emotional and psychological stresses these appointments impose on applicants. I mention these high-profile cases from major NCAA Division I men's basketball programs to illustrate the broader scope of this issue. Smaller programs and US secondary schools, which lack the same level of exposure, may be dealing with the same issues. A significant part of mitigating basketball trafficking in the United States is to interrogate and remedy how the US immigration system and its policies are contributing factors.

References

Aceto, Michael. 2002. "Ethnic Personal Names and Multiple Identities in Anglophone Caribbean Speech Communities in Latin America." *Language in Society* 31 (4): 577–608. https://doi.org/10.1017/S0047404502314040.

Adeyemo, Adeoye O. 2022. "Place, Race, and Sports: Examining the Beliefs and Aspirations of Motivated Black Male Students Who Play High School Sports." *Urban Education* 57 (1): 154–83.

Adeyemo, Adeoye O. 2023. "Black on Both Sides: Toward an Understanding of the Athletic and Career Aspirations of Black Males Who Play Sports." *Journal of Sport and Social Issues* 47 (2): 126–57. https://doi.org/10.1177/01937235221144434.

Agbor, Avitus A. 2021. "Africans and the Costs of Obtaining Visas for International Migration: A Disquisition on the Trends, Implications and Biases in the Policy Framework." *Cogent Social Sciences* 7 (1): 1827526. https://doi.org/10.1080/23311886.2020.1827526.

Aladejebi, Funké, Kristi A. Allain, Rhonda C. George, and Ornella Nzindukiyimana. 2022. "'We the North'? Race, Nation, and the Multicultural Politics of Toronto's First NBA Championship." *Journal of Canadian Studies* 56 (1): 1–34.

Alfaro, O. 1925. *El peligro antillano en la América Central: La defensa de la raza.* 2nd ed. Panama City: Imprenta nacional.

Allard, Elaine C. 2015. "Undocumented Status and Schooling for Newcomer Teens." *Harvard Educational Review* 85 (3): 478–501. https://doi.org/10.17763/0017-8055.85.3.478.

Amen Strayhorn, Kali-Ahset. 2014. "Black Panama and Globalization in the Neoliberal Era, 1990–2012." PhD diss., Emory University. ProQuest (UMI 3647013).

Ariail, Cat. 2017. "Between the Boundaries: The Athletic Citizenship Quest of Carlota Gooden." *Journal of Sport History* 44 (1): 1–19. https://doi.org/10.5406/jsporthistory.44.1.0001.

Banton, Kafu. 2000. "De qué me hablas." On *The Best of Me*. Album.

Bashi, Vilna Francine. 2007. *Survival of the Knitted: Immigrant Social Networks in a Stratified World*. Stanford, CA: Stanford University Press.

Beamon, Krystal. 2012. "'I'm a Baller': Athletic Identity Foreclosure Among African-American Former Student-Athletes." *Journal of African American Studies* 16 (2): 195–208. https://doi.org/10.1007/s12111-012-9211-8.

Besnier, Niko, Domenica Gisella Calabrò, and Daniel Guinness, eds. 2015. *Sport, Migration, and Gender in the Neoliberal Age*. London: Routledge.

Brace-Govan, Janice, and Hélène de Burgh-Woodman. 2008. "Sneakers and Street Culture: A Postcolonial Analysis of Marginalized Cultural Consumption." *Consumption, Markets and Culture* 11 (2): 93–112.

Briar Cliff University. 2023. "Looking Back: Panama Pipeline Pushed Charger Hoops to National Prominence." Family and Friends, January 30. https://www.briarcliff.edu/family-and-friends/parents/news/looking-back-panama-pipeline-pushed-charger-hoops-to-national-prominence.

Brooks, Scott N. 2009. *Black Men Can't Shoot*. Chicago: University of Chicago Press.

Brooks, Scott N., and Michael A. McKail. 2008. "A Theory of the Preferred Worker: A Structural Explanation for Black Male Dominance in Basketball." *Critical Sociology* 34 (3): 369–87. https://doi.org/10.1177/0896920507088164.

Brown, Keffrelyn D. 2016. *After the "At-Risk" Label: Reorienting Educational Policy and Practice*. New York: Teachers College Press.

Cancino, Jorge. 2018. "Trump endurece las penas para los estudiantes que se queden ilegalmente." *Univision*, August 9. https://www.univision.com/noticias/visas/el-gobierno-publica-memorando-que-pone-en-riesgo-de-deportacion-a-estudiantes-que-acumulen-presencia-ilegal.

Carbado, Devon W. 2005. "Racial Naturalization." *American Quarterly* 57 (3): 633–58.

Carter-Francique, Akilah R., Algerian Hart, and Geremy Cheeks. 2015. "Examining the Value of Social Capital and Social Support for Black Student-Athletes' Academic Success." *Journal of African American Studies* 19 (2): 157–77. https://doi.org/10.1007/s12111-015-9295-z.

Caty, Laura. 2019. "The Trump Administration's Impact on F-1 and J-1 Visas." *Immigration and Human Rights Law Review* 1 (2): 2. https://scholarship.law.uc.edu/ihrlr/vol1/iss2/2.

Center for US-Mexican Studies. 2017. "The Students We Share: At the Border—San Diego and Tijuana." UC San Diego School of Global Policy and Strategy. https://usmex.ucsd.edu/_files/mmfrp_policy%20brief_2017.pdf.

Chepyator-Thomson, Rose, Ryan Turcott, and Matthew Lee Smith. 2016. "Exploring Migration Patterns and University Destination Choices of International Student-Athletes in NCAA Division I Men's Basketball (2004–2014)." *International Journal of Sport Management* 17 (4): 576–92.

Clotfelter, Charles T. 2019. *Big-Time Sports in American Universities*. New York: Cambridge University Press.

Clouse, Thomas. 2017. "Some Crying Foul After Foreign Athletes Lead Post Falls' Genesis Prep to State Basketball Title." *Spokesman-Review*, March 9. https://www.spokesman.com/stories/2017/mar/09/some-crying-foul-after-foreign-athletes-lead-post-/.

Coleman-King, Chonika. 2014. *The (Re-)Making of a Black American: Tracing the Racial and Ethnic Socialization of Caribbean American Youth.* New York: Peter Lang.

Collins, Patricia Hill. 2000. *Black Feminist Thought: Knowledge, Consciousness, and the Politics of Empowerment.* 2nd ed. New York: Routledge.

Comeaux, Eddie. 2018. "Stereotypes, Control, Hyper-Surveillance, and Disposability of NCAA Division I Black Male Athletes." *New Directions for Student Services* 2018 (163): 33–42. https://doi.org/10.1002/ss.20268.

Congressional Research Service. 2021. *Asylum Eligibility for Applicants Fleeing Gang and Domestic Violence: Recent Developments.* Version 3. Report No. LSB10617. Updated August 6. https://crsreports.congress.gov/product/pdf/LSB/LSB10617.

Cooper, Joseph N. 2019. *From Exploitation Back to Empowerment: Black Male Holistic (Under) Development Through Sport and (Mis)education.* New York: Peter Lang.

Corinealdi, Kaysha. 2013. "Envisioning Multiple Citizenships: West Indian Panamanians and Creating Community in the Canal Zone Neocolony." *Global South* 6 (2): 87–106. https://doi.org/10.2979/globalsouth.6.2.87.

Corinealdi, Kaysha. 2022. *Panama in Black: Afro-Caribbean World Making in the Twentieth Century.* Durham, NC: Duke University Press.

Cox, Aimee Meredith. 2015. *Shapeshifters: Black Girls and the Choreography of Citizenship.* Durham, NC: Duke University Press.

Curry, Tommy J. 2021. "Expendables for Whom: Terry Crews and the Erasure of Black Male Victims of Sexual Assault and Rape." *Women's Studies in Communication* 42 (3): 287–307.

Dalton, Matt. 2016. "Shoe Money, AAU Basketball, and the Effects on College Basketball Recruiting." *Mississippi Sports Law Review* 6 (1): 108–14.

Danish, Stephen J., Albert J. Petitpas, and Bruce D. Hale. 1993. "Life Development Intervention for Athletes: Life Skills Through Sports." *Counseling Psychologist* 21 (3): 352–85.

de B'béri, Boulou Ebanda, and Peter Hogarth. 2009. "White America's Construction of Black Bodies: The Case of Ron Artest as a Model of Covert Racial Ideology in the NBA's Discourse." *Journal of International and Intercultural Communication* 2 (2): 89–106. https://doi.org/10.1080/17513050902759496.

De Paulis, Marixa Lasso. 2007. "Race and Ethnicity in the Formation of Panamanian National Identity: Panamanian Discrimination Against Chinese and West Indians in the Thirties." *Revista Panameña de Política* 4:61–92.

DiFiori, John P., Arne Güllich, Joel S. Brenner, Jean Côté, Brian Hainline, Edward Ryan III, and Robert M. Malina. 2018. "The NBA and Youth Basketball: Recommendations for Promoting a Healthy and Positive Experience." *Sports Medicine* 48 (9): 2053–65. https://doi.org/10.1007/s40279-018-0950-0.

Ditota, Donna. 2019. "Foreign SU Basketball Players Need Patience, Paperwork, Hope." *Syracuse.com,* April 11. https://www.syracuse.com/orangebasketball/2019/04/path-for-international-basketball-players-at-syracuse-requires-patience-hope.html

Donnelly, Peter, and Leanne Petherick. 2004. "Workers' Playtime? Child Labour at the Extremes of the Sporting Spectrum." *Sport in Society* 7 (3): 301–21. https://doi.org/10.1080/1743043042000291659.

Dumas, Michael J., and Joseph Derrick Nelson. 2016. "(Re)Imagining Black Boyhood: Toward a Critical Framework for Educational Research." *Harvard Educational Review* 86 (1): 27–47. https://doi.org/10.17763/0017-8055.86.1.27.

Elliott, Diana M. 1997. "Traumatic Events: Prevalence and Delayed Recall in the General Population." *Journal of Consulting and Clinical Psychology* 65 (5): 811–20.

Esson, James. 2013. "A Body and a Dream at a Vital Conjuncture: Ghanaian Youth, Uncertainty and the Allure of Football." *Geoforum* 47:84–92. https://doi.org/10.1016/j.geoforum.2013.03.011.

Esson, James. 2015a. "Better Off at Home? Rethinking Responses to Trafficked West African Footballers in Europe." *Journal of Ethnic and Migration Studies* 41 (3): 512–30. https://doi.org/10.1080/1369183X.2014.927733.

Esson, James. 2015b. "You Have to Try Your Luck: Male Ghanaian Youth and the Uncertainty of Football Migration." *Environment and Planning A: Economy and Space* 47 (6): 1383–97. https://doi.org/10.1177/0308518X15594920.

Esson, James. 2020. "Playing the Victim? Human Trafficking, African Youth, and Geographies of Structural Inequality." *Population, Space and Place* 26 (6): e2309. https://doi.org/10.1002/psp.2309.

Falcous, Mark, and Joseph Maguire. 2005. "Globetrotters and Local Heroes? Labor Migration, Basketball, and Local Identities." *Sociology of Sport Journal* 22 (2): 137–57. https://doi.org/10.1123/ssj.22.2.137.

Fanon, Frantz. 2008. *Black Skin, White Masks*. Translated by Richard Philcox. New York: Grove.

Ferber, Abby L. 2007. "The Construction of Black Masculinity: White Supremacy Now and Then." *Journal of Sport and Social Issues* 31 (1): 11–24. https://doi.org/10.1177/0193723506296829.

Frederick, Evan, James Sanderson, and Nicholas Schlereth. 2017. "Kick These Kids Off the Team and Take Away Their Scholarships: Facebook and Perceptions of Athlete Activism at the University of Missouri." *Journal of Issues in Intercollegiate Athletics* 10 (1): 17–34. https://scholarcommons.sc.edu/jiia/vol10/iss1/20.

Frenkel, Stephen. 2002. "Geographical Representations of the 'Other': The Landscape of the Panama Canal Zone." *Journal of Historical Geography* 28 (1): 85–99.

Garcia, Michael John. 2006. *Criminalizing Unlawful Presence: Selected Issues*. Order Code RS22413. Congressional Research Service. https://ilw.com/immigrationdaily/news/2006,0509-crs.pdf.

García Diaz, Modesto. 2020. "La raza afro, pilar del deporte tricolor: El somatotipo de los atletas otroga una ventaja sobre las otras etnias, especialmente en disciplinas que demanda fuerza y explosividad." *Expreso*, July 18. https://www.expreso.ec/deportes/raza-afro-pilar-deporte-tricolor-34199.html.

Gill, Emmitt, Langston Clark, and Alvin Logan. 2020. "Freedom for First Downs: Interest Convergence and the Missouri Black Student Boycott." *Journal of Negro Education* 89 (3): 342–59.

Gilmore, Amir A., and Pamela J. Bettis. 2021. "Antiblackness and the Adultification of Black Children in a U.S. Prison Nation." *Oxford Research Encyclopedia of Education*, March 25. https://doi.org/10.1093/acrefore/9780190264093.013.1293.

Golash-Boza, Tanya Maria. 2015. *Deported: Immigrant Policing, Disposable Labor, and Global Capitalism*. New York: New York University Press.

Gómez Cervantes, Andrea. 2021. "'Looking Mexican': Indigenous and Non-Indigenous Latina/o Immigrants and the Racialization of Illegality in the Midwest." *Social Problems* 68 (1): 100–117. https://doi.org/10.1093/socpro/spz048.

Gonzales, Roberto G. 2015. *Lives in Limbo: Undocumented and Coming of Age in America*. Oakland: University of California Press. https://doi.org/10.1525/9780520962415.

Goodman, Adam. 2020. *The Deportation Machine: America's Long History of Expelling Immigrants*. Princeton, NJ: Princeton University Press.

Grosbard, Adam. 2018. "Panamanian Jonathan Salazar Is Living Out His Mother's Dream with St. John Bosco Basketball." *Press-Telegram*, November 28. https://www .presstelegram.com/2018/11/28/panamanian-jonathan-salazar-is-living-out-his -mothers-dream-with-st-john-bosco-basketball/.

Guridy, Frank Andre. 2010. *Forging Diaspora: Afro-Cubans and African Americans in a World of Empire and Jim Crow*. Chapel Hill: University of North Carolina Press. https://doi.org/10.5149/9780807895979_guridy.

Hall, Stuart. 2019. *Essential Essays*. Edited by David Morley. 2 vols. Durham, NC: Duke University Press.

Harrison, Louis, Gary Sailes, Willy K. Rotich, and Albert Y. Bimper. 2011. "Living the Dream or Awakening from the Nightmare: Race and Athletic Identity." *Race Ethnicity and Education* 14 (1): 91–103. https://doi.org/10.1080/13613324.2011.531982.

Hawkins, Billy. 2010. *The New Plantation: Black Athletes, College Sports, and Predominantly White NCAA Institutions*. New York: Palgrave Macmillan. https://doi.org/10.1057 /9780230105539.

Hawkins, Billy. 2017. "Interest Convergence: A Revolutionary Theory for Athletic Reform." In *Critical Race Theory: Black Athletic Sporting Experiences in the United States*, edited by Billy J. Hawkins, Akilah R. Carter-Francique, and Joseph N. Cooper, 57–84. New York: Palgrave Macmillan. https://doi.org/10.1057/978-1-137-60038-7_3.

Hersch, Joni. 2011. "The Persistence of Skin Color Discrimination for Immigrants." *Social Science Research* 40 (5): 1337–49. https://doi.org/10.1016/j.ssresearch.2010.12 .006.

Hinderlie, Holly Heard, and Maureen Kenny. 2002. "Attachment, Social Support, and College Adjustment Among Black Students at Predominantly White Universities." *Journal of College Student Development* 43 (3): 327–40.

Horka, Tyler. 2019. "'Panamanian Prince': How Iverson Molinar Made It to Mississippi State." *Clarion Ledger*, December 13. https://www.clarionledger.com/story/sports /college/mississippi-state/2019/12/13/ncaa-college-basketball-mississippi-state-ben -howland-iverson-molinar-recruiting-panama/4348149002/.

Hosick, Michelle Brutlag. 2021. "NCAA Adopts Interim Name, Image and Likeness Policy." NCAA, June 30. https://www.ncaa.org/news/2021/6/30/ncaa-adopts-interim -name-image-and-likeness-policy.aspx.

Hutchinson Miller, Carmen. 2012. "The Province and Port of Limón: Metaphors for Afro-Costa Rican Black Identity." *Journal of Arts and Humanities* 1 (2): 1–17. https:// doi.org/10.18533/journal.v1i2.114.

Indianapolis Recorder. 1937. "'Bill' Yancey Is Idolized by Youth of Panama as Work Begins to Shape." April 3.

Instituto Nacional de Estadística y Censo (INEC). 2023. *Encuesta de Mercado Laboral, Agosto 2023.* Panama City: INEC. https://www.inec.gob.pa/archivos/P076072362023121 3154047Comentario.pdf.

International Basketball Federation. 2017. "FIBA Signs 11-Year Strategic Partnership with Iconic Basketball Brand Nike." Press release, February 27. https://www.fiba.basketball /en/news/fiba-signs-11-year-strategic-partnership-with-iconic-basketball-brand-nike.

James, Carl E. 2003. "Schooling, Basketball and US Scholarship Aspirations of Canadian Student Athletes." *Race, Ethnicity and Education* 6 (2): 123–44.

Jeffrey, Craig. 2012. "Geographies of Children and Youth II: Global Youth Agency." *Progress in Human Geography* 36 (2): 155–71. https://doi.org/10.1177/0309132510393316.

Johnson, Kevin R. 2012. "An Immigration Gideon for Lawful Permanent Residents." *Yale Law Journal* 122 (8): 2394–415.

Jones, Samuel Vincent. 2010. "The Invisible Man: The Conscious Neglect of Men and Boys in the War on Human Trafficking." *Utah Law Review* 2010 (4): 1143–88.

Jua, Nantang. 2003. "Differential Responses to Disappearing Transitional Pathways: Redefining Possibility Among Cameroonian Youths." *African Studies Review* 46 (2): 13–36. https://doi.org/10.2307/1514824.

Kentucky High School Athletic Association. 2013. "Bylaw 7. Transfer Rule–Foreign Exchange Students." Bylaws of the Kentucky High School Athletic Association. https://portal.ksba.org/public/Meeting/Attachments/DisplayAttachment.aspx ?AttachmentID=197793.

La Furcia, Ange. 2016. "Los colores de las fantasías: Estudios sobre masculinidades en Colombia: Crítica feminista y geopolítica del conocimiento en la matriz colonial." *Revista Colombiana de Sociología* 39 (1): 47–78. https://doi.org/10.15446/rcs.v39n1.56341.

Lago, Kristen. 2018. "Panama-Native Jonathan Salazar Realizes Basketball Dreams at St. John Bosco." *Spectrum News 1*, December 20. https://spectrumnews1.com/ca /southern-california/high-school-sports/2018/12/20/how-basketball-changed-one-st –john-bosco-senior-s-life-.

Lakhani, Sarah M. 2019. "Universalizing the U Visa: Challenges of Immigration Case Selection in Legal Nonprofits." *California Law Review* 107 (5): 1661–711. https://doi .org/10.15779/Z38G15TB7H.

La Prensa. 2012. "Panamá, un crisol de fibras." September 2. https://www.prensa.com /luis_buron-barahona/Panama-crisol-fibras_0_3470652921.html.

Lopez, María Pabón. 2004. "Reflections on Educating Latino and Latina Undocumented Children: Beyond *Plyler v. Doe.*" *Seton Hall Law Review* 35 (4): 1373–406.

Lopez, Nancy. 2019. "What's Your Street Race? The Urgency of Critical Race Theory and Intersectionality as Lenses for Revising the US Office of Management and Budget Guidelines, Census and Administrative Data in Latinx Communities and Beyond." *Genealogy* 5 (3): 75. https://doi.org/10.3390/genealogy5030075.

Lowe de Goodin, Melva. 2014. *People of African Ancestry in Panama, 1501–2012.* Panama City: Editora Sibuaste.

Maguire, Joseph, and John Bale. 1994. "Introduction: Sports Labour Migration in the Global Arena." In *The Global Sports Arena: Athletic Migration in an Interdependent*

World, edited by John Bale and Joseph Maguire, 1–21. London: Routledge. https://doi .org/10.4324/9781315035871.

Maguire, Ken. 2017. "Senegal Native Diagne Took Long Road to WKU." *Bowling Green Daily News*, June 1. https://www.bgdailynews.com/sports/wku/senegal-native -diagne-took-long-road-to-wku/article_7ee54bd7-a1c5-519b-b0db-37b151debcc1.html.

May, Reuben A. Buford. 2007. *Living Through the Hoop: High School Basketball, Race, and the American Dream*. New York: New York University Press.

McGuinness, Aims. 2016. *Path of Empire: Panama and the California Gold Rush*. Ithaca, NY: Cornell University Press.

McNeel, Bekah. 2017. "Game Over: St. Anthony Returns to Catholic Identity, College Prep Focus." *San Antonio Report*, August 28. https://sanantonioreport.org/game-over -st-anthony-returns-to-catholic-identity-college-prep-focus/.

Millington, Robert S. 2010. "Basketball With(out) Borders: Interrogating the Intersections of Sport, Development, and Capitalism." Master's thesis, Queen's University. http://hdl.handle.net/1974/5449.

Moreno Figueroa, Mónica G. 2010. "Distributed Intensities: Whiteness, Mestizaje and the Logics of Mexican Racism." *Ethnicities* 10 (3): 387–401. https://doi.org/10.1177 /1468796810372305.

Morgan-Trostle, Juliana, Kexin Zheng, and Carl Lipscombe. 2015. *The State of Black Immigrants*. New York: Black Alliance for Just Immigration; NYU School of Law Immigrant Rights Clinic. https://baji.org/wp-content/uploads/2020/03/sobi-fullreport -jan22.pdf.

Mosby, Dorothy Elizabeth. 2001. "Me Navel String Is Buried There: Place, Language and Nation in the Literary Configuration of Afro-Costa Rican Identity." PhD diss., University of Missouri–Columbia. ProQuest (UMI 3013004).

Mosby, Dorothy Elizabeth. 2018. Introduction to *Quince Duncan's "Weathered Men" and "The Four Mirrors": Two Novels of Afro-Costa Rican Identity*, by Quince Duncan, translated by Dorothy Elizabeth Mosby, 1–16. Cham, Switzerland: Palgrave Macmillan. https://doi.org/10.1007/978-3-319-97535-1_1.

Muh, Cameron. 2020. "Getting to Know BYU Men's Basketball Transfer Gideon George." Daily Universe, Brigham Young University, October 15. https://universe.byu .edu/2020/10/15/getting-to-know-byu-basketball-transfer-gideon-george/.

Mwaniki, Munene Franjo. 2017. *The Black Migrant Athlete: Media, Race, and the Diaspora in Sports*. Lincoln: University of Nebraska Press.

National Junior College Athletic Association. 2019. *The National Junior College Athletic Association Eligibility Pamphlet, 2019–2020*. Charlotte, NC: National Junior College Athletic Association.

NCAA (National Collegiate Athletic Association). n.d. "Nonscholastic Event Guidelines and Requirements." Accessed April 3, 2025. http://ncaaorg.s3.amazonaws.com /enforcement/ecag/ECAG_NonScholasticEventGuidelinesandRequirements.pdf.

NCAA (National Collegiate Athletic Association). 2017. "International Student-Athletes." June 14. http://www.ncaa.org/student-athletes/future/international -student-athletes.

NCAA (National Collegiate Athletic Association). 2018. "NCAA Demographics Database." http://www.ncaa.org/sports/2018/12/13/ncaa-demographics-database.aspx.

NCAA (National Collegiate Athletic Association). 2020. *2020–21 NCAA Division I Manual*. Indianapolis: National Collegiate Athletic Association.

NCAA (National Collegiate Athletic Association). 2021. *2021–22 Guide to International Academic Standards for Eligibility*. Indianapolis: National Collegiate Athletic Association.

Neal, Mark Anthony. 2013. *Looking for Leroy: Illegible Black Masculinities*. New York: New York University Press.

Neumayer, Eric. 2006. "Unequal Access to Foreign Spaces: How States Use Visa Restrictions to Regulate Mobility in a Globalized World." *Transactions of the Institute of British Geographers* 31 (1): 72–84. https://doi.org/10.1111/j.1475-5661.2006.00194.x.

Neumayer, Eric. 2010. "Visa Restrictions and Bilateral Travel." *Professional Geographer* 62 (2): 171–81. https://doi.org/10.1080/00330121003600835.

Newton, Velma. 1984. *The Silver Men: West Indian Labour Migration to Panama, 1850–1914*. Mona, Jamaica: Institute of Social and Economic Research, University of the West Indies.

Nkrumah, Kwame. 1968. *Neo-Colonialism: The Last Stage of Imperialism*. London: Heinemann Educational.

Palmer, Breanne J. 2017. "The Crossroads: Being Black, Immigrant, and Undocumented in the Era of #BlackLivesMatter." *Georgetown Journal of Law and Modern Critical Race Perspectives* 9 (2): 99–121.

Panama American. 1937a. "Bill Yancey, Ball Coach, to Arrive Here March First." February 25. Hemeroteca Biblioteca Nacional Ernesto J. Castillero, Panama City, Panama.

Panama American. 1937b. "Yancey Welcomed at Cristobal Enroute to Post on Pacific Side." West Indian News, March 2. Hemeroteca Biblioteca Nacional Ernesto J. Castillero, Panama City, Panama.

Pleso, Faye J. 2017. "Oversight and Quality Assurance of Academic Programs Under F-1 Visas." PhD diss., Walden University. ProQuest (10289408).

Priestley, George. 2004. "Antillean-Panamanians or Afro-Panamanians? Political Participation and the Politics of Identity During the Carter-Torrijos Treaty Negotiations." *Transforming Anthropology* 12 (1–2): 50–67. https://doi.org/10.1525/tran.2004.12.1-2.50.

Rahier, Jean Muteba. 2008. "Soccer and the (*Tri-*)Color of the Ecuadorian Nation: Visual and Ideological (Dis-)Continuities of Black Otherness from Monocultural *Mestizaje* to Multiculturalism." *Visual Anthropology Review* 24 (2): 148–82. https://doi.org/10.1111/j.1548-7458.2008.00011.x.

Ralph, Michael. 2007. "Prototype: In Search of the Perfect Senegalese Basketball Physique." *International Journal of the History of Sport* 24 (2): 238–63. https://doi.org/10.1080/09523360601045963.

Rhoden, William C. 2007. *Forty Million Dollar Slaves: The Rise, Fall, and Redemption of the Black Athlete*. New York: Three Rivers.

Rios, Victor M. 2011. *Punished: Policing the Lives of Black and Latino Boys*. New York: New York University Press.

Runstedtler, Theresa. 2018. "More Than Just Play: Unmasking Black Child Labor in the Athletic Industrial Complex." *Journal of Sport and Social Issues* 42 (3): 152–69. https://doi.org/10.1177/0193723518758458.

Santucci, Jon. 2018. "Nation Christian CEO Mike Woodbury Answers to Recorded Tirade Toward Former Student-Athlete." TCPalm, October 31. https://www.tcpalm .com/story/news/2018/10/31/nation-christian-ceo-answers-vulgar-tirade/1833740002/.

Sarabia, Heidy. 2015. "Global South Cosmopolitans: The Opening and Closing of the USA-Mexico Border for Mexican Tourists." *Ethnic and Racial Studies* 38 (2): 227–42. https://doi.org/10.1080/01419870.2014.887741.

Sayers, Justin. 2018. "Western Kentucky to Pay Charles Bassey's Guardian $200k as Assistant." *Courier Journal*, July 15. https://www.courier-journal.com/story/sports /college/kentuckiana/2018/07/05/wku-pay-charles-basseys-guardian-200-k-assistant /759579002/.

Sekot, Aleš, and Tomáš Pětivlas. 2014. "College Basketball in Sport Globalization." *Studia Sportiva* 8 (1): 5–12. https://doi.org/10.5817//StS2014-1-1.

Senado de la República. 2021. "Aprueba Senado garantizar impulso deportivo a indíge-nas y afromexicanas." Coordinación de Communicación Social Mexico, September 7. https://comunicacionsocial.senado.gob.mx/informacion/comunicados/582-aprueba -senado-garantizar-impulso-deportivo-a-indigenas-y-afromexicanas.

Smith, Earl. 2014. "The Athletic Industrial Complex: Conference Realignment, Race, and Title IX." In *Race in American Sports: Essays*, edited by James L. Conyers Jr., 71–83. Jefferson, NC: McFarland.

Smith, William A., Jalil Bishop Mustaffa, Chantal M. Jones, Tommy J. Curry, and Walter R. Allen. 2016. "'You Make Me Wanna Holler and Throw Up Both My Hands!': Campus Culture, Black Misandric Microaggressions, and Racial Battle Fatigue." *International Journal of Qualitative Studies in Education* 29 (9): 1189–209.

Stanmyre, Matthew, and Steve Politi. 2017. "The Fast Break." *NJ.com*, October 1. https:// www.nj.com/sports/page/the_fast_break.html.

Starr, Alexandra. 2015. "American Hustle." *Harper's Magazine*, April. https://harpers.org /archive/2015/04/american-hustle/.

Steinitz, Matti. 2022. "Soulful Sancocho: Soul Music and Practices of Hemispheric Black Transnationalism in 1960s and 1970s Panama." *Black Scholar* 52 (1): 15–26. https://doi .org/10.1080/00064246.2022.2007344.

Sterne, Valerie. 2020. *Elementary School Poverty Disparities in Texas*. Austin: Institute for Urban Policy Research and Analysis, College of Liberal Arts, University of Texas at Austin. https://utexas.app.box.com/v/school-poverty-disparities.

Sullivan, Mariah, Matt Moore, Lindsey C. Blom, and Greta Slater. 2020. "Relationship Between Social Support and Depressive Symptoms in Collegiate Student Athletes." *Journal for the Study of Sports and Athletes in Education* 14 (3): 192–209. https://doi.org /10.1080/19357397.2020.1768034.

Szok, Peter A. 2012. *Wolf Tracks: Popular Art and Re-Africanization in Twentieth-Century Panama*. Jackson: University Press of Mississippi.

Tanelorn, Jackal, and April Anderson. 2019. "Worldwide Approval (and Denial): Ana-lysing Nonimmigrant Visa Statistics to the United States from 2000 to 2016." *Mobili-ties* 14 (2): 267–88. https://doi.org/10.1080/17450101.2019.1567986.

TCAL (Texas Christian Athletic League). 2016. *2016–2017 Texas Christian Athletic League Official Bylaws*. https://issuu.com/t-cal/docs/2016-2017_tcal_official_bylaws.docx.

Thomas, Daniel J., III, Marcus W. Johnson, Langston Clark, and Louis Harrison Jr. 2020. "When the Mirage Fades: Black Boys Encountering Antiblackness in a Predominantly White Catholic High School." *Race Ethnicity and Education* 25 (7): 1–20. https://doi.org/10.1080/13613324.2020.1798376.

Thompson-Hernández, Walter. 2016. "'Oye, Qué Bien Juegan Los Negros, ¿No?': Blaxicans and Basketball in Mexico." In *Afro-Latin@s in Movement: Critical Approaches to Blackness and Transnationalism in the Americas*, edited by Petra R. Rivera-Rideau, Jennifer A. Jones, and Tianna S. Paschel, 109–30. New York: Palgrave Macmillan. https://doi.org/10.1057/978-1-137-59874-5_5.

Todres, Jonathan. 2015. "Human Trafficking and Film: How Popular Portrayals Influence Law and Public Perception." *Cornell Law Review Online* 101:1–24.

Tolison, Blaine. 2019. "Private School Founder Gets Federal Prison Term for Role in Human Trafficking." wsoc-tv, November 13. https://www.wsoctv.com/news/local/private-school-founder-gets-federal-prison-term-for-role-in-human-trafficking/1007740834/.

Turcott, Ryan, and N. David Pifer. 2018. "The Preferred Players: A Theoretical and Comparative Analysis of Men's Basketball Recruits at the ncaa's Mid-Major Level." *Journal of Contemporary Athletics* 12 (3): 151–73.

uil (University Interscholastic League). 2016. *Constitution and Contest Rules: 2016–2017*. Austin: University of Texas at Austin. https://www.uiltexas.org/files/policy/uil-ccr-2016-2017-full.pdf.

uil (University Interscholastic League). 2020. "Student Eligibility for All uil Contests: 2020–2021." Austin: University of Texas at Austin. https://www.uiltexas.org/files/policy/uil-ccr-subchapter-m.pdf.

United Nations International Children's Emergency Fund. 2018. *Estrategia nacional multisectorial de prevención de la violencia contra niños, niñas y adolescentes*. https://www.unicef.org/panama/media/691/file/Estrategia%20Nacional%20Multisectorial%20de%20Prevenci%C3%B3n%20de%20la%20Violencia%20contra%20Ni%C3%B1os,%20Ni%C3%B1as%20y%20Adolescentes%20.pdf.

US Courts. n.d. "Access to Education—Rule of Law." About Federal Courts. Accessed March 17, 2021. https://www.uscourts.gov/educational-resources/educational-activities/access-education-rule-law.

US Department of Homeland Security. 2013. "What Is Human Trafficking?" Blue Campaign, May 24. https://www.dhs.gov/blue-campaign/what-human-trafficking.

US Department of Homeland Security. 2016. "Trafficking of Student Athletes." Counterterrorism and Criminal Exploitation Update. *sevp Spotlight* 6 (1): 2. https://studyinthestates.dhs.gov/sites/default/files/SEVP%20Spotlight_APR%2016_FINAL.pdf.

US Department of Homeland Security. 2017. "International Student Athlete q&a." fru Update. *sevp Spotlight* 7 (1): 2. https://studyinthestates.dhs.gov/assets/sevp_spotlight_march_2017.pdf.

US Department of Homeland Security. 2020. *Number of f-1 Student Visa Holders in the U.S. That Received Any Amount of "Athletic Scholarship" Listed in "Student's Funding For" Section of Financials on i-20 Forms. Years 2015–2020*. Washington, DC: US Department of Homeland Security.

US Department of Justice. 2019. "Charlotte Private School Owner Is Sentenced to Prison for Scheme Involving Student Visas." US Attorney's Office, Western District of North Carolina, press release, November 12. https://www.justice.gov/usao-wdnc/pr/charlotte -private-school-owner-sentenced-prison-scheme-involving-student-visas.

US Department of State. 2020. *2020 Trafficking in Persons Report*. https://www.state.gov /wp-content/uploads/2020/06/2020-TIP-Report-Complete-062420-FINAL.pdf.

US Department of State, Bureau of Consular Affairs. n.d. "Visa Denials." Accessed March 16, 2021. https://travel.state.gov/content/travel/en/us-visas/visa-information -resources/visa-denials.html.

US Embassy in Panama. 2020. "Security Alert—U. S. Embassy Panama City, Panama." January 21. https://pa.usembassy.gov/security-alert-u-s-embassy-panama-city-panama/.

US House of Representatives, Committee on Merchant Marine and Fisheries. 1977. *Panama Canal Miscellaneous: Hearings Before the Subcommittee on the Panama Canal of the Committee on Merchant Marine and Fisheries, House of Representatives, Ninety-Fifth Congress, First Session, on C.Z. Biological Area Authorization, H.R. 3348, March 22, 1977, Problems of Canal Zone Residents and Employees, April 12, 13, 1977, Balboa, Canal Zone, January 1, 1977*. Washington, DC: US Government Publishing Office.

US Immigration and Customs Enforcement. 2020. *Student and Exchange Visitor Program (SEVP) 2018 SEVIS by the Numbers Report*. Washington, DC: ICE. https://www.ice.gov /doclib/sevis/btn/18_0501_hsi_sevp-0418-biannual-sevis-btn.pdf.

Wallace, Brandon. 2022. "Commodifying Black Expressivity: Race and the Representational Politics of Streetball." *Communication and Sport* 10 (6): 1053–69. https://doi.org /10.1177/2167479520945222.

Wallace, Javier L. 2023. "Lost in Translation: Reverted Black Panamanian Sporting Networks." *Southern Cultures* 29 (2): 24–37.

Wallace, Javier L., Langston Clark, and James E. Cooper. 2022. "Reclaiming the Conveyor Belt: Physical Education Teacher Education as a Pipeline to the Professoriate for Black Males." *Journal of Teaching in Physical Education* 41 (2): 252–59. https://doi .org/10.1123/jtpe.2021-0013.

Warde, Bryan. 2013. "Black Male Disproportionality in the Criminal Justice Systems of the USA, Canada, and England: A Comparative Analysis of Incarceration." *Journal of African American Studies* 17 (4): 461–79. https://doi.org/10.1007/s12111-012-9235-0.

Wardle, Huon, and Laura Obermuller. 2019. "'Windrush Generation' and 'Hostile Environment': Symbols and Lived Experiences in Caribbean Migration to the UK." *Migration and Society* 2 (1): 81–89. https://doi.org/10.3167/arms.2019.020108.

Warren, Jonathan W., and France Winddance Twine. 2008. "Critical Race Studies in Latin America: Recent Advances, Recurrent Weaknesses." In *A Companion to Racial and Ethnic Studies*, edited by David Theo Goldberg and John Solomos, 538–60. Malden, MA: Blackwell. https://doi.org/10.1111/b.9780631206163.2002.00045.x.

Westerman, George Washington. 1937. "The Passing Review." News of the Colored Community. *Panama American*, March 7. Hemeroteca Biblioteca Nacional Ernesto J. Castillero, Panama City, Panama.

Wetzel, Dan. 2023. "California Could Lead Another Charge in College Athlete Pay with Its Latest Proposed Bill." *Yahoo Sports*, January 19. https://sports.yahoo.com/california

-could-lead-another-charge-in-college-athlete-pay-with-its-latest-proposed-bill
-010553341.html.

White, Derrick E. 2019. *Blood, Sweat, and Tears: Jake Gaither, Florida A&M, and the History of Black College Football.* Chapel Hill: University of North Carolina Press.

Wintergreen Research. 2020. *Youth Team, League, and Tournament Sports: Market Shares, Strategies, and Forecasts, COVID-19 and Post-COVID-19, Worldwide, 2020 to 2027.* Research and Markets, October 2020. https://www.researchandmarkets.com/reports /5189499/youth-team-league-and-tournament-sports-market.

Wolch, Jennifer R. 1990. *The Shadow State: Government and Voluntary Sector in Transition.* New York: Foundation Center.

Yilmaz, Serhat, James Esson, Paul Darby, Eleanor Drywood, and Carolynne Mason. 2020. "Children's Rights and the Regulations on the Transfer of Young Players in Football." *International Review for the Sociology of Sport* 55 (1): 115–24. https://doi.org /10.1177/1012690218786665.

Yosso, Tara J. 2005. "Whose Culture Has Capital? A Critical Race Theory Discussion of Community Cultural Wealth." *Race Ethnicity and Education* 8 (1): 69–91.

Zuvanich, Adam. 2016. "St. Anthony Catholic Fires Head Coach for Playing Ineligible Player." *My San Antonio*, December 1. https://www.mysanantonio.com/sports/high -school/article/St-Anthony-Catholic-fires-head-coach-for-playing-10647902.php.

Zuvanich, Adam. 2017. "St. Anthony Coach Wins Custody Battle over Bassey." *My San Antonio*, July 14. https://www.mysanantonio.com/sports/article/St-Anthony-coach -wins-custody-battle-over-Bassey-11290027.php.

Index

Note: Page numbers in italics indicate illustrations.

athletic scholarships: academic and English requirements for, 4–5, 34; benefits to schools of, 62, 78, 82; benefits to students of, 62, 82, 92, 138–39; as charitable and necessitating gratitude, 82, 85–86, 103, 107–8; costs to students of, 3–4, 62–63, 78–79; English language learning support and, 41, 61–62, 84, 94–95, 109, 111; as neocolonial, 62–63, 85–86; in Panama, 9, 34–35, 61; power to revoke, 5, 108, 111–13, 124. *See also* supports needed by international student athletes in the United States

athletic superiority of Black people. *See* racial stereotypes of Black boys and men: as athletically superior

Auriantal, Hennssy, 99–100

Austin (Texas), 120–21

Bale, John, 62

basketball industrial complex. *See* athletic industrial complex (AIC)

basketball mixtapes, 10, 25–26

basketball tournaments. *See* Centrobasket tournament; tournaments

basketball trafficking: adultification and, 88–89; cases in the United States, 7, 125–26, 127–29, 141; complicity of athletic governing bodies in, 131–32; definition of, 5–6; lack of resources for victims of, 135, 141–42, 152; refusal to see Black males as victims and, 6–7, 135–37, 142; trauma and, 139–41, 150–51. *See also* human trafficking

Bassey, Charles, 99–100

Black athletic superiority. *See* racial stereotypes of Black boys and men: as athletically superior

Black colleges and universities. *See* historically Black colleges and universities (HBCUs)

Black culture and basketball, 8, 10, 63–64

Black male labor in basketball. *See* labor of Black males in basketball

Black Panamanian coaches and educators, 11–14, *15*, 16, 29, 162

Black people in Costa Rica, 72–73, 80

Black people in Panama: criminalization of, 8, 56; cultural groups of, 27, 53–56; racism against, 43–44, 56–57, 60, 65–67; segregation and, 55. *See also* West Indians in Panama

Brace-Govan, Janice, 64

Briar Cliff College, 14

Brooks, Scott, 10, 30, 41, 78, 80–81, 160, 165

Brown, Panama Al, 51

Buford, Reuben A., 93

Carbado, Devon, 148–49, 159

Carter-Francique, Akilah, 98, 110

Centrobasket tournament, 23–25, 30–33, 42, 45

chombos. *See* West Indians in Panama

Clark, Jamal, 72–73

Club Mercurio, 12–13

coach and player relationships: abuse and control in, 5, 97–98, 102–4, 110, 114, 128–29, 138; power dynamics in, 99–100, 104–5, 108–9, 112, 123–25, 128; regulation of by athletic governing bodies, 98, 100, 113

Colón (Panama), 3, 47–51, 64–66, 80, 162

Comeaux, Eddie, 5, 108, 112, 128

conveyer belt concept in sports, 60–61, 162

Corinealdi, Kaysha, 16, 28, 57, 121

corporate marketing and basketball, 7, 31–33, 45

Costa Rica, 73, 80

criminalization of Black boys and men, 8, 56, 65–67, 142, 147–49

Curry, Tommy, 136

de Burgh-Woodman, Hélène, 64

DHS. *See* United States Department of Homeland Security